Perspectives on Supported Collaborative Teacher Inquiry

Routledge Research in Education

Perspectives on Supported Collaborative Teacher Inquiry

Edited by David Slavit,
Tamara Holmlund Nelson
and Anne Kennedy

Routledge
Taylor & Francis Group
New York   London

First published 2009
by Routledge
270 Madison Ave, New York, NY 10016

Simultaneously published in the UK
by Routledge
2 Park Square, Milton Park, Abingdon, Oxon OX14 4RN

Routledge is an imprint of the Taylor & Francis Group, an informa business

Library of Congress Cataloging in Publication Data

Perspectives on supported collaborative teacher inquiry / edited by David Slavit,
Tamara Holmlund Nelson, and Anne Kennedy.
    p. cm. — (Routledge research in education)
    Includes bibliographical references and index.
    1. Teachers—In-service training. 2. Reflective teaching. 3. Mentoring
in education. I. Slavit, David. II. Holmlund Nelson, Tamara D. (Tamara
Dawn) III. Kennedy, Anne.
    LB1731.P459 2009
    370.71'5—dc22
    2008051505

ISBN10: 0-415-99926-X (hbk)
ISBN10: 0-203-87654-7 (ebk)

ISBN13: 978-0-415-99926-7 (hbk)
ISBN13: 978-0-203-87654-1 (ebk)

To Gisela and our wonderful sons, Max and Arthur—D.S.

To Kris, Kira, and Beck, who have all contributed in so many ways!—T.H.N.

To my husband John Lang and my three beautiful and talented nieces, Elizabeth, Lucianne, and Claire—A.K.

Contents

Figures

Tables

Preface

This book is about a form of collaborative professional development (PD) which we term supported collaborative teacher inquiry (SCTI). Succinctly put, SCTI is a general description of classroom-based research that engages teachers in dialogue and collective activity to investigate and coconstruct understandings about teaching and learning. The teachers' collaborative inquiries are grounded in evidence that emanates from their professional practice, and support for the work is accessible and applicable. Those aspects of our working definition (which is expounded throughout the book) that can separate it from the more general notion of collaborative PD are: (a) teachers surfacing a focus around a meaningful dilemma, question, curiosity, or problem of practice; (b) teacher interactions, grounded in data, in pursuit of resolutions and answers to this focus; and (c) the presence of a support structure.

Collaborative PD models are becoming increasingly widespread, sprouting up everywhere in various forms. Some forms of collaborative PD include curricular alignment or content knowledge training. Other forms of collaborative PD involve teachers in completing a mandated set of prescribed inquiry steps to measure student progress on a learning issue deemed important by the principal. Still others involve teachers in resolving issues and dilemmas important to their classroom contexts. While the latter can be a highly successful and rewarding experience, it might also become frustrating when teachers lack collaborative and/or inquiry skills necessary to move forward. As collaborative PD models become more widespread and are increasingly promoted, the potential for enacting SCTI also expands. Theoretical and empirical discussions of what constitutes support for teachers engaged in SCTI provide important contributions to furthering this work.

Unfortunately, teachers engaged in SCTI may feel as though they are navigating upstream without a paddle. Resource allocation towards more central instructional functions as well as cries of "teachers should be in the classroom teaching" are profound and reasonable barriers against actively supporting teacher inquiry. Further, in our current educational system, the everyday lives of teachers afford little opportunity to meaningfully undertake inquiry into their practice. Teachers' days are filled with "student contact time," "prep time," "grading time," and numerous other activities that quickly consume minutes and hours. Teachers engaged in inquiry on their practice are provided few oars, and often navigate against the current.

In the play *The Fantasticks*, two farmers bemoan their fatherly skills:

> *Every plant grows according to the plot.*
> *While with progeny, it's hodge-podgenee.*
> *For as soon as you think you know what kind you've got,*
> *It's what they're not!*
> *So, plant a cabbage, get a cabbage, not a sauerkraut.*
> *That's why I love vegetables, you know what you're about.*

The farmers make a powerful point regarding the mutability of human behavior, a point that pertains to the two foci of this book: educational research and teacher professional development. Both are grounded in human activity and require nuanced attention to the ever-changing behaviors, knowledge, and dispositions held by participants. These become exponentially more complicated as the number of participants and relationships between them increase. SCTI, a potential focus for both educational research and professional development, is rife with such complexities. In addition, while analyses of supports provided to teachers engaged in SCTI should consider the many dynamic aspects inherent in teachers' inquiry groups and classrooms, these analyses should also go beyond the teachers' immediate contexts. SCTI assumes that appropriate and accessible supports are available to teacher groups. However, the contexts and systems surrounding most examples of SCTI are laced with dynamic uncertainties, making support for SCTI groups difficult to pinpoint and enact.

Therefore, we must also explore the nature and place of support from the perspective of broader educational contexts. In doing so, we consider the systems and norms that shape these broader contexts. For years, researchers and educators have foraged their way through an educational context that speaks of diversity, but often bases evaluative standards on normative measures. Most educational reform, as it pertains to the classroom, is based on the premise that students 1) have differences, 2) should learn certain things, and 3) receive instruction that enables them, as individuals, to develop along targeted learning goals. The universality in #2 and the individuality in #1 form a definite tension found in #3. For example, the omnipresent large-scale tests of student achievement assume a one-size-fits-all educational model that is far different from the realities that exist in our nation's schools. Similarly, the resurgence of experimental design as the "gold standard" for educational research uses assumptions for generalization that fail to account for many of the nuanced facets of diversity that surface in most (all?) of our nation's classrooms. And the standards and rubrics for teaching and teacher professionalism established by organizations such as the National Board for

Professional Teaching Standards, as well as similar standards established by individual school districts, evaluate all teachers on a given set of measures that are assumed to fit with all educational contexts. While the preceding standards and norms have significant benefits, they also have significant limitations. However, what is often overlooked is that they are *norms* by which we navigate educational reform. Educational research, including research specific to SCTI, needs to account for these norms.

In "The River," Bruce Springsteen begins:

> *I come from down in the valley, where mister when you're young*
> *They bring you up to do like your daddy done*

In some sense, we are still young, and we still "do like our daddies done." Serious attention to public education in the United States probably began near the turn of the 20th century. But educational research to inform policy and instructional decision making didn't begin to accumulate in significant amounts until the last 30 or 40 years. While research on teaching has developed into a significantly large body of literature, a research base for *collaborative* teacher research is only currently emerging. This is despite the fact that the enactment of collaborative teacher research has been steadily increasing over the past 10 to 20 years. More specifically, theoretical discussions of SCTI are needed in the professional development and educational research literature; further, empirical evidence on the processes and results of SCTI are in greater demand. This edited work provides multiple perspectives on the frameworks that shape current SCTI projects, with accompanying empirical evidence on the processes and outcomes therein.

In addition to educational researchers investigating aspects of SCTI, this book is helpful to K–12 teachers, administrators, and other leaders actually engaged in supported collaborative teacher inquiry and who are looking for theoretical frameworks and case-based examples to inform their work. Specifically, (a) educational researchers will have an extensive set of empirically-based investigations from which to draw that frame and enact research into SCTI contexts, and (b) teacher educators and professional developers will be provided specific models of SCTI with accompanying "lessons learned" for each model.

We see the theory and research in this book as highly usable by K–12 teachers and administrators who are engaged in work of this kind. This book can also expand the knowledge base and potentially improve the practice (i.e., support the ability to provide professional development) of those who support these groups; namely K–12 teacher educators and professional developers. Our past interactions with professional development providers lead us to conclude that they can and desire to know more theory and empirical results pertaining to SCTI, and that they are hungry for empirically-based resources to provide their teachers in pursuit of their own collaborative inquiry goals. The contribution of this work is not in providing a how-to book for conducting SCTI, but a usable, intellectual, and data-based discussion of ideas central to SCTI, complete with empirically-based case descriptions.

This book began from a collaboration of a few researchers interested in the notion of support for teachers engaged in collaborative inquiry. Although coming from different points of view, contexts, and content area foci, the members of this group shared a strong belief in the need for understanding more about this research area, and were individually engaged in a variety of research initiatives involving some form of SCTI. We met on several occasions, including copresentations at educational conferences, and formed a collective sense of how to utilize our research agendas in support of the goals of this book. This edited volume is the culmination of the work of these individuals.

We want to explicitly identify what this book does not seek to accomplish. We are not trying to answer the question "Are teacher collaborative inquiry groups, such as professional learning communities and lesson study, worthwhile?" While we contribute theory and research to those seeking to address this question, we do not feel that the small number of cases in this volume can come close to providing conclusive answers to this question. Further, it is problematic to assume a shared understanding of what it means to be "worthwhile" in this context. The authors in this edited volume approach this question from various points of view and, while not conclusively addressing the question, provide perspective and data to inform the question.

Second, we are not providing a "cookbook" for how to conduct supported collaborative teacher inquiry. While various models of SCTI are found in this book, and specific recommendations for enacting SCTI can be easily gleaned from each of the cases, we do not focus on providing specific steps for how to conduct inquiry of this kind.

Third, we do not target claims that connect SCTI with specific student learning outcomes; the focus of this book is on the notion of support. But we do feel that this research goal is extremely important. In this particular climate, where accountability is supreme and collaborative teacher inquiry is in vogue, finding such information is of the utmost importance. In our own work with numerous school districts, hundreds of teachers, and dozens of collaborative inquiry groups, we have sought ways of finding direct linkages between the work of the teachers and student learning outcomes. Our problems began when we tried to identify which student learning outcomes would be of most interest. As we rejected the idea that standardized scores are meaningful measures for understanding the linkage, our problems became complex and resource demanding (we believe our situation is neither novel nor abnormal). Many of the chapters do not touch on student learning outcomes, while others provide some empirically-based discussion on the issue. We hope one day to be part of a contribution that provides richer information on linkages between collaborative teacher inquiry and student learning than that found in this volume.

Finally, we have several "thank-yous" to relay. Support for this work has been provided by a Mathematics Science Partnership grant from the U.S. Department of Education and by the National Science Foundation Grant ESI-0554579. While the opinions expressed in this document are solely those of the authors, the editors wish to thank the generosity of these agencies for their support. The editors also wish to acknowledge the support and assistance of the teachers, facilitators, and administrators associated with the professional development and research projects discussed in the various chapters in this book.

There are also many individuals we wish to acknowledge for their support and guidance throughout this process. First, each contributing author has been absolutely marvelous, going way beyond the call to ensure that this book is of the highest quality (and was brought to you on time!). We also thank our STRIDE research colleague Angie Deuel for her keen and lively mind, especially in keeping us honest, real, and upbeat. Tamara Shoup deserves our thanks for all that she Tazzes. And our research group would also not be the same without the support of Michele Mason, Linda Edwards, and Amy Pachelli. We also thank Wendi Laurence for her inspiration and insights during our formative years. Finally, we wish to thank Hilda Borko, Jim Hiebert, Randy Philipp, Jim Minstrell, and Alberto Rodriguez for their general support and specific guidance throughout various aspects of our work.

D.S.
T.H.N.
A.K.

1 Supported Collaborative Teacher Inquiry

David Slavit and Tamara Holmlund Nelson

Washington State University Vancouver

In the current era of heightened media attention to high-stakes, quantitative measures of what it means to be successful in our public schools, the actual processes, and even the people, tend to be overshadowed by the sheer power of these numeric statements. For example, according to the Third International Mathematics and Science Study (TIMSS) and the Progress in International Reading Literacy Study (PIRLS), the United States is not among the top countries in the world in regard to mathematics, science, or reading achievement. State-level tests across the United States reveal large percentages of students who do not obtain a proficient achievement rating in a variety of school subjects. While some represent a less gloomy scenario (Berliner & Biddle, 1995; Bracey, 2006), messages in the public mainstream are consistently bleak, and it is no wonder that accusations about the qualifications and professionalism of teachers are constantly raised, and that teachers feel defensive about their profession.

So what might be done about this? More specifically, what kinds of supports can be provided to teachers to raise their professional status, improve their instruction, and ultimately impact their students' development in more powerful ways? Currently, while beginning teachers usually receive some kind of professional mentoring at the early career stage, the scope of this support is usually limited in quality and variety (Smith & Ingersoll, 2004). Perhaps more importantly, the vast majority of teachers have limited access to the kind of professional nurturing that current evidence suggests is most impacting. For example, Garet, Porter, Desimone, Birman, and Yoon (2001) found that the qualities of professional development (PD) that intensify the effects on teacher instruction are: (a) the presence of ongoing teacher networks or study groups rather than workshops or conferences, (b) consistency with teachers' goals, other activities, and materials and policies, and (c) same-subject, grade, or school group participation. However, they also found that the PD teachers normally receive has (a) an average time span of activity that is less than one week; (b) a median number of 15 contact hours per PD activity; (c) no theme, coherence, or active learning opportunities; and (d) limited group participation. Not long ago, Stigler and Hiebert (1999) used TIMSS data to argue for the existence of a teaching gap in the United States. However, given the existing contexts of teacher professionalization, could it be that there is actually a professional development gap? Stigler and Hiebert suggest that this, too, may be the case:

> To really improve teaching we must invest far more than we do now in generating and sharing knowledge about teaching. This is another sort of teaching gap. Compared with other countries, the United States clearly lacks a system for developing professional knowledge and for giving teachers the opportunity to learn about teaching. American teachers, compared with those in Japan, for example, have no means of contributing to the gradual improvement of teaching methods or of improving their own skills. American teachers are left alone, an action sometimes justified on grounds of freedom, independence, and professionalism. This is not good enough if we want excellent schools in the next century (pp. 12–13).

Such a situation leads us to consider the following questions: What kinds of support do teachers need to grow professionally? How are these supports best provided to teachers?

THE NEED FOR TEACHER COLLABORATION

National curricular reform documents in the United States, in nearly all subject areas and grade levels, promote the use of small-group work and problem-based learning experiences to support student development. These recommendations are based on years of theoretical development and a burgeoning empirical base. Likewise, recent evidence suggests that teacher professional development performed collaboratively and grounded in "the work teachers do" is an effective forum for challenging existing beliefs about content, learners, and teaching, and for using data and research to reflect on, and possibly change, instructional practice (Borko, 2004; Grossman, Wineburg, & Woolworth, 2001; Little, 2003). However, in our work with teachers and school administrators, we are finding that teachers need an enormous amount of support in enacting this kind of PD, and that the nature of these supports can be both hard to identify and difficult to provide. Moreover, broader professional contexts, such as district mandates and national achievement initiatives, can also provide supports and challenges to the professional goals of teachers. In some cases, a reculturation (Fullan, 2001) is needed that goes beyond mere changes to the structures of the classroom, school, and district contexts, but works toward a fundamental change in the way both teachers and administrators interrelate, work, and even think. This can often require a deep analysis of not just the nature of the goal or activity under consideration, but investigation into the complex relationship between the activity, how individual people work, how these people work in a collective manner, and how this work dynamic can be supported.

Grossman et al. (2001) claim that American high schools have failed to create cultures of collaboration and community for the work teachers do. Louis and Kruse (1995), working in urban schools, found that teacher community was possible across K–12, but required "personal struggle and administrative commitment" (p. 21). Further, because policy discussions emphasize the outcomes of student–teacher interactions, "administrators and policymakers virtually ignore the broader context of teachers' work" (p. 4).

While the metaphor of a teacher classroom being an island of practice is far from new (Lortie, 1975), what can be overlooked is that teachers often make excursions to islands of professional development. These are usually devoid of social interaction that might include challenges to teachers' beliefs about teaching or insights into what is possible (Sarason, 1996). For example, a majority of the professional development initiatives in which teachers participate in the districts we have observed could be classified as curricular alignment activity, training on a specific curriculum or instructional technique, or content knowledge development. Teachers often have little time to inquire about and reflect on their *own* instructional practice or on their students' work.

A DISCUSSION OF SUPPORT

Nelson and Slavit (2008) describe supported collaborative teacher inquiry (SCTI) as professional development in which teacher teams build collaborative structures for the purpose of inquiring into aspects of their own instructional practice. In this work, we described two broad kinds of support as critical to SCTI:

1. Support for the collaborative teacher inquiry *process*, and
2. Enhancing the *interface* between the teacher inquiry and broader educational contexts.

Our ongoing work with teachers engaged in SCTI suggests a third important area of support:

3. Nurturing an *inquiry stance* toward teaching.

SCTI that emanates from the needs and passions of teachers often leads to an inquiry focus that is grounded in their immediate professional goals. However, care must be taken when teacher groups are forced together (such as when all third-grade teachers are asked to form a professional learning community to study reading achievement) or when time and other supports are not available to cultivate the construction of a common vision, inquiry focus, or goal. Common vision is a pathway to collective intentions. When present in SCTI, buy-in, passion, and authentic conversation can emerge. Perhaps more importantly, when SCTI is teacher-initiated and a shared sense of wonder (Wells, 1999) or inquiry stance (Cochran-Smith & Lytle, 1999; Jaworksi, 2006) are developed, dissonance, questions, and knowledge about practice can surface that can advance the individually and collectively constructed vision of high-quality learning and teaching present in the teacher group (Ball & Cohen, 1999; Lampert & Ball, 1998; Supovitz & Turner, 2000; Thompson & Zeuli, 1999). Yet, Wilson and Berne's (1999) review of exemplary research on professional development underscores the difficulty teachers have in assuming a collaborative inquiry stance. Teacher talk commonly centers on the particulars of a classroom event, complaints about administrative actions or policies, or tales of the challenges presented by particular students; seldom do teachers engage in critical, data-based examinations of teaching and learning. As a facilitation expert with whom we work has said, "teachers often don't know how to ask the curious questions."

A primary function of SCTI should be to stimulate a quest for knowledge through a close examination of classroom practices and student understanding that ultimately leads to change. If teachers are to successfully engage in activities and discussions that build on, or disrupt, their perspectives about practice and student learning, specific characteristics for supporting such actions must be identified. Teachers can participate in a collaborative inquiry process of their own volition and not seek or have access to appropriate supports, or they could be invited to participate in a collaborative inquiry but given minimal support. In these situations, the teacher community is forced to perform all aspects of the inquiry with whatever time and resources (intellectual and material) they bring to the process, a situation that can lead to less than satisfying results. On the other hand, teachers might have access to a host of supports, whether or not they initiate the inquiry process. These supports can be derived or driven by forces and individuals both inside and outside the teacher inquiry community and have the potential to directly impact the enactment of the inquiry process and influence the perception of value of the teachers' work. Specifically, we see *support for the inquiry process, enhancing the interface between the teacher inquiry and broader educational contexts,* and *nurturing an inquiry stance toward teaching* as key to professional development of this kind.

Support for the Collaborative Inquiry Process

Thompson and Zeuli (1999) emphasize that for professional development to be transformative, teachers need help with the processes of inquiry as they move through an inquiry cycle. Too often professional development efforts result in a conservative form of "tinkering" (p. 355) with existing practices; assistance is needed to explicitly surface, confront, and take action upon the dissonance created by identifying gaps between a vision of high-quality teaching and the actuality of student outcomes. A facilitator can directly support the inquiry process by providing resources that build teachers' skills in framing an inquiry focus, helping to identify data that will inform their question, and enriching teachers' understandings of data analysis. Facilitators can also play a crucial role by asking questions or raising issues that teachers might otherwise avoid, fail to see, or be afraid to make explicit. Effective team development requires attention to the interactions of each group member, and a skillful facilitator can help the group coalesce, encourage risk taking, enhance inquiry and advocacy skills, and improve motivation (Garmston & Wellman, 1999). Such interactions are what truly attack a teaching culture that reaffirms the privatization of practice.

For example, a group of secondary teachers with whom we have worked wanted to incorporate rich mathematical problem-solving tasks into their curriculum and instruction. The teachers had a local mathematics curriculum specialist who served as group facilitator and immediately provided support by identifying two specific websites that contained mathematical tasks appropriate for this purpose. The facilitator then worked with the group in the development of a problem-solving rubric to be used with the tasks, which would provide a measure of student learning for the teacher group. This facilitator had also helped the teachers build norms for positive collaboration, and provided and modeled protocols for holding discussions about student work. When the teachers were engaged in discussions of the students' work on these mathematical tasks, the facilitator pushed the group to go beyond their own characterizations of student work and "come to agreement" on how the student work would be interpreted via the rubric. The latter support proved critical in moving the group forward in their overall interpretations of the student data, and even on the general nature of data and research. Although the teachers would have obtained results on their own, the facilitator clearly provided important and specific supports to the teachers' inquiry process. As one teacher stated:

> Our facilitator was so empowering for that part and she started with me and I felt her influence in very tactful ways. She first started off in saying, "What is your cycle that you're going to go through? What are these meetings? What is it about that you're meeting? What is going on?" And we've kind of developed a cycle within this meeting structure. And then she moved it further and said, "Where's your evidence of this work going on in the classroom?" So we started looking at observations and then she said, "Okay, what's your evidence of students' growth?" and we started looking at student work ... So this is the process that we went through and it was nice to have a process that we could center our meetings around. And then she would say, "So what are you talking about when you talk about these tasks?" And she would keep pushing me further, "What is the mathematics?" I'm like, oh, yeah, that would be a good question to ask.

Enhancing the Interface between Teacher Inquiry and Broader Educational Contexts

The second kind of support we view as critical to SCTI involves relationships between the immediate teacher inquiry environment and other, usually broader, educational contexts. McLaughlin and Talbert (2006) state:

> Even the best-designed professional development resources will fall short, and the most robust professional community will dissolve, when other elements in teachers' professional context ignore, frustrate, or work at cross-purposes with the learning and change they intend. (p. 79)

These authors identify four sets of individuals prominent in these broader contexts: school administrators, teachers' organizations, professional developers, and parents and community members. Perhaps hidden in this list, we have also found university faculty providing research and other data-based information, professional organizations providing forums for teachers to engage in professional dialogue, and state and federal agencies introducing broad initiatives and mandates to play important and direct roles inside the teacher group. While we must be cognizant that teachers need to be both aware of and reactive to forces in these broader contexts, in our own work we have attempted to give equal emphasis to the teachers' ability to enter into and participate in these venues in a proactive manner. In other words, we see the interface between the teachers' work and the broader contexts as a two-way street in which teachers are both influencing and are influenced by the forces therein. While sometimes difficult to operationalize, such a perspective increases the potential vision and power of the teacher inquiry work by moving it into a broader sphere of awareness and influence.

Various individuals have the opportunity to provide support of this kind. While school administrators can provide support by structuring time within the working day for teacher groups to meet, it is also important that they explicitly value collaborative work in communications with other faculty and coparticipate in the process of sharing the vision and work of the teacher group, particularly with district administrators. Teacher groups who have an external facilitator or critical friend possess a key means of support, as this person is in a unique position both in and out of the teacher group. She or he can play an important role in seeking connections between the teachers' inquiry focus and existing department, school, or district goals, as well as advocating for a public valuing of the work of the teachers. While school and district administrators are fundamental to support of this kind, some administrators may lack the time, commitment, or ability to fully understand or become involved in the teachers' collaborative inquiry. In these cases, external facilitators can help the learning community to "build a non-threatening environment . . . keep the group together . . . and make people's contributions feel valued" (Andrews & Lewis, 2002, p. 248). But in those cases when an external facilitator is not available, the principal emerges as an even more crucial element of support for teachers engaging in collaborative inquiry (Fullan, Hill, & Crévola, 2006; Huffman, Hipp, Pankake, & Moller, 2001; Nelson & Sassi, 2005).

For example, in a middle school with which we recently worked, a group of science teachers decided to collaboratively focus on their students' abilities to write scientific conclusions that met state standards (a more thorough discussion of this case is provided in Nelson et al., this volume). To establish baseline data on students' conclusion-writing skills, the teachers analyzed results from a district-level assessment given in October. As the year progressed, the teachers agreed to use a variety of instructional strategies to help their students more fully understand the standards related to conclusion writing. Some of the teachers did this multiple times, and scored and collected student work as evidence of student needs and progress. Other teachers, not fully committed to the collaborative inquiry process, did not sample students' conclusion writing throughout the year. Additionally, a district-level summative assessment scheduled for March was cancelled that would have provided another data point for the teachers in their assessment of student growth. These circumstances left this group concerned that they would not be able to draw any conclusions regarding their students' development, and a sense of dismay and frustration began to surface. One of the teachers decided to ask the principal to directly intervene, using her position of authority, and encourage the group to proceed with the summative assessment despite the district cancellation. This principal had previously provided both support and commitment to the teacher group through the provision of professional development time and verbal school-wide recognition, and thus had a positive relationship with the teachers. When the teacher group next met, the principal suggested that the science teachers implement one final conclusion writing assessment, couching this in terms of "bringing closure to their inquiry," and offered to provide further resources in support of this process. Because this group of teachers were viewed by others in the school as an exemplar of collaborative inquiry, it was important to the principal that they have evidence of the impact of their work on student learning. The previous summer, the principal had published a brief article in a district-wide publication acknowledging and praising the work of this teacher group. Not only did this principal provide direct support to the teachers' inquiry process, she also successfully linked the teachers' work to the broader school (and even state) educational contexts, expanding the potential importance and impact of the teachers' work. In fact, in our direct experiences with over 40 collaborative inquiry groups, we have witnessed numerous examples of facilitators or critical friends, who were not necessarily the school principal, successfully link the work of teachers to broader educational contexts.

Nurturing an Inquiry Stance

The third kind of support we view as important to SCTI involves the nurturing of an inquiry stance amongst the teacher participants. To discuss this support, we make use of Jaworski's (2006) notions of *inquiry as a tool* and *inquiry as a way of being* to clarify our meaning of inquiry stance. In nearly all cases, collaborative inquiry groups seek various data collection and analytic techniques in constructing a path through a given inquiry cycle. Often this path is quite useful for identifying and addressing various problems and dilemmas important in teachers' individual or collective contexts. Hence, inquiry can be a tool used by teachers to better understand learners, practice, curriculum, or other important educational dimensions. However, Jaworski also discusses the notion of inquiry in ways that transcend its use as a tool.

Specifically, inquiry as a way of being incorporates the notion of inquiry into the very essence of teachers as professional educators, often manifested by an inherent desire to question and better understand. This disposition to ponder and seek transformation underlies the essence of an inquiry stance.

In a collaborative setting, an inquiry stance can be established or enhanced through interactions amongst the teacher participants. In these settings, teachers can display "a willingness to wonder, to ask questions, and to seek to understand by collaborating with others in the attempt to make answers to them" (Wells, 1999, p. 121). Unlike instances where teachers either reject or accept at face value ideas from others, an inquiry stance promotes knowledge negotiation (Nelson, 2005) that stimulates the examination of alternate perspectives and the questioning of one's own knowledge and beliefs in an effort to coconstruct meaning.

Teaching and beliefs about teaching are closely linked (Philipp, 2007), often requiring long-term and supported periods of reflection (Cooney, Shealy, & Arvold, 1998; Raymond, 1997). It can take years of modeling, gentle persuasion, and targeted professional development to shift some teachers' core views about teaching, even slightly. Nurturing an inquiry stance is perhaps more complex, and even controversial, since the development of an inquiry stance requires changes to an individual's very nature. Like attempts to change teachers' beliefs, supporting a stance toward inquiry requires time and reflection, particularly given that an inquiry stance is naturally related to both teaching and beliefs about teaching (Jaworski, 2006).

The previously discussed example of a mathematics specialist serving as facilitator provides a rich example where modeling the questioning process and offering a genuine curiosity toward the work of the teacher group nurtured many teachers toward an inquiry stance. However, we do not imply that simply modeling an inquiry stance is sufficient support for teachers in making a transformation in their way of being, or even in expanding on a developing stance toward inquiry. In addition, we have experienced many teachers enter into an SCTI setting with an established inquiry stance, while we have witnessed others develop one over time. Further, teachers who would not be described as possessing an inquiry stance can be excellent teachers and professional educators. However, we have found the possession of an inquiry stance to be quite important to the inquiry work of either an individual or teacher group (see Lamb et al., this volume, for a thorough discussion).

SUMMARY

Collectively, these three kinds of supports are crucial to the work of teachers engaged in collaborative inquiry. Further, these three supports provide researchers with a theoretical framework for examining the notion of support. The remaining chapters of this book provide case studies that examine the nature and impact of supports in various SCTI contexts using this theoretical lens.

PD MODELS THAT INCORPORATE SCTI

Collaborative teacher inquiry takes many forms. Little (2003), in the context of professional learning communities, refers to the "optimistic premise" of collaborative teacher inquiry, yet emphasizes that what teachers do during and as a result of participation in this kind of PD has been hidden inside a black box for quite some time. There are a variety of models of SCTI currently used in schools and districts to support teacher development. However, while the research base is currently on the rise, we still know very little about the results of these kinds of initiatives on teaching, teaching perspective, and student learning. Nor do we know much about the actual processes that define the teachers' individual and collective experiences while engaged in SCTI. However, an overview of the literature would suggest that the following characteristics of effective PD (Darling-Hammond & McLaughlin, 1995; Hawley & Valli, 1999; Little, Gearhart, Curry, & Kafka, 2003) are also characteristic of SCTI:

1. Has established norms and dispositions that allow for trust building and risk taking.

2. Is grounded in the work teachers do in support of student learning goals.

3. Engages teachers in inquiry and reflection.

4. Is collaborative, intensive, and ongoing.

5. Has access to a variety of usable, relevant supports throughout all phases of the inquiry.

6. Is meaningfully connected to other school and district initiatives.

These overarching characteristics of SCTI can be enacted in various models currently found in the professional development landscape, including communities of practice, professional learning communities, teacher teams (vertical teams, horizontal teams), coaching, lesson study, peer observation, book study, and collaborative action research. While each of these models has its own variations, and all could be performed with or without direct support, we claim that the following represent common approaches to SCTI when supports are present and processes of inquiry take place within the group.

Communities of Practice

This variation of SCTI emphasizes the social interactions of a group of teachers as they intentionally share aspects of their practice in an effort to learn and develop. Learning is usually characterized by a shift in action or a transformation of identity. The teacher group is purposeful about building relationships and supporting one another as they pursue questions around a common domain of interest (Lave & Wenger, 1991; Rogoff, 2003; Wenger, 1998).

Professional Learning Communities (PLCs)

PLCs are perhaps the most common model through which SCTI is now enacted in K–12 schools. PLCs are usually characterized by a shared vision and shared leadership toward a collective activity. PLCs make use of data around a commonly agreed-on inquiry focus to generate information, perspective, and new questions about the collective activity (Eaker, Dufour, & Burnette, 2002; Hord, 1997; Louis & Kruse, 1995).

Teacher Teams

Teacher teams can be both vertical (across grade levels) and horizontal (same grade level, perhaps across content areas). While the term *team* normally refers to the coteaching process, when teacher teams search for common perspectives and vision, raise and pursue questions, and coanalyze student work and other forms of data, this instructional model can be considered a form of SCTI, particularly when some support from school or district personnel is present.

Coaching

When conducted in a manner consistent with SCTI, a school or district will provide a coach to work with a group of teachers on an instructional issue through an analysis of data. Usually the teachers are from the same grade, grade band, or subject area. Coaching usually assumes an expert/novice paradigm and tends to draw more from the expertise of the coach, and specific classroom observations made by the coach, than from the information gleaned from more general data-analysis techniques.

Lesson Study

This popular model of SCTI generally involves a group of teachers examining curricular materials or analyzing student-learning data. Based upon these analyses, the teachers collectively decide upon a common teaching action and design a specific instructional plan. As members of the group implement the lesson, other teachers observe so that the group can collectively analyze the implementation and reflect on the entire process. Based on this analysis, further refinements to the instructional perspective and approach are made, and the process continues (Lewis, 2002; Fernandez & Yoshida, 2004).

Peer Observation and Video Clubs

Peer observation is a model that directly challenges the island-of-practice metaphor that permeates much of K–12 schooling. In this model, teacher groups perform observations in each other's classrooms as points of common experience to stimulate conversation around high-quality teaching and learning. Video clubs (Sherin, 2004) represent a similar model of SCTI, with videotape providing a lasting artifact for repeated analysis of classroom practice.

Book Study

Teachers can employ a book (or article, or any relevant piece of literature) as a stimulus for conversation around shared issues of interest or possible areas of development. Text-based protocols and facilitators can serve to enrich the dialogue. Though not necessarily grounded in data, this model does incorporate a collective reflection on practice stimulated by data-based ideas.

Collaborative Action Research

Action research is grounded in questions embedded in teachers' immediate contexts; it is inquiry into teachers' own practice, usually by pursuing the impacts of a change in one's own instructional approach or method. Performed collaboratively, the added dimensions of critical dialogue and knowledge negotiation (Nelson, 2005) can arise (Sagor, 2004).

ORGANIZATION OF THE BOOK

The following chapters represent theoretically- and empirically-based discussions of SCTI, with a particular emphasis on the nature of support provided to the teacher groups under discussion. Table 1.1 provides an overview of the composition and specific foci of the various SCTI groups included in this book. While SCTI is the thread by which all six of the case-based contributions are joined, variance exists with regard to the specific model of SCTI being discussed, teacher grade level and subject area, and school/district context. Each chapter includes: (a) an introduction and overview of the professional development model under discussion, with attention to the type of SCTI being used; (b) a thorough

Table 1.1 Overview of the SCTI cases contained in the upcoming chapters.

	2 *Lamb et al.*	*3* *McDuffie*	*4* *Nelson et al.*	*5* *Bondy et al.*	*6* *Wenger et al.*	*7* *Slavit et al.*
SCTI Model	Communities of practice	Lesson study, video club	Professional learning community	Coaching; Inclusion meetings	Distance-based networking	Professional learning community
Scope of PD	District-wide	2 math teachers	Science Dept.	School-wide	Region-wide	Science Dept.
Participation	Voluntary	Voluntary	Voluntary to mandatory	Mandatory	Voluntary	Voluntary to mandatory
Inquiry Focus	Classroom interactions, students' mathematical thinking	Mathematics discourse	Negotiating state content standards	Supporting struggling students	Problems of practice	Conclusion writing in science
Inquiry Facilitation	Professional development provider	Teachers, researcher	Teacher leaders, external facilitator	Researcher	Researchers	Teacher leaders, external facilitator
Role of the researcher	Observer	Participant	Observer – participant	Participant	Participant	Observer – participant
Composition of SCTI Team	Cohort groups (data collected from 95 teachers), 1 facilitator	2 middle school mathematics teachers, 1 researcher	11 life and physical science teachers	Grade level teams, school specialists, administrators, researcher	6 beginning teachers, researcher	2 groups of secondary science teachers, administrators
Subject Area	Mathematics	Mathematics	Science	Inclusion	Various	Science
Setting / Grade Level	Urban; K-3	Suburban; 7	Suburban; 7-8	Small Urban; K-5	Rural: K-8	Suburban; 6-12

discussion of the definition of support present in the SCTI; (c) an inside look at one or more groups of teachers as they engage in their inquiry work, illustrative of the SCTI model and descriptive of the nature of support present; and (d) concluding remarks. A concluding, unifying chapter makes use of the theoretical and empirical work in the cases to explore cross-case findings and a future vision for research and professional development work of this kind.

REFERENCES

Andrews, D., & Lewis, M. (2002). The experience of a professional community: Teachers developing a new image of themselves and their workplace. *Educational Research, 44*(3), 237–254.

Ball, D. L., & Cohen, D. K. (1999). Developing practice, developing practitioners: Toward a practice-based theory of professional education. In L. Darling-Hammond & G. Sykes (Eds.), *Teaching as the learning profession: Handbook of policy and practice* (pp. 1–32). San Francisco: Jossey-Bass.

Berliner, D. C., & Biddle, B. J. (1995). *The manufactured crisis: Myths, fraud, and the attack on America's public schools.* Reading, MA: Addison-Wesley.

Borko, H. (2004). Professional development and teacher learning: Mapping the terrain. *Educational Researcher, 33*(8), 3–15.

Bracey, Gerald W. (2006). The 16th Bracey Report on the condition of public education. *Phi Delta Kappan, 88*(2), 151–166.

Cochran-Smith, M., & Lytle, S. (1999). The teacher research movement: A decade later. *Educational Researcher, 28*(7), 15–25.

Cooney, T. J., Shealy, B. E., & Arvold, B. (1998). Conceptualizing belief structures of preservice secondary mathematics teachers. *Journal for Research in Mathematics Education, 29*(3), 306–333.

Darling-Hammond, L., & McLaughlin, M. W. (1995). Policies that support professional teacher development in an era of reform. *Phi Delta Kappan, 76,* 642–644.

Eaker, R., DuFour, R., & Burnette, R. (2002). *Getting started: Reculturing schools to become professional learning communities.* Bloomington, IN: National Educational Service.

Fernandez, C., & Yoshida, M. (2004). *Lesson study: A Japanese approach to improving mathematics teaching and learning.* Hillsdale, NJ: Erlbaum.

Fullan, M. (2001). *Leading in a culture of change.* San Francisco: Jossey-Bass.

Fullan, M., Hill, P., & Crévola, C. (2006). *Breakthrough.* Thousand Oaks, CA: Corwin Press.

Garet, M., Porter, A., Desimone, L., Birman, B., & Yoon, K. S. (2001). What makes professional development effective? Results from a national sample of teachers. *American Education Research Journal, 38*(4), 915–945.

Garmston, R. J., & Wellman, B. M. (1999). *The adaptive school: A sourcebook for developing collaborative groups.* Norwood, MA: Christopher-Gordon Publishers.

Grossman, P., Wineburg, S., & Woolworth, S. (2001). Toward a theory of teacher community. *Teachers College Record, 103*(6), 942–1012.

Hawley, W. D., & Valli, L. (1999). The essentials of effective professional development: A new consensus. In L. Darling-Hammond & G. Sykes (Eds.), *Teaching as the learning profession* (pp. 127–150). San Francisco: Jossey-Bass.

Hord, S. M. (1997). *Professional learning communities: Communities of continuous inquiry and improvement.* Austin, TX: Southwest Educational Development Laboratory.

Huffman, J. B., Hipp, K. A., Pankake, A. M., & Moller, G. (2001). Professional learning communities: Leadership, purposeful decision making, and job-embedded staff development. *Journal of School Leadership, 11*(5), 448–463.

Jaworski, B. (2006). Theory and practice in mathematics teaching development: Critical inquiry as a mode of learning in teaching. *Journal of Mathematics Teacher Education, 9,* 187–211.

Lampert, M., & Ball, D. L. (1998). *Teaching, multimedia, and mathematics: Investigations of real practice.* New York: Teachers College Press.

Lave, J., & Wenger, E. (1991). *Situated learning: Legitimate peripheral participation.* Cambridge, UK: Cambridge University Press.

Lewis, C. (2002). *Lesson study: A handbook of teacher-led instructional change.* Philadelphia: Research for Better Schools.

Little, J. W. (2003). Inside teacher community: Representations of classroom practice. *Teachers College Record, 105*(6), 913–945.

Little, J. W., Gearhart, M., Curry, M., & Kafka, J. (2003). Looking at student work for teacher learning, teacher community, and school reform. *Phi Delta Kappan, 85*(3), 184–192.

Lortie, D. C. (1975). *Schoolteacher: A sociological study.* Chicago: University of Chicago.

Louis, K. S., & Kruse, S. D. (1995). *Professionalism and community: Perspectives on reforming urban schools.* Thousand Oaks, CA: Corwin Press.

McLaughlin, M., & Talbert, J. E. (2006). *Building school-based teacher learning communities: Professional strategies to improve student achievement.* New York: Teachers College Press.

Nelson, B. S., & Sassi, A. (2005). *The effective principal: Instructional leadership for high-quality learning.* New York: Teachers College Press.

Nelson, T. H. (2005). Knowledge interactions in teacher-scientist partnerships: Negotiation, consultation, and rejection. *Journal of Teacher Education, 56*(4), 382–395.

Nelson, T. H., & Slavit, D. (2008). Supported teacher collaborative inquiry. *Teacher Education Quarterly, 35*(10), 99–116.

Philipp, R. A. (2007). Mathematics teachers' beliefs and affect. In F. Lester (Ed.), *Second handbook of research on mathematics teaching and learning* (pp.257–315). Reston, VA: National Council of Teachers of Mathematics.

Raymond, A. M. (1997). Inconsistency between a beginning elementary school teacher's mathematics beliefs and teaching practice. *Journal for Research in Mathematics Education, 28*(5), 550–576.

Rogoff, B. (2003). *The cultural nature of human development.* Oxford: Oxford University Press.

Sagor, R. (2004). *The action research guidebook: A four-step process for educators and school teams.* Thousand Oaks, CA: Corwin Press.

Sarason, S. B. (1996). *Revisiting "The culture of the school and the problem of change."* New York: Teachers College Press.

Sherin, M. (2004). Teacher learning in the context of a video club. *Teaching and Teacher Education, 20*(2), 163–183.

Smith, T., & Ingersoll, R. (2004). What are the effects of induction and mentoring on beginning teacher turnover? *American Educational Research Journal, 41*(2), 681–714.

Stigler, J., & Hiebert, J. (1999). *The teaching gap: Best ideas from the world's teachers for improving education in the classroom.* New York: The Free Press.

Supovitz, J. A., & Turner, H. M. (2000). The effects of professional development on science teaching practices and classroom culture. *Journal of Research on Science Teaching, 37*(9), 963–980.

Thompson, C. L., & Zeuli, J. S. (1999). The frame and the tapestry: Standards-based reform and professional development. In L. Darling-Hammond & G. Sykes (Eds.), *Teaching as the learning profession* (pp. 341–375). San Francisco: Jossey-Bass.

Wells, G. (1999). *Dialogic inquiry: Towards a sociocultural practice and theory of education.* Cambridge, UK: Cambridge University Press.

Wenger, E. (1998). *Communities of practice: Learning, meaning, and identity.* Cambridge, UK: Cambridge University Press.

Wilson, S. M., & Berne, J. (1999). Teacher learning and the acquisition of professional knowledge: An examination of research on contemporary professional development. In A. Iran-Nejad & P. D. Pearson (Eds.), *Review of research in education* (pp. 173–210). Washington, DC: AERA.

2 Developing Teachers' Stances of Inquiry
Studying Teachers' Evolving Perspectives (STEP)[1]

Lisa Clement Lamb, Randolph A. Philipp,
Victoria R. Jacobs, and Bonnie P. Schappelle

San Diego State University

A fundamental goal for teacher professional development is for teachers to learn how to continue learning from their practices. However, professional development is too often designed to help teachers learn to implement particular teaching techniques, often in single sessions (Hawley & Valli, 1999; Hill, 2004). Designers are beginning to understand the importance of offering professional development that engages teachers in inquiry and reflection and that is sustained, collaborative, grounded in the work of teachers, and connected to school and district initiatives (Darling-Hammond & McLaughlin, 1996; Hawley & Valli, 1999). Such professional development experiences enable teachers to continue to grow and inquire about their practices even after formal professional development has ended (Franke, Carpenter, Levi, & Fennema, 2001).

BRINGING INQUIRY INTO A COMMUNITY OF PRACTICE

Defining Communities of Practice

One way that researchers talk about supporting the collaborative and sustained nature of effective professional development experiences is through *communities of practice* (Lave & Wenger, 1991; Wenger, 1998). In a community of practice, both knowledge and experience are highly valued and learning is usually characterized by shifts in participation (Rogoff, 1997; Kazemi & Franke, 2004) or transformation of the identities of its members (Wells, 1999; Wenger, 1998). When a community of practice develops, it provides the foundation for teachers who are members of the community to, we argue, develop a stance of inquiry (described following).

Distinguishing Inquiry as a Process and Stance

In effective professional development experiences teachers are encouraged to develop a stance of inquiry (Ball & Cohen, 1999; Wilson & Berne, 1999) to effectively respond to students, and to learn in and from their practices. Nelson and Slavit (2008) found that *supported collaborative inquiry* strongly influences teachers' engagement in sustained professional development opportunities. They asserted a need for both internal and external supports for the development of the collaborative-inquiry process (see Chapter 1 for details).

Others have similarly called for teachers to focus on inquiry within professional development and in their classrooms, and we begin with distinctions regarding inquiry that may be thought of as a set of practices versus a stance. Although one may inform the other, *inquiry as a set of practices* is often thought of as an investigation that teachers conduct to answer a particular question related to their teaching practice (for example, *action research* as described by Zeichner, Klehr, & Caro-Bruce, 2000). The discrete activity of activating a set of processes to answer a particular question evokes a sense of a time element, wherein a beginning and end could well be identified in an investigation surrounding a question about which one has inquired.

In contrast, Cochran-Smith and Lytle (1999, 2001) and Wells (1999) described inquiry not as a set of actions or activities to be completed, but as a *perspective toward teaching and learning* in which key practices, processes, and ways of working are viewed as a *stance of inquiry*. Cochran-Smith and Lytle (1999) wrote, "The metaphor [of stance] is intended to capture the ways we stand, the ways we see, and the lenses we see through" (1999, p. 288). Practices that provide evidence of an inquiry stance include learning to question one's own and others' assumptions and beliefs about teaching, learning, and schooling; taking a critical stance on the work of others; and not accepting scripted materials or research as the final word on what teachers should do. Wells (1999) wrote that an inquiry stance also indicates "a willingness to wonder, to ask questions, and to seek to understand by collaborating with others in the attempt to make answers to them" (p. 121). Cochran-Smith and Lytle (1999, 2001) stated that teachers with an inquiry stance look more deeply than at test scores or correct answers for evidence of student learning; they may look for other indicators of students' understandings, including what students say and how they reason about problems or questions. It is the development of genuine curiosity about their own teaching and their own students coupled with the development of lenses for answering those questions about which they are curious that makes the development of an inquiry stance powerful.

Cochran-Smith and Lytle (1999) acknowledged that teaching from an inquiry stance is difficult, making every decision messy and potentially troubling and, further, "associated more with uncertainty than certainty, more with posing problems and dilemmas than with solving them, and also with the recognition that inquiry both stems from and generates questions" (1999, p. 294). The development of an inquiry stance provides teachers with an opportunity for generative growth (Franke et al., 2001)—a stance toward their own learning that enables them to take ownership of their knowledge; pose questions of interest to their local circumstances related to teaching and learning; generate answers to their own questions; use their classrooms, students, and colleagues as sites for learning; and realize that they can "construct knowledge through their own activity" (Franke et al., 2001, p. 656).

Relationship between Communities of Practice and Inquiry Stance

We view two indications of learning within a community of practice—shifts in participation and transformation in identity—as highly congruous with Cochran-Smith and Lytle's notion of inquiry as stance. Thus, one might expect to see the development of an inquiry stance characterized by shifts in participation and by transformations in identity, and these shifts and transformations may be visible in the classroom or outside the classroom.[2] Examples of shifts in participation are teachers posing different kinds of questions to students in an effort to learn from and with their students, or teachers discussing with other teachers their changing expectations for students' classroom participation. Examples of teachers' transforming their identities are teachers' becoming less dependent on the text as the arbiter of knowledge, questioning previously taken-for-granted practices, and becoming curious about individual children's mathematical understandings and how to extend those. These shifts in participation and transformations of identity encompass many aspects of developing a stance of inquiry. When we refer to the term *inquiry,* we use Cochran-Smith and Lytle's notion of *inquiry as stance* because development of a stance of inquiry was a goal in the professional development experience described in this chapter.

FOCUS OF PROFESSIONAL DEVELOPMENT ON CHILDREN'S MATHEMATICAL THINKING

Our goals in this chapter are (a) to provide evidence that the professional development experience described herein supported the development of an inquiry stance, (b) to identify features of the professional development experience that contributed to teachers' growth in developing an inquiry stance, and (c) to consider implications for others who are similarly engaged with teachers. To accomplish these three goals, we first describe the sustained professional development experience which existed within communities of practice focused on children's mathematical thinking.

During the past few decades, mathematics educators have gained substantial knowledge about both children's mathematical thinking within specific content domains and the power of teachers' regularly eliciting and building on children's thinking (Grouws, 1992; Lester, 2007; National Research Council [NRC], 2001). In response, Schifter (2001) and others have argued that professional development projects should include helping teachers "learn to attend to the mathematics in what children say and do" (p. 71). The communities of practice focused on children's mathematical thinking we describe were adapted from Cognitively Guided Instruction (CGI). CGI has regularly been identified as providing opportunities for teachers to grow in their beliefs, knowledge, and practice (Carpenter, Fennema, Peterson, Chiang, & Loef, 1989; Fennema, Carpenter, Franke, Levi, Jacobs, & Empson, 1996; Jacobs, Franke, Carpenter, Levi, & Battey, 2007; Villaseñor & Kepner, 1993). Researchers who initially provided this type of professional development for teachers (Carpenter, Fennema, Franke, Levi, & Empson, 2000) wrote,

> There does not exist one way of implementing CGI. Our intent is not to get teachers to adopt a set of teaching behaviors or moves. Rather, we provide a framework so teachers can think about their students' understandings of mathematics and then make instructional decisions based on the underlying principles. We strive to create *inquiry* [italics added] about teaching so teachers are thinking about why they would do certain things and how that relates to the children's learning of mathematics. (p. 4)

By providing a framework for delving into the complex practices associated with teaching and learning mathematics, CGI professional development, instead of offering specific lessons or scripted questions, supports teachers in the process of developing an inquiry stance toward teaching and learning.

METHODS

The data were drawn from Studying Teachers' Evolving Perspectives (STEP), a large, multi-year study in which we used a cross-sectional design to investigate the perspectives of teachers engaged in sustained professional development for various lengths of time. The 95 K–3 teachers, all volunteers for the professional development experience, ranged from those about to begin professional development to those who had actively participated in sustained professional development for nine years. The teachers in this study had a mean of 14–16 years of teaching experience, with a range of 4–33 years.

Data Sources and Analysis

Data sources included field notes of a subset of the professional development sessions, individual interviews conducted with participants at various points during their professional development experience, written responses to questions posed regarding student work, focus-group discussions of participants who were engaged in their first year of professional development, classroom observations, and interviews with the facilitator. The interviews were audiotaped and transcribed. In addition, the focus group discussions were audiotaped and portions were transcribed.

For data analysis, we used grounded theory methodology and open coding (Strauss & Corbin, 1998) to better understand the teachers' development of a stance of inquiry. Consistent with this methodology, we searched for recurring themes in the initial data analysis. Using these themes, we formed hypotheses and analyzed the data according to these hypotheses. With subsequent passes through the data, we revised hypotheses while we looked for confirming and disconfirming evidence. This iterative process served to empirically establish our claims.

Setting

Most of the participants came from elementary schools within a single district. Because of its success, the goals of the professional development were eventually aimed at building a cadre of teachers who could go back to their school sites and potentially influence other teachers. Participants engaged in professional development for an equivalent of about five full days per year (in either half- or full-day increments). Between professional development sessions, teachers read an article or chapter and posed problems to their students, and they brought their students' written work to the next session. During professional development sessions, teachers engaged by solving mathematics problems, reading research, and analyzing video and written student work derived from their own classrooms as well as from artifacts provided by the facilitator. With the help of their colleagues, teachers also worked to make sense of their students' thinking from the written work in ways that highlighted core mathematical ideas and children's understandings related to those ideas.

The facilitator's overarching goals for the professional development were to help teachers (a) learn how children think about and develop understandings in particular mathematical domains; (b) learn how to appropriately elicit and respond to children's ideas in ways that support those understandings; and (c) to develop an inquiry stance toward teaching and learning. Children's mathematical thinking served as the focus for interactions in the professional development. The conversations were informed by research on children's thinking, and the teachers worked together to make explicit the similarities and differences in children's strategies. Teachers were given opportunities to recognize the power of attending to the subtle details in children's strategies—details that reflected mathematically relevant differences in the understandings children bring to their problem solutions. Teachers also engaged in conversations about how mathematical tasks, classroom interactions, and classroom norms could be used to support and extend children's understandings within particular mathematical domains; although teachers shared practices, no single practice was deemed *the* practice that others should adopt. Special attention was paid to what children could do rather than to what they could not do, and teachers discussed how to reconceptualize children's struggles as opportunities to identify understandings (not misunderstandings) children held and then questions teachers could pose to elicit and build on those understandings.

Facilitator

The facilitator for the sessions we describe facilitated almost all sessions for the teachers in our large-scale study, and, in general, her approach across groups was similar. In the first few years of the teachers' participation in the professional development, the facilitator served as the district's program specialist in mathematics and science; in later years, her role was exclusively defined to support professional development experiences focused on children's mathematical thinking. Many of the activities and resources she selected are common in CGI professional development (see, e.g., Carpenter, Fennema, Franke, & Empson, 1995; Fennema, Carpenter, Levi, Franke, & Empson, 1999), but she adapted materials to account for her particular context.

EFFECTS OF ENGAGEMENT IN COMMUNITIES OF PRACTICE

In this professional development setting, teachers began by investigating and understanding children's mathematical thinking as an overarching lens. Shifts occur over the years of participation in communities of practice focused on children's mathematical thinking such that teachers increasingly take more ownership for their time together, the questions they pose to their students, and so on. Over time, teachers identify questions of interest to them, but the questions are specific to their particular contexts and students. For example, teachers choose which children they will interview but may have fine-grained questions about the particular understandings of different children. When participation in the community progresses, teachers also determine which numbers to use in problems they pose to their students[3] (and become increasingly sophisticated in their choices), how to organize learning environments to elicit and build on children's mathematical thinking, and how to orchestrate discussions—these decisions are not predetermined through a set CGI program but, rather, develop over time through engaging with other teachers focused on understanding children's mathematical thinking. Although the overarching goal of teachers in these communities of practice is to learn about and use children's mathematical thinking as a means for modifying practice so that students more fully engage in rich mathematical experiences leading to increased mathematical proficiency (NRC, 2001), the focus of each teacher's inquiry concerning her students, teaching, and classroom is specific to and determined by that teacher. Following we provide examples that highlight shifts in participation and transformation in identity and data regarding the development of an inquiry stance associated with these communities of practice. The shifts in participation reported in this study are similar to those identified in a study of a similar children's thinking professional development experience by Kazemi and Franke (2004), and we build from their findings. Kazemi and Franke (2004) identified two shifts in participation: One shift occurred when the group learned to attend to the details in children's strategies, and a second shift occurred when teachers began to hypothesize instructional trajectories for their students. In the section following, we share aspects of the professional development we deemed significant in supporting these shifts, transformations, and development of an inquiry stance.

SHIFTS IN PARTICIPATION

To provide the reader a sense for both what happened in these sessions and the differences in participation we identified between teachers beginning participation in a community of practice and teachers who had engaged in a community for two to five years, we provide a detailed picture of two professional development sessions: (a) the first of five full-day sessions to be held throughout the school year for teachers who were just beginning their first year of professional development focused on children's mathematical thinking and (b) the third of five full-day sessions of a group of emerging teacher leaders who had participated in professional development for at least two years (some for as many as five) and had been selected by school-site administrators to assume leadership roles at their sites. We share details about these two days to provide the reader with a sense for how teachers initially begin engaging with ideas from the professional development and how that work evolved to give a sense for the shifts in participation that can be identified by comparing the two sessions.

Year 1 Session

A fairly typical first day of professional development focused on children's mathematical thinking includes watching video clips, making predictions about whether the teachers' students could solve particular problems, and introducing the CGI problem-types classification (see footnote 5 for examples of the ways in which problems are classified). In the session described below, 38 K–3 teachers engaged in this first day of professional development.

Session Description

The facilitator introduced herself and shared her background as a teacher and a staff developer for the district. She noted that she would not provide a new curriculum or program but would instead share ideas that could be incorporated into teachers' current practices. She then transitioned to ask the teachers to solve a story problem in two ways. Teachers shared their strategies, and the facilitator helped them to understand one another's strategies and to make connections across strategies.

The facilitator then distributed a set of three problems (differing by grade level) and asked the teachers to predict and record whether *each* of their students could solve each problem and then to explain their class-wide predictions by problem. After teachers made their predictions and discussed them in small groups and with the group as a whole, the facilitator introduced their task to complete prior to the next session—to pose these problems to their students.

Teachers were next asked to rank order each of the following problems from easiest to most difficult and to explain their rankings:[4]

(a) Carla has 7 dollars. How many more dollars does she have to earn so that she will have 11 dollars to buy a puppy?

(b) Mr. Gomez had 20 cupcakes. He put the cupcakes into 4 boxes so there were the same number of cupcakes in each box. How many cupcakes did Mr. Gomez put in each box?

(c) Paco had 13 cookies. He ate 6 of them. How many cookies does Paco have left?

(d) Tad had 15 guppies. He put 3 guppies in each jar. How many jars did Tad put guppies in?

(e) Robin has 3 packages of gum. There are 6 pieces of gum in each package. How many pieces of gum does Robin have altogether?

(f) Hannah has 12 balloons. Jacob has 7 balloons. How many more balloons does Hannah have than Jacob?

Teachers discussed their choices, then watched a video of a kindergart-ner solving the problems. Teachers learned about various problem types by sorting problems, describing their classification schemes, watching video clips of another child solving problems (some of which she could not solve for reasons at least partially explainable by the problem type), and discussing the problem-type classification of Carpenter et al. (1999).[5] The classification is based on the ways children view the problems and the distinctions children tend to make when solving them. The facilitator then shared research findings on kindergartners' performance in solving these problems; she gave percentages correct and percentages of those who used an appropriate strategy but miscounted (Carpenter, Ansell, Franke, Fennema, & Weisbeck, 1993) to emphasize a focus on children's strate-gies rather than answers. The teachers were surprised that so many kin-dergartners solved these problems successfully. The teachers continued to watch video clips of children solving problems using various strategies and to discuss the strategies and implicit and explicit understandings reflected in the strategies.

At the end of the session, the teachers shared the ideas they would remember from the day's experience. They included notions that children think differently than adults think, students' natural strategies do not necessarily match cultural algorithms, teacher questioning is an important component of instruction, teachers in their classrooms act as observers and as researchers, and to get children to focus on the process and not on the answer is difficult.

In addition to the classroom investigations described earlier, the facilitator assigned for homework two chapters to read (Carpenter, Fennema, Franke, Levi, & Empson, 1999) about story-problem classifications and children's strategies for solving problems.

Comments

Although the facilitator organized and selected the activities and led most of the components of the first day of professional development, several features of the session provide a sense for how shifts in participation may change over time. For example, within the first hour of participation, teachers were asked to make predictions about whether and how their own students might solve problems and were then provided a framework for beginning to interpret their students' responses to the problems. The tasks provided not only immediate relevance for teachers but also a new lens for inquiring about students' mathematical reasoning. The act of asking teachers to make predictions was a first step in inviting teachers to explore their students' thinking in different ways. Often, at the beginning of professional development, teachers' predictions are incorrect, and those differences begin to engender curiosity and excitement that teachers share at subsequent sessions. When their understanding of their students' mathematical thinking grows and becomes more nuanced, the teachers' sharing (and thus their participation) takes on a more central role in the professional development.

The remainder of the first-year sessions and the second-year sessions of professional development were characterized by teachers' continuing focus on inquiring into their students' mathematical thinking, with increasing emphasis on not only understanding their children's thinking but also considering ways to encourage children to use particular strategies that would advance their thinking in developmentally appropriate ways. Although some problems and number choices may more effectively extend children's reasoning than others (and teachers assumed increasing responsibility for selecting the problems and number choices), no single correct problem or set of numbers is ideal. In CGI professional development, teachers are supported in their roles as problem posers who are curious about and attend to their children' strategies by considering profoundly how one might respond to a child after coming to understand the child's strategy. Teachers work to support learning trajectories for their students through making instructional decisions that are consistent with both their knowledge of their own students and the research base on children's mathematical thinking (Carpenter et al., 1993; Carpenter et al., 1999; Carpenter, Franke, & Levi, 2003; Empson, 1995). The work is both challenging and empowering, and teachers in the community come to appreciate the support of one another while they tackle the challenges.

Session for Emerging Teacher Leaders

We next describe a session (the third in the year) with 24 kindergarten through fifth-grade teachers who had engaged in a community of practice focused on children's mathematical thinking for at least two years (some for as many as five) and were beginning to initiate activities aligned with this professional development at their school sites. We share this session to provide aspects of the transformation of practice that occurred. The transformations included a taken-as-shared vision of teaching and learning; joint decision making; and a shared repertoire of artifacts, language, and ways of interacting.

Session Description

Prior to this session, teachers had jointly decided to host a family math night, to collaborate with another teacher at their sites, and to pose multiplication problems to their students using numbers that the teachers selected at the preceding professional development session. Several teachers had already held the family math night at their sites, and others were about to do so. During whole-group sharing, teachers discussed both logistics and outcomes. Participants then made plans to lead, at their sites, staff-development sessions during which teachers would read and discuss a problem-solving chapter from a mathematics resource book (Van de Walle, 2004). They discussed in whole group and small groups how they might facilitate such a discussion.

In grade-level groups, teachers next examined their students' work on multiplication and categorized strategies by their levels of sophistication. Each group created a poster of their students' work (grouped by levels of sophistication), including representative student work; shared their poster; and discussed the strategies shown. During the sharing, teachers explored how to facilitate movement from one level to the next level of sophistication and discussed ideas for having students share strategies, the role of notation, and the variety of algorithms for multiplication.

The teachers discussed further how they could use student work during their site-based staff-development sessions. The discussion included whether participation in the sessions should be voluntary, whether to have teachers engage in grade-level or mixed-grade groups, what features of the poster-creation task made it productive, how to reduce competitiveness among teachers, what questions a facilitator could pose to support productive conversations about the student work teachers bring to the staff-development session, how to integrate discussions of place-value understanding with the student-work discussion, and what mathematics tasks teachers could use with students to support place-value understanding.

Comments

The Emerging Teacher Leader group is characterized by a focus on supporting other teachers while continuing to learn about their own children's mathematical thinking. When compared with the roles of community members in Year 1 of professional development, the differences in participation become apparent. For example, the facilitator's role has shifted from a leader and primary decision-maker toward that of a participant—the facilitator joined a teacher-leader group during the sharing about family math nights and took on a role of contributor to discussions more so than group leader. The participants themselves took leads in discussions and, to a great extent, determined the direction of the conversations. Further, the discussion about their students' multiplication strategies began with a taken-as-shared understanding of children's strategies and attention to details of strategies and a common goal of fostering students' increasingly sophisticated strategies. Thus, shifts in participation included shifts in roles the participants adopted, the shared leadership taken within the community, and the shifts in discussion about student work from "muddling-through" strategies to considering multiple paths for facilitating increasing sophistication in strategies.

TRANSFORMATION OF IDENTITY

A second characteristic of the development of a community of practice is a transformation of identity, whereby participants begin to view themselves as both problem posers and problem solvers; they begin to view their students and colleagues as sites for learning and see their own knowledge base as one that can continually grow through their interactions with their students and with their colleagues. For example, one teacher provides evidence of her identity transformation in her recognition that she can negotiate a challenging teaching moment by drawing upon her children's-thinking lens:

> We had some great fun with measurement this week. The kids were supposed to measure things around the room so that we could have a way of "talking about their size" and comparing them. One kid used yardsticks (what she already knew) and when the yardstick was too short, she started adding on bears! I freaked out [because I did not know what to do]. I've never done measurement [by giving kids choices in how they would measure things around the room], so I just asked a zillion questions and we had a dynamic discussion!! It's funny how questioning helps me solve problems and situations with the kids when

I feel powerless, stumped, or confused myself. I'm always learning with this! (teacher engaged in a community of practice for 3 years)

The teacher's comments reflect curiosity about her students' thinking, recognition that she has the power to investigate that thinking, and realization that the work of teaching is filled simultaneously with challenges and opportunities to learn. When this teacher noted, "It's funny how questioning helps me solve problems and situations with the kids when I feel powerless, stumped, or confused myself," she indicated a recognition that her identity as a teacher had begun to evolve in ways that enabled her to ponder questions about teaching that, prior to her professional development, she would likely have avoided. Note that this teacher was willing to create a learning environment that was based on making public her students' mathematical reasoning, but in so doing, she found herself in a pedagogical quandary that, at least momentarily, left her feeling powerless and confused. She found her way through this challenge, however, and we contend that the experiences within the community of practice provided support for the codevelopment of the teacher's practices and her identity. When her identity evolved, she believed even more in making space for her students to reason mathematically, and so she provided more such occasions. These occasions seldom come with a road map for knowing how to build on students' mathematical reasoning, but when she became more confident in her ability to work with these situations, she was more willing to trust where her evolving identity as a teacher was leading her. In this way her changing practice and her identity transformation supported each other. We also note in this teacher's response a passion about what she and her students are learning. Wells (1999) wrote:

> Where everyone is involved in personally significant inquiry, there is an additional satisfaction and excitement in sharing what one is doing with others, in hearing what others are doing, and in discovering how these doings and understandings can be related. Herein lies the pleasure as well as the motive for collaboration. (p. 122)

This teacher confirmed her satisfaction and excitement in inquiring about her students' learning and her eagerness to share her "doings" with others by enthusiastically sharing this classroom interaction without prompting from others in the community.

DEVELOPMENT OF AN INQUIRY STANCE

An inquiry stance is not necessarily one that grows solely with teaching experience, and, as our data show, it takes years to develop, even within communities of practice. We asked 95 grades K–3 teachers to respond to questions about three samples of Grade 2 students' written work when solving this multiplication problem: *Todd has 6 bags of M&Ms. Each bag has 43 M&Ms. How many M&Ms does Todd have?*, and to a video of a Grades 1–2 classroom wherein three strategies were shared in response to the problem: *There are 19 kids in class today. 7 have hot lunch. How many brought cold lunch?* The written responses were analyzed for, among other purposes, indications of an inquiry stance. In particular, we identified three categories of responses—those that provided evidence of a robust stance of inquiry, those that provided evidence of a limited stance of inquiry, and those that provided no evidence of a stance of inquiry. The patterns that emerged provide a sense for the time and support teachers need to develop such a stance and the recognition that teaching experience alone is insufficient for that development. In identifying instances of an inquiry stance, we looked for one or more of the following: (a) "wondering" language that may come in the form of posing questions about students' strategies or sentences that began, "I wonder whether," or "I am curious about . . ."; (b) tentative language to capture the notion that alternative explanations may exist for a set of student work; and (c) hypotheses about how students might solve future problems as both an indication of their curiosity about students' future work and their weighing of multiple alternatives. The results are provided in Table 2.1.

We consider several findings noteworthy. First, whereas about three-fourths of the Advancing Participants and almost all of the Emerging Teacher Leaders provided at least some evidence of a stance of inquiry, fewer than one-fourth of the Initial Participants provided any such evidence. Further, no Initial Participants and only one-fifth of the Advancing Participants but more than half of the Emerging Teacher Leaders provided evidence of a robust stance of inquiry. The results show that a community of practice focused on children's mathematical thinking does, in fact, support the development of an inquiry stance. However, stances of inquiry evolve over time, and although some changes took place within the first 2

Table 2.1 Depth of an Inquiry Stance

	Initial Participants (n = 31)	Advancing Participants (n = 31)	Emerging Teacher Leaders (n = 33)
Robust stance	0%	19%	58%
Limited stance	23%	55%	39%
No evidence of a stance of inquiry	77%	26%	3%

Note. Initial Participants were experienced teachers about to engage in professional development focused on children's mathematical thinking, Advancing Participants had engaged for two years, and Emerging Teacher Leaders had engaged for four or more years. All three groups had a mean of 14–16 years of teaching experience.

years, more robust changes required more than two years of involvement in a community of practice.

The following quote from an interview with an Emerging Teacher Leader provides a sense for the rich returns of a community that seeks to support inquiry:

> [Participating in the professional development for the last several years has] totally changed who I am as a teacher, as a math teacher. . . . It's just opened up this whole new curiosity that there's no way I would have had otherwise, and I sometimes wonder, "Would I have burned out of teaching?" I think this [participation in the professional development] to some degree has . . . saved me as a teacher. I think maybe teaching math is what's kept me in teaching. It has been the best thing . . . that I've done. It's being a part of this and having the time to talk to other teachers and learn from [the facilitator] and learn from each other. (teacher engaged in a community of practice for 6 years)

This teacher shared the role that the community of practice played in both developing her curiosity (stance) as a teacher and supporting her learning. The powerful statements about how the community supported her passion for staying in the profession speak to the need for teachers to have opportunities to engage as inquirers within communities of practice focused on children's thinking and are representative of the benefits that accrue through such experiences. In our research, we have also found that teachers engaged in a sustained community of practice focused on children's mathematical thinking as compared with nonparticipating teachers were (a) better able to attend to the details of children's mathematical thinking and to interpret children's mathematical understandings (Jacobs, Lamb, Philipp, Schappelle, & Burke, 2007; Jacobs, Lamb, Philipp, & Schappelle, 2008); (b) more likely to articulate instructional goals based on the specifics of children's mathematical thinking (Jacobs et al., 2007); and (c) more likely to articulate, for a struggling student, detailed support that provided space for the child's thinking to emerge (Jacobs et al., 2008); further, the participating teachers learned mathematics content from the professional development, even though developing teachers' mathematical content knowledge was not the primary goal of the professional development (Philipp, Schappelle, Siegfried, Jacobs, & Lamb, 2008).

SUPPORT FOR TEACHERS' DEVELOPMENT OF AN INQUIRY STANCE

In the preceding sections, we shared examples of a shift in participation, a transformation of identity, and evidence of the development of an inquiry stance to indicate the power of communities of practice focused on children's mathematical thinking. However, the process for how the communities grew and were nurtured is complex, and in this section, we share three features of the professional development that appeared to contribute to the teachers' and the communities' development: the children's-mathematical-thinking lens of the professional development; the facilitator's role as perceived colleague in developing a high-functioning, collaborative community; and the role of forces external to the communities of practice in supporting the inquiry environment.

First, the focus of the professional development on children's mathematical thinking, informed primarily by the CGI literature, provided a lens through which teachers could inquire about their own students' thinking and related issues of teaching. Some features of this set of professional development experiences are typical for professional development focused on students' mathematical thinking. A significant research base has shown the effectiveness of CGI in changing teachers' knowledge, beliefs, practice, and inquiry stance (for an overview, see Wilson & Berne, 1999).

Second, although the investigation into children's mathematical thinking is an important component of professional development that supports teachers in becoming inquirers in their classrooms, the role of facilitator is likewise important in supporting the development of a community of practice. We could have considered other features of the professional development (such as the nature of the tasks, the role of student work, and the like), but because all those factors were mediated through the facilitator and her ability to develop an inquiry community, we highlight her role.

Finally, we report on the external stakeholders' roles in providing significant, but often not discussed, supports. Forces external to the community play an important role in whether and how teachers engage with ideas in their communities of practice. The history with regard to external support for the inquiry environment is not straightforward, and support came from various external stakeholders over the years. We describe the kinds of support the facilitator and the teachers in this community received from external sources.

CHILDREN'S-MATHEMATICAL-THINKING LENS

This professional development focused on children's mathematical thinking and used frameworks from the CGI literature. It included (a) using the research base on children's mathematical thinking to inform discussion of individual student's thinking and classroom situations (either from video clips or from the participating teachers' classrooms), written student work (typically collected by the participants), individual student interviews, articles, or chapters, and (b) tasks that connected to the research base and to the teachers' classrooms to be completed between sessions. These features of the professional development provided opportunities for teachers to become curious about their own students' thinking and how it might develop, thus providing opportunities to develop a stance of inquiry toward their students and classrooms. Thus, for example, the facilitator shared frameworks related to students' mathematical thinking but did not share prescriptions for how teachers should engage with their students. Teachers engaged in conversations that drew on the research base, but decisions about how to incorporate the ideas were left to each teacher to ponder and determine.

During Sessions

Whether discussing early-number development, place value, fractions, or early algebra, the facilitator based the community of practice on research focused on children's mathematical thinking in the relevant area. The descriptions of the sessions in a previous section provided a sense for the extent to which the research base was utilized. For example, in a Year 1 session, the teachers were asked to classify a set of problems in at least two ways before the facilitator shared a research-based classification scheme of problem types (Carpenter et al., 1999; see footnote 4 for a brief description of problem types).

One teacher shared in a detailed way how the knowledge base of problem types had played out in her understanding of her students:

> I think that a lot of what I have learned is just simply how children think—just realizing that what I always thought, "This problem, this problem, this problem are all the same. Why don't you guys get it?"— that the children are completely looking at it in a different way. It's really helped me realize, as I watch their little wheels turn, that they are not seeing it as the same [problem] that I am and with the same relationship to other things that I see. To them, [each problem type] is something new and different—the different types of problems. They really do look at them and approach them differently. And that's been really good for me to see because it's kind of opened my eyes to realize that instead of beating my head against the wall, I've got to realize that I'm teaching something different. (Teacher engaged in Year 1 of professional development)

Although this teacher had more than 18 years of teaching experience, she acknowledged that the children's-thinking lens was providing her with opportunities to notice features of different types of problems and of her children's thinking related to those problems that in previous years of teaching she had not considered. Teaching experience alone was insufficient to orient the teacher toward thinking about aspects of problems for which children's approaches differed from hers. Her comments illuminate the reflexive relationship between the research base and her ability to inquire into her students' thinking—that is, the research base gave her a lens through which she could begin to ask and answer more detailed questions about her own students. First, she was able to answer a question that she had long held (i.e., Why do my students inconsistently solve what I view as all the same types of problems?). Second, implied in her comments is that in opening her eyes, she now has the opportunity to ask different questions of her students; to inquire in a different, more nuanced way, about their strategies; and to have a language for sharing strategies with her community members. In essence, the research base enables her to "wonder" more deeply about her students.

Between Sessions

One major benefit of the sustained professional development is that the teachers could engage with a variety of tasks between sessions. These tasks most often took the form of engaging students in problem solving and collecting their written work to discuss during the next session, conducting individual student interviews, and reading related literature—all of which helped teachers inquire about their own students' mathematical thinking. The gathering and then sharing of what they learned from these tasks served four purposes. First, the sharing provided a venue in which to compare their children's thinking and strategies with those observed by other teachers and to debrief about what they learned. This debriefing often took the form of sharing surprises and developing hypotheses or asking questions about what they learned, which often sparked a previously unexperienced curiosity about students and teaching. Second, the debriefing held teachers accountable to the inquiry community, and so although teachers had busy schedules, they incorporated the engagement of students in problem solving and collecting their written work, the conducting of interviews, or the reading of chapters into their days, in part because they would be returning to the community to share. Third, the tasks provided a way to continue conversations at school sites between sessions because teachers were more likely to share what they were learning about their students' mathematical thinking when they had similar tasks with which to engage their students. Fourth, the tasks provided a common and meaningful context around which teachers could discuss issues of teaching and learning. The tasks thus provided an opportunity for teachers to explicitly connect what they were learning in the professional development with their classrooms and students and, thus, contributed to shifts in participation by way of forging a common set of experiences from which to communicate.

When teachers began to scrutinize student work and conduct student interviews, they were able to learn more about their students. One teacher shared her surprise that a child whom she considered to be quite low in mathematical performance could actually solve several problems with large numbers. She stated:

The low child in particular—I didn't expect him to do some of these double-digit problems. I didn't think he would be able to use the bigger numbers, but he still got 3 out of 5 right! I was amazed that he could do multiplication and he could do dividing out for division. Every test we take he gets an Unsatisfactory, less than 50% on math, so it is interesting that he does have ability. (teacher engaged in Year 1 professional development)

The between-sessions tasks served as a way for this teacher to learn something about this student that, after 25 years of teaching, surprised her. As Cochran-Smith and Lytle (2001) noted as evidence of an inquiry stance, this teacher was able to look beyond traditional tests and include the interview as an indicator of learning. This opportunity to talk with her students provided a way that she had never previously experienced to inquire into her children's mathematical thinking. The unexpected response from a student she perceived as low may have caused some disequilibrium, which provided her an opportunity for learning (Ball & Cohen, 1999).

FACILITATOR AS PERCEIVED COLLEAGUE

The facilitator's role is one that has received scant attention in the literature (for exceptions, see Franke & Kazemi, 2001; Stein & Mundry, 1999); we focus on one aspect—the facilitator as perceived colleague—that appeared to support the development of a community of practice, which fostered the growth in teachers becoming inquirers into their own classrooms. The role we identified is far from sufficient, however, in considering all the qualities one would want in a professional development facilitator. For example, the facilitator needs general skills such as selecting appropriate tasks, facilitating discussions by asking questions and keeping participants on the subject, planning, time management—certainly necessary features of any successful professional development initiative. We, however, consider an aspect often overlooked—perhaps because it is not a skill per se but a stance toward professional development—and we think that this role is both significant and complementary to the goals of CGI.

First, as an indication of the value to teachers of the communities of practice described herein, across all years of teachers' participation, the teacher dropout rate is less than 10%, very low when one considers the competition for teachers' time. When asked about her own perceptions of the reasons for high rates of continued participation in the sustained professional development and the documented differences between teachers who had engaged in this sustained professional development and those who had not, the facilitator shared her belief that the success was in large part due to the teachers perceiving her as "one of them." The facilitator went on to share:

A teacher years ago said, "You know what? The reason I like coming to see you is because you are one of us, and you always make us feel like you are one of us." . . . I think that you are not as successful as a staff developer if they don't believe that you are in a classroom. . . . The day that a teacher doesn't feel that I am one of them, I no longer will be effective. . . . I consciously think about it. (personal communication, February 4, 2008)

The facilitator's role as a perceived colleague played out along two complementary dimensions: She (a) understood and explicitly acknowledged the lives of teachers, including honoring and drawing upon their expertise, and (b) conveyed a stance of inquiry. Because of these features of the facilitation, the teachers established communities of practice in a relatively short period of time, enabling them to take risks, to freely ask questions about their interactions with students, and to acknowledge when they themselves did not know (but were curious about) something. The facilitator's development of these communities supported teachers' willingness to engage deeply with other teachers to develop an inquiry stance.

Facilitator Understood and Explicitly Acknowledged the Lives of Teachers

During each session we attended, the facilitator made explicit references to teachers' lives, their busy schedules, the work they do, the stresses of testing, the role of the textbook, and so on. The facilitator's comments ranged from the potentially mundane (but nevertheless consistent with understanding their busy lives) to the engaged work of teaching. She made a point to (a) honor their current practices and (b) recognize the frustrations and feelings of loss of efficacy that may accompany attempts to change practices. Many teachers experienced what Cochran-Smith and Lytle (1999) described as the difficult and uncertain nature of practice associated with the development of an inquiry stance, and the facilitator had to respond to the feelings.

Honoring Current Practices

In a Year 1 session, the facilitator shared a comment that indicated her respect for the teachers' current practice: "Oftentimes when we want to make changes, we change everything at once. I want to caution you to try things and learn things, and don't throw things out. Many of the things you do *are great*." The facilitator acknowledged the work that the teachers were already doing and expressed hope that they would engage with the ideas in the professional development by incorporating what they learn with that work. The comment again identified her as one who understood teaching and the expertise that teachers brought to the professional development. In an interview we conducted during Year 1 professional development, a teacher with 26 years of teaching experience referred to the facilitator's comment:

> I have always loved to teach math, but I felt like there is so much to cover. And do I really need one more thing? How am I ever going to work this in? I kind of came into [the professional development] with that sort of attitude, and right away when [the facilitator] said, "We are not trying to change your program. We are trying to give you tools and things you can incorporate into what you are already doing," it sort of made my anxiety about it and that wall go down and go, "Okay, s*he knows that*." (teacher engaged in Year 1 professional development)

In this teacher's reflection, she shared the significant role that the facilitator's understanding of her life as a teacher played in her willingness to initially engage in the professional development. Interestingly, through interviews and classroom observations, we know that by the end of the first year of professional development, this teacher had already begun to change her practice and had committed to deeply changing her practice in the future. However, the facilitator's honoring of her current practice served to situate the teacher's practice and her identity as a teacher in the context of the professional development. This kind of acknowledgment by the facilitator enabled the teachers to engage with ideas and become curious about their students' thinking without having to worry that new ways of teaching were going to be forced upon them. Additionally, teachers realized that their practices were not going to be judged in a negative light. Paradoxically, this knowledge induced teachers to express their frustrations, which they did indeed experience in attempting to align their teaching practices more with what they learned about their students' understandings.

Recognizing Frustrations and Feelings of Loss of Efficacy

Across all sessions, the facilitator responded to teachers' frustrations. For example, in response to a teacher's frustration with facilitating students' abilities to make connections between and among strategies, the facilitator responded, "We haven't been trained well in how to do that; it is hard to see and make all those connections." The facilitator's use of the first person, *we*, indicated that she included herself as one of the teachers who lacked such opportunities, and she went on to elicit from teachers how they supported their students in making connections across strategies. By using *we*, she explicitly granted the teachers the freedom to share *not* being able to do something well and showed that through sharing and paying attention teachers can seek ways to respond, not through *consultative* communication (Slavit & Nelson, this volume) but through inquiring together.

Additionally, in a Year 1 professional development session, several teachers shared that, even as veteran teachers, they were identifying not only the surprising abilities of children they considered to be low in mathematical understanding, but also past teaching practices that may not have supported their students. For example, one shared:

> I have always used the base-10 blocks and realized that some of the kids were not ready for the base-10 blocks because they could not break apart the 10. I feel badly because [in the past] I did not allow those direct modelers to draw enough, and I also did not allow the kids who did not need to [use manipulatives] to draw the pictures. (teacher engaged in Year 1 professional development)

One way to consider this teacher's comment is as an opportunity for learning, in part because of the disequilibrium invoked upon reflecting on her past practices (Ball & Cohen, 1999). However, the reflection is also emotionally charged and appeared to carry with it a loss of efficacy for the teacher. The facilitator responded:

> You are trying to get comfortable right now and it's hard. You have to know that the time you are investing now will help them to take off later, and it's hard because you are finding out so much about your kids, some of which you may not have wanted to know. . . . The difference is you are now aware. Now you can recognize all those different levels, and so you can find ways to meet those needs.

The facilitator's response acknowledged some of the remorse that teachers felt once they began to inquire into their children's mathematical thinking. In particular, because the teachers developed a lens for focusing on what students understand that went beyond identifying whether the students produced correct answers, teachers realized that they had sometimes overestimated and other times underestimated their children's understandings. Although this newfound knowledge was encouraging to some teachers, especially when they realized the variety and sophistication of strategies their children could use, it also carried with it the burden of recognition of all that they had incorrectly assumed in the past, and for some, the looking back was painful. The facilitator was explicit about acknowledging those troubling aspects associated with the codeveloping changes in practice and stance of inquiry and how that discomfort now could serve teachers to continue to change. Later in the conversation, the facilitator again acknowledged the hard work of the teachers in grappling with this new knowledge:

> As teachers, we tend to make a lot of assumptions. What I am hearing is that you are now in tune with your kids. You may be learning things you did not want to know. I remember when I used to take out the textbook and teach, and I was never sure who I was teaching and what

their needs were. You know more about your kids, and you will be able to address their needs. It really makes my day to listen to you and to hear the depth at which you are able to talk about your kids. That says a lot about all of you, and I am really excited.

The risks, challenges, and frustrations teachers often faced when they inquired about their students' understandings were evident here, and the facilitator recognized and supported them through these challenges.

Facilitator Conveyed a Stance of Inquiry

The facilitator was also explicit with teachers about her own development and expressed features of an inquiry stance through (a) her sense of wonder and genuine curiosity about her teachers, students, and their interactions; and (b) her posing questions central to her role as a teacher and facilitator. Relating to her stance of inquiry, she consciously sought to not present herself as an expert. For example, she stated, "I don't want them to think that I am the expert. I don't know everything, and I want them to know that I am still learning and that I have a lot to learn" (personal communication, February 4, 2008).

The facilitator often shared ideas about which she had no answers, had recently learned, or had found surprising when she learned them; she usually followed these examples with a commitment to inquiring more and described how she planned to engage (or had engaged) in that inquiry. In all her professional development sessions and interviews, the facilitator exhibited a wonder and curiosity about her own, her teachers', and students' learning, and she raised questions and sought answers to those questions.

As an example of her curiosity about teachers' practices, the facilitator talked of coteaching a multiplication lesson in a class for children with special needs: She knew that teachers of special-needs children were coming to the professional development and that she lacked expertise in teaching these children; she was curious about learning more and made efforts to do so. Additionally, when discussing fraction understanding and when to share fraction symbols, the facilitator shared her surprise in what she had learned from inquiring into her students' thinking: "It was fascinating to me to find that waiting on sharing the symbols was more supportive for [the students] than if I introduced them early on." Further, in a session with teacher leaders in grade-level groups about to analyze student work and categorize it by levels of sophistication, the facilitator acknowledged her perceived shortcoming and her stance toward continuing to learn:

I want to share my frustrations. I have you share student work, but I do not feel that I, as a facilitator, make it as valuable as it can be. I want to talk about how to get more bang for our buck. I want to help teachers get more from it.

Her reflection about her own facilitation (and again, her use of the first person plural, *our*) encouraged the teacher leaders to openly reflect on similar frustrations and to consider features of the facilitation to which they should attend when engaging teachers at their own sites. After these teacher leaders had engaged in the task of analyzing student work and sharing with colleagues for 2½ hours, one teacher leader volunteered, "I think it was one of the best student-work discussions we've had; I don't know if it was because we put the strategies into a hierarchy. It caused us to think hard about the hierarchy." Although this teacher leader's comment is not conclusive evidence, the facilitator's comments at the beginning may have served to heighten teacher leaders' awareness of their roles as participants and of the features of the discussion that promoted their own inquiry. In any case, the facilitator's comment served to position her as an inquirer (and thus one who actively reflects on her actions).

We hypothesize that the facilitator's open statements about inquiring into her own practice served to model the notion that becoming more expert means not only that one has acquired more knowledge, but also that one recognizes that having questions is as important as having answers in developing an inquiry stance. In this way, the facilitator continually portrayed herself not as one thinks of an expert in traditional terms but more as among accomplished novices, "skilled in many areas and proud of their accomplishments, but they realize that what they know is miniscule compared to all that is potentially knowable" (Cognition and Technology Group at Vanderbilt as cited in NRC, 2000, p. 48). The Cognition and Technology Group continued, "This model helps free people to continue to learn even though they may have spent 10 to 20 years as an 'expert' in their field" (NRC, 2000, p. 48). The facilitator's expression of her stance of inquiry encouraged the teachers to risk sharing their questions in a way that was valued and, in many ways, *expected* as part of their role in a community of practice.

ROLE OF EXTERNAL FORCES: DISTRICT OFFICE SUPPORT

Forces external to the community of practice play an important role in whether and how teachers engage with ideas within the community. Funding decisions, for example, affect whether teachers have opportunities to participate in professional development, and so principals and superintendents are instrumental in determining whether professional development takes place and for how long, whether substitutes are provided, and so on. But other factors include principals' awareness of and commitment to ideas shared in professional development, which can influence teachers' willingness to take up ideas. Similarly, the degree of alignment of textbooks and district assessments with professional development can influence teachers' engagement in professional development opportunities. Slavit and Nelson (this volume) acknowledged the role that stakeholders such as superintendents, principals, and others play in the support for teachers' communities of inquiry. Similarly, other researchers have found that teachers' perceptions that their principals supported reform-oriented, standards-based instructional practices were associated with positive changes in teachers' reported attitudes and practices (Heck, Banilower, Weiss, & Rosenberg, 2008).

In this professional development experience, the history with regard to external support for the inquiry environment is not straightforward, and support came from various external stakeholders over the years. Initially, the district provided support for the professional development by allowing the district's elementary mathematics and science program specialist (the facilitator described earlier) to provide this professional development. The facilitator had herself participated in professional development on children's mathematical thinking and for two years was supported by the district to then provide professional development for volunteer teachers (such that by the end of Year 2, more than 140 teachers had participated, in groups of 30 to 35). In Years 1 and 2, the facilitator provided five days of professional development for each participant, in addition to fulfilling the other responsibilities of her position. The district provided reference books and substitute teachers (paid from government funds used to support teachers' development) for all participating teachers.

In Year 3, the district's Curriculum and Staff Development Directors wanted to move forward with other priorities for the district, and so funding the CGI professional development became a concern. However, four principals from the schools in which a subset of the 140 teachers were trained recognized the benefits to their teachers and students. In Year 3, these principals agreed to pay the salary of the facilitator for the days she planned and provided CGI professional development and to pay the substitutes for their teachers, all volunteers. The facilitator thus continued to provide CGI professional development for teachers. By the end of Year 3, other principals in the district wanted their teachers to have opportunities to engage in the professional development, many of them acknowledging the requests from their teachers for continued participation. The Assistant Superintendent in charge of Curriculum and Instruction then changed the facilitator's position so that in Years 4 and 5, she was supported to conduct professional development solely focused on children's mathematical thinking. In Year 5, the facilitator also created a group of emerging teacher leaders so that, between meetings, the teacher leaders could support the growing number of teachers at each site. While the facilitator continued her professional development work in Year 5, she also met with the Assistant Superintendent of Curriculum and Instruction to discuss how the district might continue to support the teachers. The Assistant Superintendent suggested that incorporating some of these ideas into the district's scope and sequence (and consequently into their district assessments) would provide a structural way to support the goals of the professional development. In

Year 6, the facilitator continued her professional development work and co-led the revision of the district's mathematics scope and sequence for Grades K–7, and the corresponding district mathematics assessments.

We consider several features of the external support to be noteworthy. First, for three years (Years 4–6), the district fully funded a position for the facilitator to support teachers' professional development focused on inquiring into children's mathematical thinking. This support included the salary of the facilitator and resource books for each teacher participating in the professional development; principals paid for their teachers' substitutes during Years 4–6. During Year 3, however, because of the district's need to move forward with other priorities, support for the CGI professional development was in jeopardy; were it not for the commitment and support from four principals in Year 3, the CGI professional development in the district might have ended. However, not only was the principals' and teachers' knowledge of the benefits of the support for their students essential, but also the district leaders' willingness to listen to its principals and teachers and to respond with support in the form of funding for a full-time position for a CGI professional development facilitator was crucial and, some might conclude, exceptional. Without support from all these key stakeholders, continued support from the district office would likely have dwindled, if not disappeared.

CONCLUSIONS AND IMPLICATIONS

In the United States, opportunities for sustained professional development are not built into the professional lives of teachers. A small percentage of teachers identify and pursue opportunities for sustained professional development, but even those experiences end. Because of the paucity of opportunities for teachers in the United States to grow from structured professional development experiences, a greater focus must be placed on supporting teachers to learn how to continue to learn from their practices. The professional development described in this chapter successfully supported teachers in developing a stance of inquiry, thereby empowering the teachers in such learning. We provided an example of the ways in which, over time, teachers' roles within the community of practice shifted to become more central and an example of how a teacher's identity transformed such that she took more ownership of her construction of knowledge; we provided evidence that when the number of years of participation in a community of practice focused on children's thinking increased, the teachers developed more robust stances of inquiry. In the inquiry communities we described, the teachers (all volunteers) developed a reflexive relationship between the research base on children's mathematical thinking and an inquiry stance. When the teachers gained more knowledge, they became interested in answering questions specific to their classrooms and students, and the teachers were themselves able to generate the knowledge to answer them. Significantly, teachers chose to continue the professional development for several years. Even after four or more years of professional development, they recognized the need for further inquiry into aspects of their class-rooms and students, both recognizing that they had more to learn and seek-ing to continue their learning—in essence, they developed an inquiry stance within their communities of practice. Following we summarize the three features of the professional development that supported teachers' inquiry and consider the implications of each feature.

Three Features of the Professional Development

We identified three features of the professional development that appeared to be especially important to teachers' development of an inquiry stance. First, a focus of the professional development on children's mathematical thinking has a well-documented research base showing that this type of professional development supports teachers' learning along a variety of measures and serves as a basis for teachers' inquiry. We found that teach-ers became curious about and surprised by their students' reasoning and began to adopt an inquiry stance (Ball & Cohen, 1999; Cochran-Smith & Lytle, 2001). The professional development helped teachers look at children differently by providing them a new lens for investigating their students' mathematical thinking.

Within each session, the facilitator worked to support teachers' reflection about whether and how their students would solve particular problems, and between sessions, teachers engaged with their students' reasoning about the problems. During and between sessions, teachers began to wonder about their children's mathematical thinking, which spurred their development of hypotheses and a desire to learn more from their students. The frameworks provided in the research base generated teachers' curiosity about their own students' mathematical thinking, which provided a venue for examining how the details in children's strategies illuminate each child's mathematical understandings. These examinations support teachers in considering impli-cations for extending their children's mathematical understandings.

Our finding that a focus on children's mathematical thinking supports teachers in becoming inquirers into their own classrooms corroborates sim-ilar findings and continues a long line of documentation of the importance of this work. Thus, one promising avenue for others interested in support-ing teachers' development of an inquiry stance may be to begin with what is known about students' understandings in particular content areas and how it can be leveraged to help teachers inquire about their own students' understandings.

Second, the role of facilitator was highlighted, and what we deemed to be vital features of her practice were shared. Research related to the role of the facilitator is scarce, and so we offer a starting point for considering features of a facilitator's practice that appear to support teachers in building a community of practice. The facilitator's role as perceived colleague was enacted in her explicit references to understanding the lives of teachers and teaching and in expressing an inquiry stance. In particular, those who are interested in supporting teachers may want to consider the challenges and frustrations teachers experience when developing an inquiry stance and associated changes in practice and how facilitators might respond to those.

Finally, in line with Nelson and Slavit's (2008) findings, the role of external stakeholders appeared to play a central role in providing opportunities for teachers to become inquirers into their own practices. The facilitator, initially trained by a university researcher, then supported the professional development of hundreds of teachers for more than six years (without funding from external, university-based research grants). Through the years of support, either central-office district leaders or principals (and often both) made substantial commitments of resources and verbal support that maintained the ongoing availability for the communities of practice focused on children's mathematical thinking. Those interested in supporting communities of practice may want to seek relationships with these external stakeholders, by inviting them to sessions, regularly sharing the work of the community, identifying ways to tie the work of the community to the district's goals, and so on. Without the district's support, maintaining teachers' participation in sustained professional development for four years and more would have been difficult, if not impossible; yet support for ongoing, sustained learning is essential for the development of an inquiry stance.

NOTES

1. Preparation of this paper was supported by a grant from the National Science Foundation (ESI-0455785). The views expressed are those of the authors and do not necessarily reflect the views of NSF.
2. Although the community to which we refer when we write about a *community of practice* is the professional development community, we assert that the effects of the development of the community will be realized in not only the professional development sessions but also teachers' own classrooms and interactions with others outside the professional development setting.
3. During a professional development session, teachers may be given a problem and asked to select numbers to use for their students. For example, *Maria has rocks in her collection. How many more rocks will she need to have rocks altogether?* Selecting numbers that support children in becoming increasingly sophisticated in their strategies is a challenging skill that develops over time.
4. We provide the actual problems here because, in some transcripts we include in this chapter, teachers refer to the analysis of these problems.
5. When comparing problems (a), (c), and (f), for example, many adults, including teachers, tend to think of these as subtraction problems, but children often view them differently. Teachers learn the value of categorizing problems

not by operations but in ways that distinguish how young children might model them—by identifying the location of the unknown and by considering whether the problem involves action. In general, problems for which the *result* is unknown are easier for young children to model and solve than problems for which the *change* is unknown, making (c) easier to model than (a). Additionally, problems with *action* tend to be easier for students to model and solve than problems with *no action*. So, in general, young children more easily solve (c) and (a), which have action, than (f), which has no action.

REFERENCES

Ball, D. L., & Cohen, D. K. (1999). Developing practice, developing practitioners: Toward a practice-based theory of professional education. In L. Darling-Hammond & G. Sykes (Eds.), *Teaching as the learning profession: Handbook of policy and practice*. San Francisco: Jossey-Bass.

Carpenter, T. P., Ansell, E., Franke, M. L., Fennema, E., & Weisbeck, L. (1993). Models of problem solving: A study of kindergarten children's problem-solving processes. *Journal for Research in Mathematics Education, 24*, 427–440.

Carpenter, T. P., Fennema, E., Franke, M. L. (Producers), & Empson, S. B. (Director). (1995). *Cognitively Guided Instruction* [Videotapes (7)]. Madison, WI: Wisconsin Center for Education Research.

Carpenter, T., Fennema, E., Franke, M., Levi, L., & Empson, S. (1999). *Children's mathematics*. Portsmouth, NH: Heinemann.

Carpenter, T., Fennema, E., Franke, M., Levi, L., & Empson, S. (2000). *Cognitively guided instruction: A research-based teacher professional development program for elementary school mathematics*. Research Report 003, Madison, Wisconsin: National Center for Improving Student Learning and Achievement in Mathematics and Science.

Carpenter, T. P., Fennema, E., Peterson, P., Chiang, C., & Loef, M. (1989). Using knowledge of children's mathematics thinking in classroom teaching: An experimental study. *American Educational Research Journal, 26*, 499–531.

Carpenter, T. P., Franke, M. L., & Levi, L. (2003). *Thinking mathematically: Integrating arithmetic and algebra in elementary school*. Portsmouth, NH: Heinemann.

Cochran-Smith, M., & Lytle, S. (1999). Relationships of knowledge and practice: Teacher learning in communities. In A. Iran-Nejad & P. D. Pearson (Eds.), Review of research in education (Vol. 24, pp. 249–306). Washington, DC: American Educational Research Association.

Cochran-Smith, M., & Lytle, S. L. (2001). Beyond certainty: Taking an inquiry stance on practice. In A. Lieberman & L. Miller (Eds.), *Teachers caught in the action: Professional development that matters* (pp. 45–58). New York: Teachers College Press.

Darling-Hammond, L., & McLaughlin, M. W. (1996). Policies that support professional development in an era of reform. In M.W. McLaughlin & I. Oberman (Eds.), *Teacher learning: New policies, new practices*. New York: Teachers College Press.

Empson, S. (1995). Using sharing situations to help children learn fractions. *Teaching Children Mathematics, 2*, 110–114.

Fennema, E., Carpenter, T. P., Franke, M., Levi, L., Jacobs, V., & Empson, S. B. (1996). Mathematics instruction and teachers' beliefs: A longitudinal study of using children's thinking. *Journal for Research in Mathematics Education, 27*, 403–434.

44   *Lisa Clement Lamb et al.*

Fennema, E., Carpenter, T. P., Levi, L., Franke, M. L., & Empson, S. B. (1999). *Children's mathematics: Cognitively Guided Instruction: A guide for workshop leaders*. Portsmouth, NH: Heinemann.

Franke, M. L., Carpenter, T. P., Levi, L., & Fennema, E. (2001). Capturing teachers' generative change: A follow-up study of professional development in mathematics. *American Educational Research Journal, 38*, 653–689.

Franke, M. L., & Kazemi, E. (2001). Learning to teach mathematics: Focus on student thinking. *Theory into Practice, 40*(2), 102–109.

Grouws, D. A. (Ed.). (1992). *Handbook of research on mathematics teaching and learning*. New York: Macmillan.

Hawley, W. D., & Valli, L. (1999). The essentials of effective professional development: A new consensus. In L. Darling-Hammond & G. Sykes (Eds.), *Teaching as the learning profession: Handbook of policy and practice* (pp. 127–150). San Francisco: Jossey Bass.

Heck, D. J., Banilower, E. R., Weiss, I. R., & Rosenberg, S. L. (2008). Studying the effects of professional development: The case of the NSF's local systemic change through teacher enhancement initiative. *Journal for Research in Mathematics Education, 39*, 113–152.

Hill, H. C. (2004). Professional development standards and practices in elementary school mathematics. *The Elementary School Journal, 104*, 215–231.

Jacobs, V. R., Franke, M. L., Carpenter, T. P., Levi, L., & Battey, D. (2007). Professional development focused on children's algebraic reasoning in elementary school. *Journal for Research in Mathematics Education, 38*(3), 258–288.

Jacobs, V. R., Lamb, L. C., Philipp, R., Schappelle, B., & Burke, A. (2007, April 12). Professional noticing by elementary school teachers of mathematics. In A. Ellis (chair), *Missing links in the implementation of mathematics education reforms: "Attention-focusing" and "noticing."* Symposium conducted at the annual meeting of the American Educational Research Association, Chicago, IL.

Jacobs, V. R., Lamb, L. C., Philipp, R. A., & Schappelle, B. P. (2008). *Responding on the basis of children's mathematical thinking*. Manuscript in preparation.

Kazemi, E., & Franke, M. L. (2004). Teacher learning in mathematics: Using student work to promote collective inquiry. *Journal of Mathematics Teacher Education, 7*, 203–235.

Lave, J., & Wenger, E. (1991). *Situated learning: Legitimate peripheral participation*. Cambridge, UK: Cambridge University Press.

Lester, F. K. (2007). *Second handbook of research on mathematics teaching and learning*. Charlotte, NC: Information Age Publishing.

National Research Council. (2000). *How people learn: Brain, mind, experience, and school*. Washington, DC: National Academy Press.

National Research Council. (2001). *Adding it up: Helping children learn mathematics*. Washington, DC: National Academy Press.

Nelson, T. H., & Slavit, D. (2008). Supported teacher collaborative inquiry. *Teacher Education Quarterly, 35*(1), 99–116.

Philipp, R. A., Schappelle, B. P., Siegfried, J. M., Jacobs V. R., & Lamb, L. C. (2008, March 24). *The effects of professional development on the mathematical content knowledge of K–3 teachers*. Paper presented at the annual meeting of the American Educational Research Association, New York, NY.

Rogoff, B. (1997). Evaluating development in the process of participation: Theory, methods, and practice building on each other. In E. Amsel and K. A. Renninger (Eds.), *Change and development: Issues of theory, method, and application* (pp. 265–285). Mahwah, NJ: Erlbaum.

Schifter, D. (2001). Perspectives from a mathematics educator. In Mathematics Teacher Preparation Content Workshop Program Steering Committee, Center for Education, National Research Council (Eds.), *Knowing and learning mathematics for teaching: Proceedings of a workshop* (pp. 69–71). Washington, DC: National Academy Press.

Stein, M. K. & Mundry, S. (1999). Professional development for science and mathematics teachers: Dilemmas of design. *High School Magazine* 7(2), 14–18.

Strauss, A., & Corbin, J. (1998). *Basics of qualitative research: Techniques and procedures for developing grounded theory* (2nd ed.). Thousand Oaks, CA: Sage Publications.

Van de Walle, J. A. (2004). *Elementary and middle school mathematics: Teaching developmentally* (5th ed.). New York: Allyn & Bacon.

Villaseñor, A. J., & Kepner, H. S. J. (1993). Arithmetic from a problem-solving perspective: An urban implementation. *Journal for Research in Mathematics Education, 24*, 62–69.

Wells, G. (1999). *Dialogic inquiry: Toward a sociocultural practice and theory of education.* Cambridge, UK: University Press.

Wenger, E. (1998) *Communities of practice.* Cambridge, UK: Cambridge University Press.

Wilson, S., & Berne, J. (1999). Teacher learning and the acquisition of professional knowledge: An examination of research on contemporary professional development. *Review of Research in Education, 24*, 173–209.

Zeichner, K., Klehr, M., & Caro-Bruce, C. (2000). Pulling their own levers. *Journal of Staff Development, 21*(4), 36–39.

3 Mathematics Curriculum Implementation via Collaborative Inquiry

Focusing on Facilitating Mathematics Classroom Discourse

Amy Roth McDuffie

Washington State University Tri-Cities

In recent years, as part of an effort to investigate and identify aspects of instruction associated with supporting students' understanding and learning, researchers and educators have focused on the role of classroom discourse in engaging students in thinking, reasoning, and communicating understandings (Cazden, 2001). Many of these recommendations can be generalized across all content areas. For example, to incorporate these processes in mathematics instruction, teachers need to pose meaningful problems and questions, listen to students' thinking, evaluate students' responses and work, and decide when to clarify, model, or explain and when to encourage students' explanations and/or student-to-student discussions (cf. Ball, Lubienski, & Mewborn, 2001; Martin, 2007; National Council of Teachers of Mathematics [NCTM], 1991, 2000). Given that these practices have not necessarily been a part of the more didactic teaching style exhibited in the United States historically (Stigler & Hiebert, 1999), experienced and novice teachers often find that they are not prepared to engage students in meaningful classroom discourse. In mathematics, this situation becomes more urgent given the National Science Foundation's (NSF) funding of the development of mathematics and science curricular materials specifically designed to incorporate these processes in teaching and learning (Hirsch, 2007). Consequently, teachers, professional developers, and university teacher educators need to explore approaches that develop knowledge and skills needed for facilitating discourse in mathematics.

In this chapter, we examine one teacher's (Ms. Rada; teachers' names are pseudonyms) inquiry into her practice in the context of her work implementing discourse-rich curriculum materials while participating in the described professional development activities. Ms. Rada and another teacher joined with a university mathematics teacher educator (the author) to form a collaborative inquiry team (CIT). The core professional development activities were situated in the teachers' practices in the sense that they included planning, implementing, and analyzing the teachers' lessons. In addition, the CIT members participated in other professional development opportunities available in the region during the year of their work.

THE COLLABORATIVE INQUIRY TEAM'S PERSPECTIVES AND PROFESSIONAL DEVELOPMENT APPROACH

Background of the Collaborative Inquiry Team

The CIT consisted of Ms. Rada (7th-grade mathematics teacher, 10 years' experience), Ms. Leman (7th-grade mathematics teachers, 18 years' experience), and Amy Roth McDuffie (author, a mathematics teacher educator and researcher). The CIT members had known each other prior to forming the CIT through interactions at regional mathematics education meetings. Rada and Leman's middle school (sixth through eighth grades) had approximately 770 students with 12% ethnic minority and 27% free and reduced meals. Each teacher taught five of six class periods each day, with approximately 30 students in each class.

In the spring prior to our work, Rada approached Leman and me about forming an inquiry team. Rada had accepted a teaching position for the upcoming fall at the same school where Leman was teaching. Rada sought her new position primarily because she felt that her former district was not endeavoring to implement instruction consistent with national and state mathematics standards (NCTM, 2000), and she wanted to be in a more progressive school and district. Her new school had adopted *Connected Mathematics* (*CMP*, Lappan, Fey, Fitzgerald, Friel, & Phillips, 1998), a reform-oriented set of middle school mathematics textbooks, the prior year. Rada viewed *CMP* as more aligned with her perspectives on teaching and learning mathematics, particularly given her focus on classroom discourse. In addition, Rada appreciated the opportunity to teach at the same school as Leman, who was recognized in the region for her teaching expertise. While Rada was implementing *CMP* for the first time during the study, Leman was in her second year of implementing *CMP*, had piloted and advocated for adopting the *CMP* materials for her school district two years prior, and had attended workshops offered by the *CMP* publisher. Thus, Rada's decision to engage in inquiry on her practice was sparked by her new teaching position with a well-respected colleague and using curriculum materials quite different from those she had used previously. Rada and Leman requested that I join their team so that they could benefit from my background in mathematics education and broader perspectives that I might offer as an outsider to the school and district. I agreed and asked permission to document and study our work.

Based on previous professional interactions, the CIT members perceived that the team shared similar perspectives on teaching and learning mathematics. Each member espoused views consistent with a vision of mathematics education set forth by the NCTM *Standards* (1989, 2000), which included valuing students' active participation in problem solving and explaining their thinking. During interviews prior to our collaborative work as well as subsequent interactions during the study, Rada and Leman indicated that they believed students brought many ideas and strategies to mathematics learning, and that a teacher's primary role was to provide meaningful opportunities for students to build understandings.

Collaborative Inquiry on Practice

This study examined the collaborative, inquiry-based professional development activities with a focus on the following question: How did Rada's participation in the CIT support her inquiry into fostering mathematical discourse in her classroom and help her to make meaning of her other professional development activities relative to her inquiry? In investigating Rada's inquiry on practice as part of the CIT, two categories of activities emerged: work *inside* and *outside* of Rada's classroom. The *inside* activities included the CIT's intensive study of lessons with the *CMP* materials, such as planning, implementing, analyzing, and reflecting on teaching and learning. I considered these activities *inside* her classroom because all of the CIT work was based in Rada's immediate context of work with her curriculum materials, her students, and colleagues from her school. The *outside* activities included participating in a National Board Certification support group and a district-organized middle school mathematics teachers' book study group. The following sections describe these inside and outside activities in the collaborative inquiry process.

Work Inside the Classroom

Our inquiry work driven by activity inside the classroom was centered in our collaborations throughout *teaching cycles*, with each cycle including planning, implementing, and reflecting on instruction (Smith, 2001). In planning our work, the CIT agreed to implement recommendations from research on characteristics of effective professional development. Studies have found that professional development experiences are more likely to be effective when they are:

- Sustained and intensive;
- Focused on an academic content area (e.g., mathematics);
- Focused on instructional planning and principles underlying the curriculum;
- Grounded in hands-on opportunities for active learning;
- Integrated into the daily life of the school;
- Aligned with and tailored to other reform efforts, local curricular goals, and teachers' goals for students' learning (i.e., coherent) (Garet, Porter, Desimone, Birman, & Yoon, 2001; Penuel, Fishman, Yamaguchi, & Gallagher, 2007).

In structuring our work, the CIT adapted two forms of professional development with the intent to situate teachers' inquiry into practice with a *site-based and curriculum-linked* approach (Penuel et al., 2007): lesson study and video clubs. Researchers who have investigated lesson study (e.g., Bass, Usiskin, & Burrill, 2002; Fernandez, 2005; Lewis, 2002;

Wang-Iverson & Yoshida, 2005) describe it as involving teachers and possibly *knowledgeable others*, such as an accomplished colleague, university faculty, or district administrator, collaborating to: (a) formulate goals for student learning and development; (b) meticulously plan a "research lesson" to enact these goals; (c) conduct the research lesson with one team member teaching and other members gathering evidence on student learning; (d) debrief and discuss the research lesson; and (e) revise the lesson. Fernandez (2005) found that lesson study provided a venue for teachers to discuss, experiment with, and change instruction as they investigated content and pedagogy in their lessons. Similarly, video clubs involve teachers meeting to watch, discuss, and analyze excerpts of videotaped-lessons from their classrooms (Sherin, 2004). Sherin argued that video clubs provide teachers opportunities to gain stronger understandings of their own practice by providing more time to consider decisions than the immediacy called for during teaching, more focused views of classroom teaching and learning issues (e.g., the nature of questions) often obscured by attention to the multiple demands of teaching in real time, and access to communities of teachers and their classrooms as they explore their practice.

After I briefly reviewed the preceding approaches, the CIT discussed how we would collaborate as a team. The CIT members decided to blend lesson study with video clubs. The blended approach was a result of recognizing that scheduling limitations often would prohibit the teachers from observing each other's teaching in real time. In addition, we wanted to have video records of the lessons so that we could go back and analyze parts of lessons in more detail. Finally, while I served as a *knowledgeable other*, the teachers were not interested in inviting additional teachers or others to join the team because they wanted to focus only on their grade's curriculum and they wanted to experience the process in a small, safe group before opening their practice for others to observe.

For each cycle, we met to plan a lesson (all team members, approximately three meetings, two hours each), enact the lesson while video-recording (one teacher and researcher, approximately three days, one hour each day for each teacher), and analyze the videotaped lesson (all members, approximately two meetings, two hours each). Working throughout the school year, the CIT completed three cycles, and each cycle occurred over approximately three months. As the CIT planned for our work together, each teacher identified a focus area for inquiring about and improving her practice. At this point, Rada decided to focus on engaging more students in classroom discussions and empowering students to validate or question each other's reasoning and solutions.

Given that the curriculum materials were central to the inquiry process, I shall describe briefly the *CMP* materials used. Consistent with other NSF-funded materials, *CMP* was designed to reflect current research on mathematics instruction by emphasizing problem solving, reasoning, communicating ideas, and making connections (Dossey, 2007). Each unit comprised a series of "investigations" for students to explore. The teacher's edition included support for structuring lessons with a format of: *launching* the lesson with an engaging problem, *exploring* a problem (often students collaborate in small groups), and *summarizing* the lesson. The summary portion focused on students sharing problem-solving strategies, highlighting important mathematical concepts and processes learned, and building connections among strategies and concepts that students shared. The authors did not write the materials in a scripted form for teachers to follow, but instead presented the materials as a resource with options for teachers' decision making to meet students' needs. The materials included possible questions for teachers to pose, strategies and struggles students might share, mathematics content for teachers' learning, and essential concepts and processes on which to focus (Dossey, 2007).

Implementing these materials required that teachers take on new roles, "moving from always being the one who does the mathematics to being the one who guides, questions, and facilitates the learner in doing and making sense of the mathematics" (Lappan, Phillips, & Fey, 2007, p. 75). Changing to this role presents new demands on teachers and is challenging (Gamoran, Anderson, Quiroz, Secada, Williams, & Ashmann, 2003). Rada recognized this challenge, and it motivated her to collaborate with the CIT in implementing *CMP*.

Outside Professional Development Activities

Professional development activities that occurred *outside* Rada's classroom also served as a prominent part of the context and influenced Rada's inquiry into her practice. These activities included the National Board (NB) certification process and a middle school book-study group. First, I shall describe the NB certification process briefly; more detailed information is available from the *National Board for Professional Teaching Standards* (NBPTS, 2006a). Teachers who apply for NB certification submit a portfolio of classroom practice and demonstrate content knowledge through a timed exam administered at a testing center. Rada and Leman participated in an NB candidate cohort organized through my university (I served as the NB cohort facilitator) to support teachers in the process of applying for NB certification. Teachers worked throughout the school year to complete their portfolio, and the CIT members met with the NB cohort group approximately twice each month. The portfolio for the Early Adolescent Mathematics Certificate area (the certificate both teachers were seeking during the study) consisted of four entries: one classroom-based entry that included student work as evidence, two classroom-based entries that required video recordings (e.g., one focused on whole-group discussion and one focused on small-group work), and one entry that documented accomplishments outside of the classroom (NBPTS, 2006b). Rada and Leman frequently referenced and discussed the portfolio entries in meetings with the CIT. As the year progressed, Rada and Leman decided to use some of the CIT's work with lessons and video analysis for portfolio entries, and consequently, lesson study work and NB portfolio efforts merged with overlapping purposes.

A second type of inquiry-oriented professional development activity that supported the actions of the CIT was a book-study group. This group included approximately 15 middle school mathematics teachers in Rada's school district that elected (participation was not required in any way) to meet once each month. I was invited to join the group as a participant but did not facilitate the discussions. The group discussed readings from two books: *Teaching Problems and the Problems of Teaching* (Lampert, 2001) and *Elementary and Middle School Mathematics: Teaching Developmentally* (Van de Walle, 2001). The Lampert book, which was completed over the course of the year, served as the primary source for discussions, while the Van de Walle book was used as a resource for both mathematics content and pedagogical ideas when issues arose in discussions. For each meeting, the group agreed on a reading assignment. The assignment typically consisted of one chapter from each of the Lampert and Van de Walle books. Although one teacher was assigned to coordinate the group's work, all members participated equally.

RESEARCH METHODS

I applied Simon's (2000) conception of a *teacher development experiment,* which calls for working with teachers and documenting the nature of our work and the teachers' practices *while* supporting their professional development. I provided input and support as a participant in the CIT while researching the teachers' experiences using a qualitative case study approach to interpret participants' experiences and interactions (e.g., Bogdan & Biklin, 1992; Corbin & Strauss, 2008; Stake, 1995).

Data were collected throughout each teaching cycle. Data sources consisted of field notes, audiotapes (with transcription) of planning and analysis meetings, video recordings (with transcription) of lesson enactments, e-mail correspondences, curriculum materials, teachers' written work for their NB portfolio entries, and student work. The teachers were interviewed at the beginning and end of the school year, using a modified version of Cognitively Guided Instruction's pedagogical beliefs protocol (Peterson, Fennema, Carpenter, & Loef, 1989), to understand their beliefs as they began work with the professional development team.

Initially, all data were analyzed by analytic induction (Bogdan & Biklen, 1992). Using open coding (Corbin & Strauss, 2008), patterns of similarities and differences were identified for the role of the CIT, the *CMP* materials, the NB, and the book-study group in influencing Rada's and Leman's practice during the teaching cycles. After the initial analysis, I conducted a more fine-grained analysis by focusing on the nature of the support Rada experienced in inquiring about mathematical discourse. These included the CIT interactions as well as text-based resources, such as *CMP* materials, NB Standards and portfolio guidelines, and book-study sources. Within each of these broad categories, based on emerging patterns from preliminary analysis, I coded data for specific subcategories that might influence Rada as she inquired into mathematical discourse in her classroom. Subcategories included interactions that supported lesson planning and reflections, references to resources to inform text-based analysis, and the nature of CIT member contributions. In addition, I looked for evidence of similar or different status among the group members as a potential influence on CIT support (e.g., overtalking or interrupting by one member more than another, close listening, attending to/building from others' ideas, and equal or unequal participation in discussions).

In considering text-based resources, the *CMP* curriculum was the primary artifact utilized by the CIT during lesson study sessions. Therefore, I analyzed *CMP* materials for text that might influence or support Rada in her inquiry, such as suggested prompts to use in discussions. In addition, when the *CMP* materials were referenced in CIT discussions, I traced these references to gain a sense of which aspects of the materials emerged as important to the inquiry focus. Other text-based resources included the NB materials and the books used for the book-study group. In tracing these references, I looked for specific examples of perspectives on teaching and learning mathematics, pedagogical approaches, and/or resources to build content understandings that may have served as pivotal ideas for Rada's inquiry into practice. I employed member checking (Stake, 1995) to support the trustworthiness of the data analysis by sharing preliminary findings with Rada and Leman.

RADA'S CHANGING PRACTICE THROUGH INQUIRY

As evidenced in a larger study (Roth McDuffie, 2008), Rada experienced substantial changes in how she facilitated discussions with *CMP* lessons in her classroom. Just as the CIT was beginning to collaborate, Rada's classroom consistently exhibited an Initiation-Response-Feedback (IRF; also referred to as Initiation-Response-Evaluation [IRE]) discourse pattern (Cazden, 2001) with follow-up explanations from Rada. IRF has been a prominent classroom discourse pattern for decades, especially in mathematics classroom. With this pattern, the teacher poses a question, a student responds, and the teacher offers feedback or an evaluation of a response (e.g., "Good."). This interaction pattern does not tend to encourage students to engage in higher-level reasoning nor to share their thinking and reasoning (Cazden, 2001).

In the winter, after identifying her inquiry focus on discourse and initiating work with the CIT, I found that Rada's classroom discourse patterns shifted substantially. Rada regularly elicited explanations from students, focused their reasoning and communication, and prompted students to ask questions of others. In addition, after establishing classroom norms for discourse, Rada frequently and explicitly reminded the class of expectations to share strategies, listen to others' approaches, and respectfully challenge and/or build on other students' ideas. This shift continued into the spring. The change in classroom discourse patterns led to students' contributions determining the direction of discussions, rather than Rada dominating talk in lessons (Roth McDuffie, 2008).

PROFESSIONAL DEVELOPMENT ACTIVITIES INFLUENCING RADA'S INQUIRY ON PRACTICE

In discussing supported collaborative teacher inquiry (SCTI), Slavit and Nelson (this volume), highlight forms of support that are critical to teacher inquiry, including: (a) support for teachers' inquiry processes and (b) support for interfacing between teachers' inquiry and broader educational contexts. As I considered Rada's inquiry, I found that the support was directed primarily on her inquiry process, rather than on interfacing her efforts with broader educational contexts, although opportunities for the latter did exist. In the following sections, I shall focus primarily on the activities that influenced Rada's inquiry and the nature of their support.

From Inside the Classroom: Activities that Supported Rada in Experimenting with and Examining Her Practice and Areas of Her Practice that Could Be Improved

In investigating the role and nature of the CIT's support for inquiry, I found that the CIT critically influenced Rada from *inside her classroom* as she: collaboratively used *CMP* with the CIT as a resource for lessons, problems, and suggestions that aligned with her focus on classroom discourse; gained new perspectives on mathematical discourse by examining her colleague's (Leman's) practice; deliberately planned to implement new strategies for facilitating discourse through collaborative work with the CIT; and gained new insights about her practice by analyzing and reflecting on videos of discourse in her classroom with the CIT. First, I discuss the roles and status of CIT members, and then I explore how the CIT provided support to Rada's inquiry into fostering mathematical discourse in her classroom.

CIT Members' Roles and Status in Supporting Rada's Inquiry

Recognizing that the nature of the interactions and roles within the CIT might account for the CIT's influence on Rada's inquiry, I investigated patterns of status, contributions, and participation in CIT interactions. In studying these interactions, I found that all three members shared an equal status overall. For instance, the members shared discussion time quite equally.

While members often interrupted and talked over each other during discussions, all members exhibited this pattern with a similar frequency. Moreover, these types of utterances occurred when the members were enthusiastic and/or inspired by each other's comments. Thus, interruptions and talking over seemed to indicate approval and appreciation for another's ideas, rather than disregard.

The content of each member's contributions was also similar in many ways. For example, when planning lessons, all members frequently asked questions, such as "How will this activity help students to make sense of the mathematics?" Yet, in examining differences in members' verbal contributions, somewhat unique roles emerged. Rada was energetic and often served as *the motivator* for the CIT's work. Recall that she initiated the forming of the CIT. Rada also called for team meetings and sent e-mails suggesting meeting agenda, even when there was usually a clear purpose and topic already established. Rada also went beyond expectations in preparing for meetings. For instance, after we had discussed potential supplemental materials at one meeting, she already had gathered and reviewed these resources by the next meeting. The motivator title is not meant to imply that Rada served as a facilitator of meetings. The CIT recognized that facilitators are often needed for professional development efforts, but given the small size of the team and the fact that all participants shared in its ownership, the CIT never identified a need for a facilitator, and no member emerged as such.

Leman was the most experienced teacher on the team and served as *the wise practitioner.* Not only did Leman have the most classroom experience, she had the most experience and training with *CMP.* Leman also had a remarkable memory for approaches she had tried, other lessons in the materials that might impact a lesson under study, and experiences with students learning specific concepts. An example of a typical contribution from Leman in which she shared ideas from past experience will be presented later in the discussion about the "Designing Algorithms" lesson. Indeed, Rada recognized Leman for her expertise in the classroom prior to our CIT work, as described earlier.

As a university mathematics educator and researcher, I focused more on research and theory behind standards-based teaching in mathematics education, and thus was regarded as *the knowledgeable advisor.* I selected *advisor* rather than *other* (as used in lesson study models) in that Rada and Leman often turned to me for advice based on research and to reflect the fact that I was more involved in team activities than a knowledgeable other usually is in lesson study. Often Rada and Leman directly asked, "Is there research on how children understand this idea?" or questions focused on pedagogy related to specific mathematics content. The research-based ideas I contributed included information on common misconceptions or challenging ideas in mathematics, approaches to questioning and facilitating discourse, information about developmental trajectories to inform planning regarding students' prior knowledge and/or future needs for mathematics, and rationale for pedagogical approaches or curricular sequencing of topics. Another function I served as an advisor was to refocus discussions on students' learning. For example, frequently when previewing materials for a lesson, I asked, "How do you think students will approach this problem?" to anticipate what might happen in a lesson. Similarly, in postlesson discussions, I asked, "Why do you think the students solved it that way?" A third function I served was as a resource in mathematics content. For example, in a lesson involving similar triangles and proportionality, the teachers were not confident about some of the mathematical terms (e.g., when to use *similar* and when to use *congruent*), and they turned to me to clarify and solidify understandings.

Our roles came together to fill needs for the team overall. In fact, at some point during the year, we each shared the jobs of motivator, wise practitioner, and knowledgeable advisor, depending on the situation. Thus, while we each served in one of these roles more often (or more predictably), no one member held that role exclusively. We began the year as colleagues and, over the course of the year, mutual respect for the expertise each member brought to the team developed further and was evident in interactions.

Using Curricular Materials that Promoted Classroom Discourse

At every planning meeting, the CIT began with an overall review of the upcoming unit followed by analyses of specific lessons. The CIT utilized these curricular materials to discuss specific approaches to facilitating discourse in *CMP* lessons. I found that *CMP* supported Rada in considering approaches that emphasized reasoning and discourse, and yet the materials alone were not sufficient to induce change. Support received during the collaborative inquiry process was extremely important to her eventual changes in instructional practice. Specifically, Rada needed interactions with colleagues focused on developing deeper understandings of both mathematics content and the recommended pedagogical approaches in order to implement the materials (Boaler, 2002; Gamoran et al., 2003; Remillard, 2005; Stein, Smith, Henningsen, & Silver, 2000). For example, for a class observed in November, Rada had read the materials to plan the lesson and participated in three CIT meetings that focused on planning this lesson and understanding the unit from which the lesson came. However, in the CIT meetings prior to this lesson, strategies for facilitating discourse had not yet become the focus of discussion. The discussion centered more on the mathematics content of scaling and proportionality, representations to use to help students' understand proportional thinking, and anticipating possible students' approaches, reasoning, and misconceptions. As discussed earlier, Rada's classroom discourse patterns in the fall did not encourage students' explanation and reasoning, but these practices were evidenced later in the winter. Thus, although the materials provided guidance and opportunities for Rada to use mathematics discourse in teaching with *CMP*, these ideas were not implemented, and additional support targeted at facilitating discourse was needed, as discussed following.

Gaining New Perspectives on Mathematical Discourse by Examining Leman's Practice

Although the NB requirements and book-group readings (described in more detail in the section "From Outside the Classroom") focused Rada's attention on mathematical discourse, examining Leman's practice through videotaped observations seemed pivotal to Rada's gaining ideas for approaches to effectively facilitate classroom discourse. Leman used the same curricular materials, stayed on a similar schedule, and worked with students who were from the same school, the same grade, and had similar family and cultural backgrounds. Hence, Rada viewed Leman's teaching with the assumption that if Leman could achieve a classroom culture and student interactions founded on engagement in mathematical discourse, then Rada could achieve a similar outcome. Moreover, by examining Leman's practice, Rada gained specific ideas for questioning strategies in lessons that she had taught or would be teaching. Thus, the problem of transferring ideas and approaches from Leman's practice to Rada's practice (i.e., imagining how a given approach would work in her classroom) was not an added challenge to implementing change for Rada.

The following excerpt from a CIT meeting illustrates a specific example of how Rada was influenced by Leman's practice. The meeting occurred on November 24, and the focus of the meeting was to view, analyze, and reflect on Leman's video from November 6. The conversation occurred as they viewed a video of Leman questioning a student about how he solved a problem involving proportionality with similar triangles. The excerpt showed how the CIT members looked for and identified forms of discourse that avoided "telling" students the answer, an idea that Rada had explored in earlier reading.

Leman: And you can hear the kids now, coming in [orally contributing], they're chiming in [with student-to-student interactions, discussing a student's work at the board].

Roth McDuffie: And [you (Leman) are asking] clarifying questions [rather than explaining the correct answer].

Rada: Yeah, now his drawing wasn't actually drawn [correctly]. And so, instead of telling him, "Hey! Look at what you've got right there!" you asked him, "Is that the same way?" and he went, "Oh" [realizing he needed to revise his drawing].

Roth McDuffie: Yes, [and this was done by] not telling him.

Rada: Because he's making sense of it himself. He's starting to understand that he's got to draw it accurately according to the relationships up on the board.

Rada observed the value of students' revising their own work and making sense of their approaches and mistakes, rather than simply being told how to correct their work by the teacher. These ideas were not new to Rada at this point, given her previous reading, but she had not yet made sense of how they might work in her practice.

Conversations such as this one with the CIT helped Rada to gain specific examples for facilitating discourse with the lessons she taught and with similar students. Indeed, at this meeting, the CIT began to view Rada's video from November 5 when she still exhibited IRF patterns of discourse. Toward the end of the meeting, Rada reflected on her video and recognized that her class did not have the same level of teacher questioning and student-to-student interactions as Leman's class. Rada reflected, "After watching yours [Leman's November 6 video], I'm thinking mine's [November 5 video] not so great" (CIT meeting, November 24). Rada then decided that she did not want to use her November 5 video as her NB portfolio entry for whole-class discussion, and instead, she wanted to work on how she facilitated discourse before videotaping another class for this entry. This example illustrates how NB prompted a focus on classroom discourse, but it was not until Rada worked with the CIT and examined her practice inside the classroom (via video) that the issue became a problem of inquiry to pursue.

Deliberately Planning to Implement New Discourse Strategies

The CIT's planning discussions addressed many aspects of teaching and learning, including deciding whether to use small groups, whole-class discussion, or individual work; generating questions and prompts for lessons; and anticipating students' responses and approaches. For example, in a planning meeting on January 3, the CIT discussed a lesson focused on students' developing algorithms for adding and subtracting fractions. After reading information from the teacher's guide, Rada prompted the CIT to discuss *CMP*'s recommendation for sharing and discussing the algorithms the students developed. She initiated the question and then shared her reasoning for why the whole group discussion might be effective:

> I was trying to look at that [the lesson "Designing Algorithms"] and thought why would you do that as a [whole-] class discussion? [Answering her own question, Rada continued . . .] You'd do it because that's the first time algorithms come up. So . . . it would be too hard [without a class discussion]. . . . There are so many different ways of designing their own algorithms. [A whole-class discussion would help] to get everybody to acknowledge theirs and then bring them to, "Okay, that's a really good one. Is there another one [that someone else has shared] that's more useful?"

I affirmed Rada's thinking and added comments regarding efficiency in algorithms:

> You want kids to see an abundance of strategies because you don't want them to just be locked into their view without seeing what other people are doing. You need a whole group discussion so they can see all of these different approaches and open up their thinking . . . to either come up with a way of doing it if they haven't come up with one [an algorithm] on their own, or to expand and find a better one or a more efficient one.

Leman continued the conversation with advice on facilitating this discussion, based on her experience teaching the lesson the previous year:

> What I suggest you do, if you do this as a whole group, is that you have a sheet of paper to the side, or the white board, and that you, as you come up with algorithms . . . have a group present their algorithms and have them come up with a group agreement after you lead them through the probing and pushing questions [questioning and clarifying their approach], making sure it is a true algorithm. Okay? Then you post it up there so that you have this running record of these different ways. Because kids are going to come up with different approaches and ways to add fractions [and you want to be able to compare and connect the different approaches later] . . . [In questioning the groups] you have to stop and as a teacher, follow it through . . . and say, "I don't understand. You need to convince me." . . . [When I taught this] I was amazed at the number of ways that they came up with.

The discussion continued and the CIT began to focus more on how the students might approach the problem and corresponding questions the teacher might ask. While discussing ideas, the CIT continually referenced the *CMP* teacher's guide. Leman shared her experiences teaching the lesson the previous year and reflected that she wished that the materials provided more guidance as to how students might develop algorithms:

> I can see the kids coming up with an algorithm for when the denominators are all the same, you just simply add the numerators. That's probably going to be the very first one that [students] come up with. And you [talking to Rada] may have to pose to them, "Well, what if the denominators aren't the same? What are you going to do then? How do you do that?" . . . They [CMP] expect these kids to come up with [more than one algorithm] . . . It [the book] says, "Write up a final version of each algorithm" [p. 48]. They are expecting the kids to come up with more than one way to do this. . . . There are times when I wish I had more examples [of what kids might do with these problems]. And

I can't imagine a brand new teacher who has never taught [knowing what to do with this lesson].

Rada taught this lesson on January 16, implementing Leman's suggestion by requiring each group to produce a poster-sized display that showed their algorithms. In this lesson, she used questioning to elicit students' conjectures and explanations and student-to-student discourse as each group presented their work. The posters were then displayed around the room for students to compare and reflect on the various algorithms.

Although this discussion did not provide Rada with much information beyond what the teacher's guide offered, sharing and hearing ideas about this lesson seemed to be important to Rada in preparing to teach the lesson. Asking students to develop their own algorithms was different from Rada's practice of demonstrating and explaining a standard algorithm to students, and Rada seemed more confident and ready to attempt this approach after this discussion with the CIT. The CIT's process of talking through the lessons and conducting "thought experiments" for how the lesson might proceed, what students might do, how to implement the recommendations in the teacher's guide, and how the mathematical ideas are progressively developed served an important role for Rada as she inquired into discourse. The supports she received from her colleague, a critical other, and the instructional materials were all important to this aspect of the inquiry.

Gaining New Insights through Video

In a meeting on December 5, the CIT discussed Rada's November videotape that she was considering using for her portfolio entry on small group instruction. Rada directed the CIT to look for evidence that she was meeting various NB requirements related to student engagement. The CIT discussion then focused on these areas by identifying incidents in the video that might serve as evidence for the NB requirements. Through this process of identifying specific aspects of facilitating discourse, the CIT helped Rada to recognize examples of her own practice when she demonstrated these strategies so that she could build on her own success. In other words, the CIT's discussion featured her successful attempts in order to encourage her to develop these aspects of her practice further. The outside-the-classroom influence of the NB portfolio prompts for whole-class discussion and the inside-the-classroom activities of the CIT converged to support Rada's analysis and reflection on her discourse practices.

To illustrate how the CIT discussions encouraged Rada, I first shall provide some context for the videotaped lesson we analyzed. Throughout a lesson on October 30, Rada exhibited a questioning pattern of IRF followed by her explanation to the students with some follow-up questions to point students toward a specific procedure, as was typical of her practice in the fall. About 40 minutes into the lesson, Rada was working with a group who struggled with finding a scale factor. To find the scale factor, they needed to compute the ratio of two corresponding sides of two triangles that measured 12.66 meters and 3.25 meters, respectively. Rada determined that the decimal values were confusing the students, so she decided to prompt students to consider first a similar problem with whole numbers and then apply the same strategy to the problem with the decimal numbers. While questioning the students, she asked them to explain how they arrived at the answer, rather than only asking for numerical or one-word answers:

Rada: If I take the decimal off here [making the quantities 12 and 3, respectively], could you tell me how much it's increasing by, or what factor? [Initiation to elicit an answer to the calculation.]
Students: Four. Four. [Response.]
Rada: Four? And how would you get that? [Initiating for an explanation, questioning a correct response.]
Student 1: Because 12 divided by 3 is 4. [Response to explain a procedure.]
Rada: So 12 divided by 3 is 4. So if I take my finger off, and now I have 12.66, and 3.25, can you use that same reasoning? [Question to prompt students to apply their reasoning to a similar problem.]
Student 2: Yeah. [Response.]
Rada: Okay, so what would you do? [Initiating, prompting students to reason through the problem and explain.]
Student 2: 12.66 divided by 3.25. [Response to explain a procedure.]
Rada: Okay, go ahead and do that. [Initiation to perform the calculation.]
Student 3: 3.90 is what we got, too. [Response.]

As we viewed this video at a CIT meeting on December 5, Leman and I noticed the change in the nature of Rada's questioning and pointed out this shift to Rada, using her questions in the preceding interaction as evidence. Below is an excerpt of this CIT discussion about Rada's approach to questioning and students' engagement that resulted from her approach:

Leman [with Roth McDuffie agreeing]: Oh my gosh, you've got so much probing going on. . . . [Note: the NB portfolio guidelines prompted candidates to evidence probing of students' responses.]
Rada: I'm glad we [videotaped this lesson]. . . . And you zoomed in on them, and then you backed up to see their faces [referring to Roth McDuffie capturing the students' engaged expressions as the students figured out the problem].
Leman: And look at them. Look at all three of them. They are *so* there. That's your best facilitation of a group. . . .
Rada [with Leman and Roth McDuffie agreeing]: And they are taking responsibility for . . . themselves [and understanding how to solve the problem].

Although Rada rarely asked students to explain their reasoning in the fall, when the CIT helped her to identify a successful incident, Rada saw how she could implement this strategy. Rada recognized the benefit of this approach for her students' learning, and this experience encouraged her to develop this questioning strategy further. The CIT's use of examples from Rada's own practice helped Rada to understand how she could implement different discourse practices and made Rada feel more confident about doing so.

As the CIT held more meetings to plan and analyze teaching and learning, the level of complexity that Rada demonstrated in analyzing her own teaching and decision-making increased. On December 5, the CIT discussion centered on asking students to explain their thinking and how students became more engaged as they made sense of the problem for themselves. By January 13, Rada's comments indicated that she was more focused on facilitating discourse based on students' thinking and understandings, rather than just seeking explanations. Rada deliberately planned questions to pose in whole-class discussions, which students to select to share, which aspect of the solution to probe further, and when to examine a different approach. In a meeting immediately following a class in January, Rada reflected,

> [I planned to ask the question,] "What made you think you were right?" I wanted to use this [question], and I didn't, I don't think. [I did say,] "I see what you've done. How can you check that with somebody else?" This one, I was trying. I was going to use [the first question] with [Student 1], but then she volunteered to go up there and show [how her group solved the problem with decimals instead of fractions]. . . . [So instead I asked] "How could you show it a different way?" [to see if Student 1 could connect her approach to fractions]. And I thought about it at that point, but see the class is getting sick of her [because she often volunteers to share her strategies that are different from the rest of the students' strategies], and she had put it on a circular graph [instead of a rectangle, as the problem stated]. . . . She said, "Oh my gosh! I did it on a pie graph." And the other kids [said], "No. It's a rectangle. The [pizza] is a rectangle." But if she was doing it with percents and decimals, the pie graph probably made sense to her. And so I kind of wanted to ask her why she tried the pie graph [but I did not]. I didn't want to go in that direction and lose everybody [and have the other students saying], "Well, [there's Student 1 taking over the discussion again]."

In sum, it was not clear that Rada recognized that many of the discourse facilitation strategies were not present in her classroom discussions. The teacher "explaining why" had been part of Rada's practice for several years, and it seemed that it had not occurred to her that she was almost always the source of the explanations. Through work with the CIT, Rada recognized the value of students communicating their reasoning, gained ideas for how to facilitate discussions, and began implementing questioning strategies to encourage students' discourse in her classroom.

In regard to supporting Rada as she analyzed and reflected on her practice, the CIT primarily functioned by identifying examples of effective questioning (even when limited examples were available) and then building on successful experiences. As Rada experimented with and implemented new questioning strategies, the CIT's discussion focused on more complex issues associated with facilitating mathematical discourse. Through frequent meetings and focus directly on Rada's practice, the CIT provided developmentally-appropriate support, taking on issues as Rada was ready to address them and incorporate them in her practice.

From Outside the Classroom: Activities that Provided Rada Different Perspectives and Ideas for Facilitating Mathematical Discourse

An essential first step toward changing practice was for Rada to identify an area of inquiry in her practice. As an experienced teacher who had been recognized by colleagues and principals as being a good teacher, identifying an area for improving practice is not an obvious or clear process. The NB process and the books Rada read as part of the book-study helped her recognize that facilitating classroom discourse was an area of her practice that needed attention, and these activities opened up possibilities for improving her teaching and her students' learning.

In regard to the effect of the NB process, the portfolio entry on whole-class mathematical discourse focused Rada's attention on how she facilitated learning during this instructional mode. This entry required the teacher to describe, analyze, and reflect on facilitating discussions (NBPTS, 2006b). The NB portfolio guidelines required Rada to demonstrate that she posed questions and prompts to elicit thinking and reasoning, encouraged and fostered verbal exchanges, and built off of students' questions, conjectures, and interactions (teacher-student and student-student) in promoting students' learning (NBPTS, 2006b).

As discussed earlier, specific NB guidelines focused Rada's attention on how she facilitated discourse during several CIT meetings. The teachers decided that they wanted to use the CIT work, using approaches from lesson study and video clubs, to complete their NB portfolio video-based entries. They recognized that the two processes were compatible, and so they decided to select video entries from among the CIT's videotaped lessons. An outcome of this decision was that the NB prompts and guidelines served as criteria of proficiency for facilitating classroom discourse and framed our analysis and discussions of the videotaped lessons. Thus, the outside influences of the NB merged with the CIT's efforts to form a symbiotic support to Rada's inquiry on discourse.

Indeed, the NB cohort met approximately twice each month, and thus I considered whether interactions with this cohort supported Rada's inquiry. However, it was not evident that these meetings played a key role for Rada in changing her practice. Her cohort provided feedback on her written entries, primarily in the form of copyediting, but I did not find instances of Rada referencing ideas or reflections gleaned from the NB cohort. Indeed, in my observations of NB cohort meetings, I found that most discussion focused on meeting NB requirements and producing high-quality portfolio entries, rather than on improving teaching and learning. As discussed previously, reading NB guidelines for portfolio entries and using the NB prompts in video analysis were important supports to focus Rada's attention on discourse practices, but the actual meetings and interactions during the NB meetings did not substantially influence Rada.

The book-study group provided a second outside-the-classroom influence on Rada's inquiry. Rada's reading of professional literature with the book-study group had a substantial impact on her professional growth trajectory. Similar to experiences with the NB process, reading the literature seemed to influence Rada more than her participation in the book group. I did not find evidence that she referenced particular ideas or discussions that emerged from the book group; instead, Rada referred to the readings directly. For example, Rada's inquiry on her own practice of facilitating mathematical discourse directly related to two chapters of Lampert's (2001) book. One chapter focused on establishing classroom norms and an environment that fosters discourse, and another chapter discussed specific approaches for facilitating a whole-class discussion. In the winter and spring, Rada implemented Lampert's ideas regarding establishing classroom culture by explicitly and repeatedly stating norms for participation in class and encouraging students to comment on other students' explanations. In addition, in a lesson in January, Rada directly discussed with her students Lampert's ideas about using pen for writing in mathematics. Lampert required students to use pen so that they could keep record of all of their thinking and the problem-solving process. Rada explained that she wanted her students to write in pen while doing mathematics, just as Lampert had with her students:

> If you change your mind [when working on a problem], then just put a line through it and then fix whatever you're doing. Just like you do when we're doing investigations when you find out that it's wrong or that part of it's wrong or you want to add to it . . . do it in pen. Okay? [I was] reading a book . . . about this teacher that was working with this, I think they were 5th-graders, and she has them do everything in pen . . . and the kids can't erase it. . . . If the kid doesn't cross it out, you can see their thinking. And you can see where they've changed their mind and decided to do something else . . . and you can see exactly how they were solving it.

Reading Van de Walle's (2001) book in the book group also underscored the idea that effectively facilitating classroom discourse to promote students' learning in mathematics was an essential part of teaching practice. Van de Walle's ideas were consistent with those of Lampert regarding classroom discourse, and yet this book provided an additional, independent source that promoted these ideas.

Rada did not reference particular ideas or discussions that emerged from the book-study group. Instead, the primary role of the book-study group was to motivate Rada to read the literature because she did not want to attend the meetings without being prepared. Rada had indicated that she always intended to read professional literature more, but she seemed to need a push to make reading a priority, and the book-group meetings provided that push. A secondary influence was that the book group validated ideas presented in readings, and hearing her colleagues' positive responses to the ideas supported Rada. The collaborative nature of this support was important to Rada as she decided to take the risks involved with trying different approaches in her classroom.

These activities were important to the previously described changes in the discourse in Rada's classroom. Specifically, the outside-the-classroom activities of preparing for her NB portfolio entry on whole-class discussion and reading the books in the book-study group produced a consistent message for Rada: facilitating whole-class discussion that engages all students, encourages teacher-to-student and student-to-student interactions, assumes that students will communicate conjectures and explanations, and values students' reasoning and approaches (not just answers) are essential parts of effective mathematics teaching and learning.

An interview at the end of the year and several follow-up conversations following the study focused on Rada's perceptions of from whom or what she received support for her inquiry. Rada's statements in these conversations served to validate my findings regarding the limited, but important, role the outside-the-classroom activities served. During the conversations, Rada explained that she drew from her work with the CIT far more than from her experiences with the NB cohort or from her discussions in the book group. She remarked that the other groups might have been more of a resource in the absence of the CIT, but given the influence of the CIT as the year progressed, she did not value and dedicate as much attention to the NB cohort or book group. Rada said that the most important role these other groups served was to provide a structure to maintain consistent work on her NB portfolio entries and to continue to read the chapters of the books.

SUMMARY OF FINDINGS

My findings and Rada's and Leman's perspectives (based on member checking) suggested that the CIT offered more support for implementing new practices and reflecting on their effectiveness than any other activity, and the CIT also served as the matrix that held other sources of influence together to support Rada's inquiry. The CIT's culture and work inside the classroom seemed to be a critical reason that the team was highly influential. Although the CIT members shared equal status, as colleagues with more in common than different in how they each contributed to discussions, they each also seemed to hold a unique role in the group. Rada initiated the team, called for meetings, and brought a level of energy and enthusiasm to our work that was unmatched by others. Leman offered substantial wisdom from practice due to her detailed reflections on 18 years of classroom experience and her prior experience with *CMP*. Roth McDuffie served as a resource for research and theory about teaching and learning, a mathematics content specialist, and one who kept the conversations focused on students' learning. The equal status and unique but complementary roles resulted in a productive, focused, and improvement-oriented team.

The CIT activities and the curricular materials supported Rada in inquiring about and improving mathematics discourse in her classroom. The NB portfolio required an entry that examined mathematical discourse during a whole-class discussion. While Rada began work on this entry, she was reading and discussing books with the book study group that emphasized the importance of mathematical discourse for teaching and learning (Lampert, 2001; Van de Walle, 2001). The books caused Rada to reflect on her practices in facilitating discussions in her class, wondering to what extent she was truly involving her students in discussing mathematical ideas and in building on each other's ideas during discussion. As Rada used her curriculum materials, she recognized that the teacher's guide emphasized discussion-based approaches. Lesson materials in the teacher's guide included a summary section with suggestions that encouraged classroom discourse built on students' conjectures and explanations and provided possible prompts to use in these discussions. However, Rada's practice in the fall evidenced how these prompts were not sufficient for Rada to incorporate high-level mathematics discourse in her classroom. Although these influences helped to initiate and form the inquiry focus, they were not the primary support for Rada.

As she viewed a video of Leman's teaching (which included more student reasoning) and then viewed her own teaching with the CIT (this video was selected as a potential portfolio entry to feature whole group discussion), she and the other CIT members observed that Rada remained the center of the discussion in her video, and her students' participation was limited to short responses (usually providing an answer to a problem without explanation). At this point, Rada decided to focus on transforming this norm for discourse in her class. As part of this process, she drew support from the CIT to plan lessons, for which mathematical discourse remained central to learning. The CIT supported Rada in designing key questions and approaches that encouraged discussion around important mathematical concepts. In reflecting on lessons, the CIT helped Rada to identify key aspects of her teaching that improved her facilitation of mathematical discourse. The issues the CIT tackled with Rada evolved as Rada advanced in her inquiry; the CIT adapted to provide support that was developmentally appropriate to where Rada was in changing her situated discourse.

It should be noted that the findings presented were a window into the process, and at no point did any of the CIT members indicate that the work on discourse was finished. Consistent with Slavit and Nelson's (this volume) discussion about the cycle for teacher inquiry, the process of implementing new approaches and evaluating practice continued with new issues emerging as other strategies became part of Rada's regular repertoire.

DISCUSSION AND IMPLICATIONS

The support from the *outside* complemented the *inside* support for the collaborative inquiry of Rada and the CIT. The outside influences (the NB process and reading the books from the study group) helped Rada to identify a focus area for inquiry and improvement in her practice. Drawing from these outside sources, Rada developed a perspective that facilitating classroom discourse is worthwhile and important for learning and gained a general understanding of strategies to use in facilitation. In addition, the NB prompts and questions provided specific criteria for what constituted effective discourse in mathematics for Rada and the CIT to consider implementing in Rada's practice. The inside influences (the *CMP* materials and the CIT work) provided ideas directly connected to Rada's planning and analysis of daily practice that became foundational to the inquiry process. Although all of these supports were important, it seemed that the CIT's interactions and inquiry-focused culture provided the catalyst for change to occur. The CIT encouraged questioning of practices, risk taking to identify areas for improvement and to try different strategies, and using evidence from practice to guide analysis, reflection, and design of new approaches. The CIT members maintained a collaborative stance and a shared vision of teaching and learning mathematics, and members' roles and expertise in the CIT synergized the inquiry process to promote deep learning about mathematics discourse and the development of discourse practices.

Earlier, I described how the CIT's support evolved in alignment with Rada's development as she endeavored to change her practice. All of these modes of influence combined to support a developmental trajectory that described Rada's learning through the inquiry process (see Figure 3.1). First, Rada learned about alternative approaches to teaching that focused on mathematical discourse, and she recognized and identified her goal to examine and change her practice by improving how she facilitated classroom discourse, endeavoring to meet NB criteria. Second, Rada initiated steps to change her practice. Third, Rada recognized benefits from the first steps, further implemented and refined strategies (including taking on more complex issues) in facilitating discourse. The fourth step did not seem to occur for Rada, but had the potential of occurring at some point. In this study, the steps in the trajectory were not entirely discrete, but rather overlapped and built on each other over time.

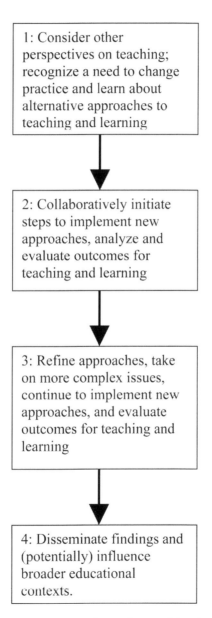

Figure 3.1 A developmental trajectory for professional development.

In examining this trajectory as it might apply to other teachers' learning, I found that the first step was a critical element to engaging in inquiry and transforming practice. Using video to examine and analyze Leman's and Rada's own practice, deliberately planning for discourse with the *CMP* lessons, and framing the CIT's work from NB criteria and readings all contributed to Rada developing an image of effective discourse practice. Considering the ubiquity of the U.S. tradition of teaching mathematics in a more didactic approach (Stigler & Hiebert, 1999), generating an awareness of alternatives is a necessary step for many teachers. It is possible that other resources could serve as supports to steps in the trajectory. For example, a teacher could learn about alternative approaches from independent professional reading, university courses, workshops and/or seminars, or examining curricular materials the teacher is not currently using. Helping to uncover a need for change and developing an image for another way of practicing are essential supports for the inquiry process.

In regard to the next two steps in the trajectory (see Figure 3.1), this study indicated that a key support was working with a *collaborative* team from *inside the classroom*. The collaborative culture and each member's unique role in the team were important in establishing a productive, focused, and improvement-oriented climate for change. While maintaining a focus on discourse, Rada, as the *motivator*, Leman, as the *wise practitioner*, and Roth McDuffie, as the *knowledgeable advisor*, employed these roles as we analyzed Rada's lessons as well as videos of Rada's and Leman's practice to produce ideas and approaches that we immediately tested and refined as part of the inquiry process. Conducting the work inside the classroom created a working laboratory for investigating practice. The collaborative culture, combined with contextualizing our work from inside the classroom, enabled the CIT to help Rada identify key teaching and learning moments in lessons, reflect on learning outcomes, suggest teaching options, and plan for future lessons.

Approaches such as lesson study (Fernandez, 2005), video clubs (Sherin, 2004), professional learning communities (Little, 2003; Little, Gearhart, Curry, & Kafka, 2003) and coaching (West & Staub, 2003) could each (or possibly in combination, as in this study) serve as structures to provide this support from inside the classroom. It seems that outside influence could continue to inform learning during these steps as well in that as ideas are refined, teachers could review relevant literature to pursue alternative teaching approaches and/or gain more in-depth insights on students' learning. However, merely adopting a professional learning structure does not seem sufficient for catalyzing the inquiry process. The culture of the team and the context of the work also should be considered.

Step 4, "Disseminate findings and potentially influence broader educational contexts," was not achieved in this study. Support to influence broader educational contexts is an important outcome for teachers' inquiry in that by influencing broader contexts, teachers' inquiry efforts are more likely to be transformative for practice and reach beyond their practices to improve schooling (Slavit & Nelson, this volume). Rada's foci and priorities were on changing her practice and completing the NB certification process, and not necessarily on affecting broader educational contexts. Changing one's own practice requires substantial energy and commitment, and completing NB requirements in the midst of that change adds another layer of complexity and effort. When I mentioned possible opportunities for disseminating her work to influence broader contexts (e.g., presenting at conferences and/or sharing ideas within her school district), Rada seemed interested and indicated that she might consider sharing her work with teachers in the future, but responded that she felt consumed with her current foci and could not think about anything else at the time. It seemed that she first needed to focus on her own development. Rada perceived that she was undertaking substantial risk inside her classroom and needed to be more confident in her changed practices before she would be willing to share her efforts with others. It is quite possible that Step 4 will be part of Rada's future professional trajectory.

Research findings on characteristics of effective professional development approaches (e.g., Garet et al., 2001; Penuel et al., 2007) align with findings from this study for what contribute to the teacher's development. However, this study highlighted the need for both outside-the-classroom and inside-the-classroom supports, and how these formed a symbiotic support system as a teacher progressed through a trajectory of learning and development. Moreover, the inside-the-classroom support emerged from the collaborative culture, the complementary roles of team members, and the meaningful context in which the work was situated. Although a case study such as this one does not suggest that all teachers would follow the same trajectory identified in Rada's case, considering this trajectory and the support needed throughout the professional development process may help educators (teachers, professional developers, university teacher educators, and administrators) to better prepare and provide for ongoing teacher learning.

REFERENCES

Ball, D., Lubienski, S., & Mewborn, D. (2001). Research on teaching mathematics: The unsolved problem of teachers' mathematical knowledge. In V. Richardson (Ed.), *Handbook of research on mathematics teaching* (pp. 433–456). Washington, DC: American Educational Research Association.

Bass, H., Usiskin, Z., & Burrill, G. (2002). *Studying classroom teaching as a medium for professional development.* Washington, DC: Mathematical Sciences Education Board of the National Research Council.

Boaler, J. (2002). *Experiencing school mathematics: Traditional and reform approaches to teaching and their impact on student learning.* Mahwah, NJ: Lawrence Erlbaum Associates.

Bogdan, R., & Biklen, S. (1992). *Qualitative research for education: An introduction to theory and methods.* Boston: Allyn & Bacon.

Cazden, C. (2001). *Classroom discourse: The language of teaching and learning.* Portsmouth, NH: Heinemann.

Corbin, J., & Strauss, A. (2008). *Basics of qualitative research: 3e.* Los Angeles: Sage.

Dossey, J. (2007). Looking back, looking ahead. In C. Hirsch (Ed.), *Perspectives on the design and development of school mathematics curricula* (pp. 185–199). Reston, VA: National Council of Teachers of Mathematics.

Fernandez, C. (2005). Lesson study: A means for elementary teachers to develop the knowledge of mathematics needed for reform-minded teaching. *Mathematical Thinking and Learning, 7*(4), 265–289.

Gamoran, A., Anderson, C., Quiroz, P., Secada, W., Williams, T., & Ashmann, S. (Eds.). (2003). *Transforming teaching in math and science: How schools and districts can support change.* New York: Teachers College Press.

Garet, M., Porter, A., Desimone, L., Birman, B., & Yoon, K. (2001). What makes professional development effective? Results from a national sample of teachers. *American Educational Research Journal, 38*(4), 915–945.

Hirsch, C. (Ed.). (2007). *Perspectives on the design and development of school mathematics curricula.* Reston, VA: National Council of Teachers of Mathematics.

Lampert, M. (2001). *Teaching problems and the problems of teaching.* New Haven, CT: Yale University Press.

Lappan, G., Fey, J., Fitzgerald, W., Friel, S., & Phillips, E. (1998). *Connected Mathematics.* Prentice Hall.

Lappan, G., Phillips, E., & Fey, J. (2007). The case of connected mathematics. In C. Hirsch (Ed.), *Perspectives on the design and development of school mathematics curricula* (pp. 67–79). Reston, VA: National Council of Teachers of Mathematics.

Lewis, C. (2002). *Lesson study: A handbook of teacher-led instructional change.* Philadelphia: Research for Better Schools.

Little, J. W. (2003). Inside teacher community: Representations of classroom practice. *Teachers College Record, 105*(6), 913–945.

Little, J. W., Gearhart, M., Curry, M., & Kafka, J. (2003). Looking at student work for teacher learning, teacher community, and school reform. *Phi Delta Kappan, 85*(3), 184–192.

Martin, T. (Ed.). (2007). *Mathematics teaching today.* Reston, VA: National Council of Teachers of Mathematics.

National Board for Professional Teaching Standards. (2006a). Retrieved August 11, 2007, from http://www.nbpts.org/.

National Board for Professional Teaching Standards. (2006b). NBPTS mathematics/early adolescence certificate area. Retrieved August 11, 2007, from http://www.nbpts.org/for _candidates/certificate_areas?ID=8&x=44&7=9/.

National Council of Teachers of Mathematics. (1989). *Curriculum and evaluation standards for school mathematics.* Reston, VA: Author.

National Council of Teachers of Mathematics. (1991). *Professional teaching standards for school mathematics.* Reston, VA: Author.

National Council of Teachers of Mathematics. (2000). *Principles and standards for school mathematics.* Reston, VA: Author.

Penuel, W., Fishman, B., Yamaguchi, R., & Gallagher, L. (2007). What makes professional development effective? Strategies that foster curriculum implementation. *American Educational Research Journal, 44*(4), 921–958.

Peterson, P., Fennema, E., Carpenter, T., & Loef, M. (1989). Teachers' pedagogical content beliefs in mathematics. *Cognition and Instruction, 6*(1), 1–40.

Remillard, J. (2005). Examining key concepts in research on teachers' use of mathematics curricula. *Review of Educational Research, 75*(2), 211–246.

Roth McDuffie, A. (2008, March). *Mathematics curriculum implementation via collaborative inquiry: Focusing on facilitating mathematics classroom discourse.* Paper presented at the American Educational Research Association Annual Meeting, New York City.

Sherin, M. (2004). Teacher learning in the context of a video club. *Teaching and Teacher Education, 20*(2), 163–183.

Simon, M. (2000). Research on the development of mathematics teachers: The teacher development experiment. In A. Kelly & R. Lesh (Eds.), *Handbook of research design in mathematics and science education* (pp. 335–360). Mahwah, NJ: Lawrence Erlbaum Associates.

Smith, M. (2001). *Practice-based professional development for teachers of mathematics.* Reston, VA: National Council of Teachers of Mathematics.

Stake, R. (1995). *The art of case study research.* Thousand Oaks, CA: Sage.

Stein, M., Smith, M., Henningsen, M., & Silver, E. (2000). *Implementing standards-based mathematics instruction: A casebook for professional development.* New York: Teachers College Press.

Stigler, J., & Hiebert, J. (1999). *The teaching gap.* New York: The Free Press.

Van de Walle, J. (2001). *Elementary and middle school mathematics: Teaching developmentally* (4th ed.). New York: Longman.

Wang-Iverson, P., & Yoshida, M. (2005). *Building our understanding of lesson study.* Philadelphia: Research for Better Schools.

West, L., & Staub, F. (2003). *Content-focused coaching: Transforming mathematics lessons.* Portsmouth, NH: Heinemann.

4 The Influence of Standards and High-Stakes Test-Related Documents on Teachers' Collaborative Inquiry

Tamara Holmlund Nelson, Anne Kennedy, Angie Deuel, and David Slavit

Washington State University Vancouver

In the United States a standards-based movement in education surfaced in the 1980s and then coalesced as a dominant force in changing the way educators think about curriculum, instruction, and student learning. Standards are now used to provide teachers and administrators guidance on the establishment of general grade-level content and performance expectations. Over time, such recommendations have become more focused and specific; standards, particularly at the state level, are no longer seen as general guidelines, but contain very specific learning targets that children are expected to reach by certain grade levels.

In this context, the National Science Education Standards (NSES, 1996) presented a new vision for science education and provided guidelines for teaching, content, assessment, and professional development. The extent to which these national standards have impacted teaching and learning is not clear. The National Research Council commissioned a number of science educators to examine the influence of the NSES on classroom teaching and student achievement; they found evidence that teachers are familiar with the NSES, yet scant evidence to show that much has changed in middle and high school classrooms (National Research Council, 2003). As in other content areas, state science standards soon followed the publication of the NSES. These have had a more direct impact on the work of teachers, as high-stakes tests tend to be more related to state standards than national standards. In Washington State, science standards were developed in 1997 as guidelines for the scientific content, inquiry, and applications that should be taught in grades K–10. Students' performance toward meeting these standards, known as the Essential Academic Learning Requirements (EALRs), began to be assessed through state-level tests at grades 5, 8, and 10. The Washington Assessment of Student Learning (WASL) in science was first administered in 2003 at the 8th- and 10th-grade levels and, as of this writing, a passing score will become a high school graduation requirement in 2013. Teachers in the state volunteer each year to work on developing new test items for the science WASL and to determine the range of various proficiencies: advanced, proficient, basic, below basic (Office of Superintendent of Public Instruction [OSPI], 2008). The state education agency has developed and presented informational sessions at different conferences across the state intended to introduce teachers to the new standards, explain the testing format and links to the EALRs, respond to teachers' questions and concerns, and keep teachers updated on new developments. Grade Level Expectations (GLEs) were produced in 2005 that expanded upon the EALRs to specifically define learning expectations for grades K–2, 3–5, 6–8, 9–10. With the GLE publication, teachers had access to a document that directly stated a vision for science education in Washington State and connected this vision to specifically defined learning expectations and testable content.

In this chapter, we examine the ways in which these various standards-related documents and associated tests were used by one group of science teachers undertaking collaborative inquiry in a professional learning community (PLC). As researchers and professional development providers, we worked with middle and high school science and mathematics teachers for five years in two ways. First, we participated in a 13-member PLC charged with planning and implementing a professional development (PD) project that helped teachers form PLCs and undertake collaborative inquiry into their students' learning and their teaching practices. In the second year of that PD project, we began a long-term study of teachers' PLC participation, the interactions between the PLC and the larger school, district, and state contexts, and the relationship between teachers' PLC work and student learning. In this chapter we specifically consider how the increasing emphasis on state standards and testing supported, challenged, and otherwise influenced one middle school science teachers' PLC activities and interactions.

The context in which a PLC exists exerts a significant influence on various aspects of teachers' collaborative inquiry, such as their inquiry focus or the data they analyze. The context also has the potential to provide meaningful support. In Washington State, we have found that teachers' collaborative inquiry is significantly shaped by the state standards described earlier and the criterion-referenced, high-stakes WASL. This is especially true in science, where the work of middle school teachers is bracketed by the state tests given in the fifth and eighth grades. Additionally, the science content standards are promoted as *the* science curriculum and, therefore, can be construed as support for teachers in making instructional and assessment decisions. Alternately, numerous reports in the popular press and in the research literature examine how a focus on high-stakes testing can shift the standards-based context from supportive to evaluative; as such, *standards* may be reduced to *test content* and *teaching for understanding* reduced to *teaching to the test* (Hargreaves, 2008; Pedulla, Abrams, Madaus, Russell, Ramos, & Miao, 2003). As McLaughlin and

Talbert (2006) caution, "[H]igh-stakes accountability systems feature narrow tests of student achievement that limit teachers' ability to learn about students' understanding and learning and too often restrict their focus to easily measurable outcomes" (p. 114). Our research provides insight into the tension between the standards as a support and high-stakes tests as a constraint that a group of middle school science teachers faced when undertaking collaborative inquiry.

PRISSM: THE PROFESSIONAL DEVELOPMENT PROJECT

An Overview of the PD Model

The Partnership for Reform in Secondary Science and Mathematics (PRiSSM) was a three-year professional development project involving approximately 150 teachers in six rural and suburban school districts in the Pacific Northwest. The first year of PRiSSM focused on building the capacity of lead teachers to engage in collaborative inquiry work. The final two years involved the implementation of site-based PLCs, led by the lead teachers, in the 22 PRiSSM schools. PRiSSM was designed to support teachers in the development of a common vision of high-quality learning and teaching while engaged in collaborative inquiry on a focus of their choosing. The large arrows in Figure 4.1 represent the generalized inquiry path teachers were encouraged to follow. The small arrows represent how most inquiry groups followed recursive loops into previous stages of the cycle rather than moving successively through each stage.

In general, PRiSSM was formulated as a supportive structure and process to help teachers do the work they felt they needed to do, whether it was something that emerged from their own classrooms or influenced by school improvement plans, district initiatives, and state standards. Rather than provide teachers with a focus, such as children's mathematical thinking (see Lamb, this volume) or inclusion (see Bondy, this volume), PRiSSM was designed to help teacher groups identify one area of teaching and learning that was important in their own setting. Then, using the inquiry cycle as a guide for their collaborative work, teachers could draw upon various forms of data to inform both their vision of quality relevant to their identified focus, determine student needs and possible teacher interventions, collect data on the impact of this action, and determine the implications for their next steps. Lead teachers learned about and practiced these inquiry processes during three week-long summer academies. In the second summer, lead teachers also learned ways to facilitate an expanded PLC with other science and/or mathematics teachers from their school (and, in some cases, across schools). In the third summer, additional teachers were designated as leaders, and attended the summer academy with the original PRiSSM lead teachers.

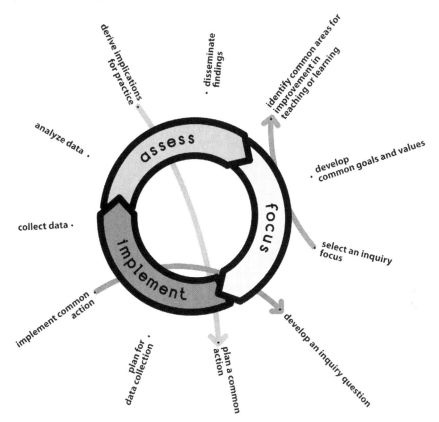

Figure 4.1 The PRiSSM inquiry cycle.

Support for Teachers' Collaborative Inquiry

Three areas for support have been previously identified (Chapter 1 of this volume) as central to teachers engaged in collaborative inquiry. The first of these, support for the inquiry process, addresses the assistance teachers may need at any stage of the cycle represented by Figure 4.1. As will be described, PRiSSM provided many of these supports. Second, support for the interface between the inquiry work and broader educational contexts was also an element of the PRiSSM support model, although this type of support was less a generalized feature of the model and more a set of tailored actions by the PRiSSM facilitator dependent upon a PLC's context. Finally, the need for explicit support for the development of an inquiry stance emerged over time. Implicit in the design of PRiSSM was a conception of teachers' "knowledge-in-practice" as described by Cochran-Smith & Lytle (1999), in that we began with "what teachers believe and what they are doing or trying to do in their own classrooms" (p. 270). Over time, we saw the need for a facilitator "who coaches or guides a group in the process of learning how to reflect and/or to conduct inquiry on practice" (p. 271). While implicit in the protocols, norms, and processes that the PRiSSM PD promoted, ways of developing a wondering perspective (Wells, 1999) or inquiry stance were not explicitly addressed in the summer academies.

Figure 4.2 is a theoretical model for understanding teacher professional development work (adapted from Carroll & Mumme, 2005; Cohen, Raudenbush, & Ball, 2003) which we will use to further delineate the kinds of supports PRiSSM provided. Starting with the inner circle of Figure 4.2, which represents the classroom, support was given to enrich the teachers' skills and perspectives associated with classroom practice. While the focus of PRiSSM was to develop capacity for collaborative inquiry, it was also felt that the teacher leaders needed to do so within the scope of effective teaching practices. However, this was the least emphasized level of support, consisting of analysis of videotaped classroom teaching segments, engagement in and discussion of mathematics and science learning activities by the teachers during week-long summer institutes, and one-on-one coaching conversations between facilitators and teachers.

PRiSSM PD activities, which predominantly related to the middle circle of Figure 4.2, centered on the teachers' engagement in collaborative

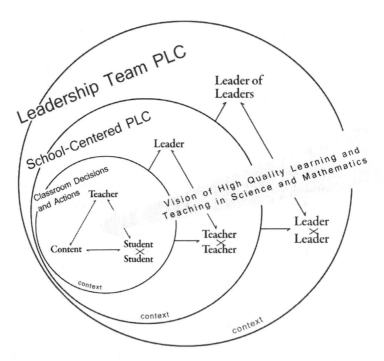

Figure 4.2 Theoretical representation of teachers' professional development through professional learning communities.

inquiry, with the content of the inquiry focused on classroom teaching and learning. Two broad sets of activities comprised the bulk of support for the inquiry process. First, specific activities were designed to support the lead teachers' abilities to facilitate collaborative inquiry with their colleagues in their schools. These included the modeling of community building activities, engagement in and protocols for discussions of high-quality learning and teaching, and attention to the development of group norms (Garmston & Wellman, 1999). The second set of activities that supported teachers' engagement in inquiry involved lead teachers' development of specific inquiry skills; during the summer academies, the teachers were introduced to various aspects of the inquiry cycle depicted in Figure 4.1. For example, protocols for collectively examining classroom-based student work and analyzing large-scale, quantitative data (such as state test results) were modeled for and used by the teachers.

Throughout the school year, teachers were also provided with support for making connections between their collaborative inquiry within the PLC and the school, district, and state contexts within which they were situated. The middle and outer circles of Figure 4.2 represent where this type of support would reside—in other words, within the PLC itself and, for many lead teachers and for the PRiSSM facilitators, in the activities of the Leadership PLC. It was through functioning outside of the PLC that facilitators, especially, could help school and district administrators recognize connections between PLC work and other initiatives. Additionally, facilitators (and lead teachers, in many occasions) could bring information from people and about projects going on outside the PLC in to the PLC. Across the three years of PRiSSM, facilitators were assigned to specific PLCs. While they were able to support the inquiry process, such as helping lead teachers to build a collaborative community, define an inquiry focus, or deal with logistical issues, facilitators also provided assistance that bridged between PLC work and resources, people, and events outside the PLC. For example, facilitators and other project staff were called upon to locate research articles, find data-collection tools, access information on school and district data, suggest targeted classroom activities or instructional practices, or try to locate specific workshops or courses that would allow teachers what they needed to continue their investigations. Further, facilitators and other project staff connected teachers to other individuals engaged in similar work. As the project progressed, many lead teachers developed their own network of resources to support their work (see Slavit et al., this volume). Due to their positions outside of the classroom, many of the facilitators were also able to negotiate consistencies or inconsistencies between a PLC's inquiry focus and larger school and district improvement efforts. In some cases, facilitators acted as communication conduits between teacher teams and school leaders, and other times they promoted teacher work at the district level as an important component of overall reform efforts.

Because PRiSSM was developed with an eye toward sustainability, attention was given to school and district administrator involvement from the outset of the project. District liaisons were established to support project work and planning, and numerous formal and informal meetings with school principals and key district stakeholders were held that were informational, proactively planned to address a specific district issue, or reactive to a problem occurring in a school or district that was usually related to inconsistencies between the teachers' inquiry work and the vision and goals of the school or district. Time was devoted during summer academies for targeted discussions of project goals and activities with school and district administrators, including administrator participation in the teachers' planning sessions. Administrator attendance at the summer institutes was high, with the exception of two of the most rural districts. Beginning- and end-of-year district events were also attended by administrators. These were designed to develop broader project awareness and buy-in by articulating project goals and activities to non-PRiSSM teachers. These events also provided a showcase for PRiSSM teachers to talk about the results, challenges, and successes of their inquiry activities. Finally, PRiSSM project staff encouraged lead teachers to take active roles in state mathematics and science education initiatives, including the presentation of their inquiry findings at regional and national venues. Collectively, these supports were intended to assist teachers in the difficult, complex journey that is teacher collaborative inquiry.

Activities during the PRiSSM summer institutes focused less specifically on the development of teachers' inquiry stance. There was an ongoing effort to generate conversations amongst the teachers about their beliefs and values for teaching and learning. This helped the lead teachers raise questions within their small group; however, this rarely translated to critical conversations in the larger PLC group in the school settings. Additionally, while each PRiSSM facilitator was either a mathematics or science specialist and a member of the project's steering committee, they had varying degrees of experience with and understanding of the notion of an inquiry stance. Thus, some were able to pose and model probing questions that pushed or challenged teachers' thinking about teaching, learning, and learners, while other facilitators predominantly supported the inquiry process. Further, the amount of time each facilitator was able to devote to an individual PLC varied greatly; it was more difficult for a facilitator to assist teachers in moving toward an inquiry stance when she or he could attend only a few meetings in a year.

PRiSSM and the Standards-Oriented Context

PRiSSM built upon Cohen and Ball's (1999) definition of the classroom environment as the interaction amongst teacher, content, and student. Drawing from Fullan, Hill, and Crevola (2006), we can refine this image by explicitly defining content as standards or clear learning objectives based upon standards. The teacher's role is expanded to include not only teaching this content, but constantly assessing students' thinking in relation to these clear learning objectives. As Fullan et al. state, this assessment provides precision—feedback to the teacher on each child's needs with respect to those objectives. Further, the assessment also provides for personalization that allows for informed, subsequent instructional decisions and actions based on each child's needs. The assessment can also provide feedback to students about gaps between learning objectives and student understandings. PRiSSM supported teachers in collaboratively examining the interactions amongst teacher, content, and student in relation to a particular aspect of student learning. In identifying this focus, teachers could potentially clarify their own ideas about what a learning goal or standard meant and, especially, what it would sound or look like if a student attained that goal. Herein lay opportunities for precision, as teachers' understandings of their expectations for learners, in relation to a standard or goal, are negotiated and necessarily become less tacit and more explicit. There are also opportunities for teachers to learn more deeply the content itself, as they may find that their existing understandings are insufficiently nuanced for defining the specifics of student understanding.

RESEARCH DESIGN AND METHODS

This case study (Merriam, 1998) of the Grays Bay PLC is one of five cases we have followed since September 2005. For this analysis, we draw from qualitative data collected from September 2005 through September 2008. The unit of analysis is the social interactions and activity in the Grays Bay PLC as related to state standards. We specifically consider how state standards (especially the GLEs) and documents related to the state test (e.g., reports of students' results, released test items, scoring guides, sample student work) influenced the activities and dialogue of the Grays Bay PLC teachers as they engaged in various stages of the collaborative inquiry cycle. In this case, *influenced* might mean supported, constrained, impacted, directed, restricted, and/or challenged at different times or to different members of the PLC.

Participants and Setting

The Grays Bay PLC (all names of people and places are pseudonyms), set in a mid sized school district of approximately 13,000 students, began as a PRiSSM-supported effort but eventually became part of a district-mandated initiative. The PLC began in the fall of 2005 with two PRiSSM lead teachers (Leon and Corinne) and four other voluntary participants: a seventh-grade life science (Leon) and an eighth-grade physical science teacher from Bay Middle School and two seventh-grade (including Corinne) and two eighth-grade teachers from Grays Middle School (the moniker *Grays Bay* reflects the participation of teachers from both of these schools). These teachers represented two out of three middle schools in the district. Beginning with the 2006–07 school year, all teachers at both schools were required to participate in a PLC; this expanded the group to eleven members, three of whom were new teachers (Corinne and another original PLC member left the district). Four of these eleven participated in the original PLC. This membership remained consistent in 2007–08, and one teacher was replaced in 2008–09.

In the first year of the PLC, leadership primarily came from the two PRiSSM teachers, Leon and Corinne. In subsequent years, Leon and Andrea (original PLC members) and Jessica and Hugh (each first-year teachers in 2006–2007) took on most of the leadership responsibilities. While they attempted to distribute leadership across all members, these teachers assumed most of the responsibility for making progress in their inquiry. Other teachers made strong contributions and also worked behind the scenes to interface with their principals, develop agendas, and access resources.

In the spring of 2006, Leon, Andrea, and Jessica from Bay Middle School were invited to join our research project as coresearchers, based on their interest in developing their leadership. This entailed a greater level of participation in data collection than the other teachers, such as participating in interviews, classroom video recordings and observations, and focus-group meetings with nine other coresearchers from other schools.

Data Collection and Analysis

A wide variety of qualitative data have been collected for three years at Grays Bay. In the first year, Leon and Corinne audiotaped all PLC meetings and collected artifacts from PLC meetings and district professional development activities relevant to the PLC work. In addition, they participated in two semistructured interviews and at least two classroom observations. In subsequent years, Leon, Andrea, and Jessica continued to audiotape PLC meetings and other relevant planning meetings amongst these lead teachers, collect artifacts, and participate in two interviews and two classroom observations (video-recorded) each year. They meet occasionally with one of the authors (Tamara) to discuss PLC progress. Tamara attended approximately 70% of their PLC meetings in the second and third years as well as about half of their district-level professional development days. All audio recordings were transcribed, and field notes were taken at various meetings.

Additionally, the principal at Bay Middle School, the district science and mathematics directors, and the assistant superintendent all participated in semistructured interviews.

Other data come from PRiSSM activities. As insiders to the PD development, we have artifacts and audio and video recordings from summer academies and annual PRiSSM Showcases; progress reports submitted by PLCs and facilitators; and information about the district context from principals and other administrators who attended the PRiSSM summer academies.

Our analysis has been ongoing, with case reports developed twice each school year. This allows us to employ a constant comparative method (Glaser, 1969; Merriam, 1998) as a research team and identify themes that persist over time. For the research focus presented in this chapter, we used open coding (Strauss & Corbin, 1998) predominantly on PLC transcripts, field notes, interviews with teachers, Showcase presentations, and PLC artifacts from the three years designated previously. After conceptual categories were identified, axial coding of these data along with classroom observations and district information helped inform the richness of the conceptual categories. The construction of data displays helped us look for patterns across time and larger themes (Miles & Huberman, 1994). Three categories emerged as most persistent in the data: the standards and test-related documents as (a) guidelines and initial sources of student data that shaped the inquiry focus (see Table 4.1); (b) resources for the implementation and data analysis phases of the inquiry cycle; and (c) frameworks for teacher learning. The test-related documents that were of particular use to the teachers were released test items, scoring guides, and scored samples of student responses (also called anchor papers) for each level of proficiency: advanced, proficient, basic, below basic. Interpretations of the teachers' collaborative work were member-checked by the three teacher coresearchers from Grays Bay.

Table 4.1 Grays Bay PLC Inquiry Focus by Year

School Year	Inquiry Focus
2005–2006	Improving students' abilities to write scientific conclusions
2006–2007	Improving students' abilities to write scientific conclusions A systems approach to instruction
2007–2008	How does using models/modeling as an instruction-assessment tool affect students' understanding of natural systems?
2008–2009	Improving students' abilities to write scientific conclusions Improving students' abilities to plan scientific investigations

TEACHERS' COLLABORATIVE INQUIRY IN
A STANDARDS-BASED CONTEXT

The Grays Bay middle school science PLC provides a rich example of the intersections between teachers' collaborative inquiry and the contextual forces exerted by state standards and high-stakes testing. In our analysis of data from the first year through the beginning of their fourth year as a PLC, their collaborative inquiry processes were significantly influenced by the state standards, the state test, and, especially, test-related documents intended to provide links from the standards to the test. We use the Grays Bay case to show the potential supports, opportunities, constraints, and dilemmas presented by state standards and tests for teachers' collaborative inquiry. This case particularly illustrates the challenges teachers faced in interpreting state standards and the support that test-related documents provided for data collection and analysis. Additionally, the Grays Bay case provides an opportunity to examine the intersection of teachers' inquiry stance, standards and high-stakes tests, and teacher learning.

The Grays Bay PLC and the State Context

In the first year of site-based PLC work (2005–06), the teachers met 15 times after school for 1.5 to 3 hours each. After that, meetings occurred twice per month on the district's late-start days; each meeting lasted approximately 80 minutes. The group met at Bay Middle School only during the 2006–07 school year to better facilitate the somewhat reluctant participation by three of the Bay teachers. In 2007–08, they alternated schools; this continued in the fall of 2008. The PLC had an occasional PRiSSM facilitator in the first year (2005–06) and a different facilitator (Judith) who attended at least half of their meetings in 2006–07. PRiSSM support ended in the spring of 2007, and they no longer had a dedicated facilitator. Beginning in 2006–07, the principal at Bay Middle School visited the PLC meetings when possible to observe but did not serve as a facilitator.

The Grade Level Expectations (GLEs) for science (OSPI, 2005) were published in 2005 as a *curriculum* to guide teachers' and districts' understandings about the expected progression of students' development of targeted science concepts and skills. Thus, in their first year as a PLC, the teachers possessed a brand new document to inform their investigation into their teaching and their students' learning. Additionally, the state test (the WASL) had been administered to eighth-grade students for three years, and test items and scoring guidelines were beginning to be released on the state's website. The format of these released items is scenario-based. A description from the OSPI website states:

> The two system scenarios briefly describe a natural system then ask students about the inputs, outputs, and transfers of matter, energy,

and information in the system. The three inquiry scenarios describe a student investigation then ask students to analyze the investigation, including writing a conclusion and planning a new investigation. Application scenarios describe a student solution to a human problem then ask students to analyze the solution, including designing a solution to a new problem. (OSPI, 2007)

These test-related documents (released items, scoring guides, and anchor papers, including samples of students' responses) proved to be a tool teachers used across the years.

Shaping the Inquiry Focus

In 2005, WASL results were shaping school-level conversations and school improvement plans across the state. At Grays and Bay middle schools, their students' science scores explicitly influenced their collaborative inquiry focus. When the PLC came together at the beginning of the 2005–06 school year, they learned that WASL results from the previous spring showed specific weaknesses in students' abilities to addresses questions related to constructing scientific explanations (part of the inquiry strand of the GLEs). This resulted in teachers deciding to focus on improving students' abilities to write scientific conclusions for their collaborative inquiry. Corinne described how their inquiry question drew from an item analysis of WASL results in conjunction with classroom-based evidence:

> Eighty percent of the kids, if we just gave them a multiple-choice test, would meet standard. But when we looked at adding writing into the equation, only about 20 to 30 percent were actually meeting standard . . . And plus we just knew from working with our students that when they were writing they weren't supporting their conclusions with evidence, they weren't asking questions, they were all over the board. So that's how we came to our question. (PRiSSM Showcase, May 4, 2006)

In this way, student data from the state test supported teachers' development of a PLC focus that was meaningful to them and validated in the larger landscape of state standards.

When the PLC expanded in the fall of 2006 to include all the seventh- and eighth-grade science teachers from both schools, they referenced the improvement in their science scores and set a school improvement goal to again increase the percent of students achieving "proficient":

> Leon: More students are meeting standards in the inquiry strand than in previous years . . . currently 58.8% of students met standard doing inquiry, so last year's 8th graders. Inquiry scores are above the state

average in science for our school, and . . . so what do we think is the cause of this, and that has to do with our teachers' actions, intentional deliberate articulation of GLEs that address inquiry by classroom teachers. That would include our science fair work as well over the last few years, focus on alignment of inquiry with regard to which grade level is responsible for teaching what, specifically as it pertains to scientific method, increased use of student design, investigations focused in inquiry, and I think that's what we've been doing, kind of more deliberate labs and stuff like that, and of course the conclusion work. (PLC meeting, October 10, 2006)

Once again, this school-level goal for increasing the number of students attaining proficiency on the WASL translated to their PLC inquiry, as conclusion writing was an important part of high-stakes testing. The original PLC members felt there was more to learn about how to help students craft and make meaning of scientific conclusions, and the new PLC members were willing to explore this area.

Concurrent with their discussions about conclusion writing, Grays Bay PLC members identified a second area of weakness for their students, based on the state test results. They were concerned about how poorly their students did on the systems section of the test (i.e., their understandings of scientific concepts). Thus, as they negotiated their inquiry focus for the year the test results played a large role in their decision-making process. Leon, the PLC leader, directed their attention when he stated:

Last year we worked in that little slice of inquiry called conclusion writing, and did a bang up job obviously, because look at how much our kids improved, and I think what we did is in large part why we saw those gains, but it looked like there were a lot of minuses in the systems strand, and now we are at this very precarious juncture of what do we do next. We need to narrow a focus. How do we approach this idea of systems, and what does that mean to us? (PLC meeting, October 10, 2006)

When negotiating their inquiry focus in 2006–07 and again in 2007–08, they referred to the standards document—the overarching Essential Academic Learning Requirements and the more specific Grade Level Expectations—to try to understand the state's vision. For example, in the following excerpt from a PLC meeting in fall, 2006, the teachers were trying to understand what a systems approach to all science content meant:

Larry: I think a nice place to start would be identify a common vocabulary and what that means—
Margaret: In terms of a system, then that might help us with a common vocabulary to start to think more system like, every time you go to a new unit you can go what's the input here, what's the output. . . .

Larry: Consistent words, consistent vocabulary, is there a consistent vocabulary, I'm looking for one of the OSPI science—

Katherine: [The GLE] handbook, in the back it breaks it down by grade, 8th grade, 10th grade.

Judith: They're also in the GLEs, so they tell you what, in any lesson you teach, if you purposely think about where's the system, what's the system, so it's talking about plants, oh, the plant is the system, what are the inputs, so it could be energy input, it could be—(October 10, 2006)

The systems EALR, however, proved to be too general to translate into a collaborative inquiry focus. As the PLC included teachers of both life and physical sciences, they could not identify GLEs that were applicable to both subject areas. Also, they could not get state test data that would help them understand specifically what their students were struggling with in each content area. Nancy expressed their frustration:

> I would like the systems questions divided out into individual strands . . . so I know specifically what I need to improve on, to me that's very powerful . . . I know it's impossible at the moment, I've been shot down many times, but I still want that to be looked at by the district . . . we can get all the data back on our kids, but we can't find out if this was a physical science question, 78% didn't get this part of it, because to me that's valuable information, I can say, "Wow, 78% of my students didn't get that part of it." That's on me, but until I can find out what specific statements my kids are struggling on year, after year, after year, it's hard to fix what you don't know is broken. (PLC meeting, October 10, 2006)

Nancy's comment about being "shot down" refers to her and others' attempts to ask state level directors for more specific information about the areas where students failed or succeeded. Partly due to their frustration at not being able to identify the content areas that needed attention, they decided to focus on both students' understandings about conclusion writing and systems.

At the end of the 2006–07 school year, they explored a new focus for the next year. Still concerned about the systems EALR, they again sought a way to identify an inquiry focus. They spent time identifying students' needs with respect to the GLEs, and again referenced the state standards:

> Some of what we could be looking for could be from the regular content, but also there could be some questions in there related to the modeling GLEs, here—"create a model or computer simulation to investigate and predict the behavior of objects," another one, "explain the advantage and limitations of investigating with a model." For those models that do that, we can also ask those kinds of questions that would help with

that particular GLE. I'm not so sure models, [if] they could [or] they should be our focus, but they could be the primary vehicle by which not only integrated with assessment but also get at the content, the systems stuff. (PLC meeting, May 18, 2007)

They recognized that the content encompassed by the systems GLEs were problematic for their students; so, in an attempt to make this more concrete, they spoke of integrating a process-oriented GLE about the use of models into the systems focus. However, over the next year they experienced difficulties in operationalizing this focus. Thus, while the systems GLE was problematic for students, it proved equally problematic for teachers as they struggled to clearly define learning goals and related classroom-based assessments that would address the standard. Without this clarity, it was difficult for teachers to frame an inquiry question that could be investigated.

For each of the four inquiry foci developed during this study, the teachers exclusively used the state standards, student test data, and test-related documents to negotiate and identify an inquiry focus. While grounding collaborative inquiry in well-defined standards is appropriate, in the next section we will show how the difficulties they faced in making meaning of these state standards ultimately led to the restriction of their inquiry to areas where the state provided clarity through the test-related documents.

A Framework for the Inquiry Processes

The standards and, even more so, the state test-related documents provided a framework for the PLC inquiry. The teachers used different documents as resources: the released test items translated into formative assessments; the anchor papers and scoring guides helped them develop common instructional activities that resulted in classroom-based data; and the scoring guides also served as an initial framework for construction of their own data-analysis tool. They built upon and extended the scoring guides and test items as their vision for student learning (related to conclusion writing, in particular) became more developed. Over the years, the teachers used the released test items as diagnostic and benchmark assessments in their classrooms, as recommended by the state. Initially these items were used just as the state released them, but over time the teachers began to make revisions based upon their analyses of their own students' responses. Andrea explained:

I think if we could take a week or so and really work on those benchmarks and then once we've given them, take another week or so and work on them again, I think they would be more representative of what we want the kids to know. It would be a much better assessment. We kind of, we didn't really throw them together but we worked with what we had and we did the best we could, and we find a lot of problems with them. [When] you don't feel confident entirely about the tool then you don't feel confident about the data you get from the tool. . . . The "Grass is Greener" [scenario] is a really good example of that . . . but that took many many sessions of giving it and scoring it and going, well, you know that question, we decided to switch from multiple choice with the manipulated variable to having them fill it in. And we learned a whole lot about, gee, they don't really entirely know that. When they could pick A, B, C, or D they were much more confident or we got better scores. So when we do choose to use our time to work on the benchmarks then they are valuable tools and we are valuing the data we get from them. (Interview, September 17, 2008)

When there were usable released test items and other documents, as there were for the conclusion writing and planning an investigation foci, teachers in the PLC were able to administer common classroom assessments, analyze the data from those assessments, and plan learning activities to address the students' needs that emerged from the analysis.

On the other hand, when there was little support from test-related documents, the progress of the PLC inquiry was severely handicapped. Specifically, the state provided limited support for the development of a framework for their focus on systems and models and they struggled, and eventually failed, to construct classroom-based assessments associated with these standards. For example, in 2007–08, after conducting a curriculum topic study (Keeley, 2005) on models, examining the models commonly used in their life and physical science courses, and piloting a common assessment tool to uncover students' ideas about the uses of models in science, some of the group members felt ready to move forward with an inquiry focus on models. Others, however, were unable to conceptualize the instructional intentions of the concept of models, and the PLC was unable to make meaning from the classroom-based student data they had collected. During an April, 2008, PLC meeting when the group reflected on their lack of progress in understanding what their focus on models meant, Jessica stated, "I feel like some of the crisis we've had this year is this sort of crisis of soul. You know? What is it that's most important in what we do and their learning?" Andrea later provided further insight into their challenge:

I think we could have pounded that one through and come up with our own sort of scoring guide or rubric, or definitions and then a rubric, and then some assessments and stuff. But every time we came up with something somebody would lead us back to square one. If I heard "everything is a model" one more time I was going to scream! That would always run us back to the beginning, it was this circular logic. I think that is why we decided to switch to the concrete this time. There are definite standards for grading a conclusion, there are definite standards for grading "plan an investigation." . . . I'm hoping that maybe in a year or two we can start pushing that topic again, because I think it's a valuable worthwhile thing, but we just, we didn't have anything to hang our hats on, we didn't have anything that felt concrete from the state that helped our investigation of that topic. (Interview, September 17, 2008)

This lack of a framework meant they did not have a starting point—that is, their ideas about the use of models in life and physical science were unbounded and they were unable to define what students should know or be able to do in this respect. Thus, in 2008–09 they decided to again focus their inquiry on conclusion writing and planning an investigation, two areas where the state provided numerous released test items, scoring guides, and anchor papers.

When there was little support from state test-related documents, as for their focus on systems and models described earlier, little progress was made in the collaborative inquiry. However, even when test-related documents were available, the teachers devoted significant time to making sense of the state expectations as expressed in the GLEs. The meaning of any one GLE was not obvious and the teachers drew upon their own understandings and expectations for student work, along with the explications provided through the scored student responses to test items (anchor papers), to create a deeper understanding of the GLE. For example, in the early weeks of the first year the teachers used the anchor papers to formulate an idea of the expectations for scientific conclusion writing as expressed in the GLE document. At a November, 2005, PLC meeting, they collectively analyzed some of these papers:

Leon: Well here's a fifth grader's answer, just to get us kind of warmed up here. These are annotations of students' responses and so if they scored them they have blanks so I guess you can kind of practice and then look at how the professional scorers have done this. Ahh, so like this one kid, the conclusive statement which is, well, in the fifth grade, rather than saying, "answer the investigative question," it was something about the prediction. Tell whether the prediction is right or wrong or something like that. So this kid said, "The kid's prediction was right," and they got a point for saying that. . . . Then, they call this thing "the lowest supporting data," which when I looked on [the website], it must have been the next grade up—an eighth grade thing, rather than saying the lowest and the highest they were very specific. So in this scoring sheet, I put [the lowest supporting data] as the two hours and [the highest supporting data as] the twelve.
Brooke: Oh I wondered what that was.
Leon: You could do it, I guess, as the six hour or some other combination. Maybe I should have left it as the lowest supporting and the

highest. Seems like a pattern. What they want them to do when they talk about the data is show the lowest point and the highest point. (PLC meeting, November 11, 2005)

The previous dialogue illustrates how teachers were using scoring guides in conjunction with an anchor paper to better understand what the learning targets (GLEs) were. Their discussion served as a means for clarifying how students were expected to use data to support a given prediction on the WASL. In this case, the test-related documents were used to provide clarification for the standards. The previous conversation also shows that teachers sought meaning for the learning target beyond the scoring of released items by consulting available information from a state website, but that this was inadequate in answering their questions. In the second year, teachers were still trying to clarify the expectations stated in the scoring guide for conclusion writing as evidenced in this excerpt from a PLC meeting:

Larry: What's the standards for explanatory language?
Leon: Good question.
Andrea: We don't know, we're not going there today.
Leon: Somehow it needs to connect the data with the answer. That's the best we can give you right now. (November 15, 2006)

Over time, in comparing professionally scored responses with their own scoring, the teachers began to formulate an understanding of what the state test was expecting students to do and, at the same time, to voice their own ideas.

While students' abilities to write scientific conclusions and plan an investigation were significant portions of the state test and, as such, well-supported by test-related documents, the teachers also considered these as important learning goals for students. Jessica asserted to her colleagues:

That's why the conclusions, we could really focus on that because there was a really universal tool. I mean in addition—at least for me—in addition to having to write in these four points [for the WASL], easy to assess but I was like, kids need to be able to make an argument, give evidence and declare how their evidence supports what they think. I mean that's life. You know? And so there was this real, like, "That is important!" (PLC meeting, April 16, 2008)

Thus, while the WASL shaped their inquiry focus each year, and the scoring guides and other test-related documents supported their data collection and analysis, the teachers' collaborative work targeted a richer outcome than just helping students pass the state test. They were confident that it was important to hold students to more rigorous expectations than those laid out by the test-scoring guides. Andrea emphasized:

I feel that it's wrong for my kids to be little automatons that can answer conclusions, I really, really, really have a problem with that. I think that embedded in a WASL conclusion are skills that are necessary for them in the wide world, in the science world, in language arts class, and I would like to focus on those skills that they can take with them, put in their pocket and say I know how to do these things, rather than I know how to answer a conclusion on the WASL. (PLC meeting, November 15, 2006)

Despite their explicit focus on improving students' abilities to pass the WASL, the Grays Bay teachers were not merely seeking a way to improve students' test scores. They also tried to make sense of the state standards and, while this occurred in the context of the test when rubrics and anchor papers were available, they also surfaced and examined their own beliefs and values in light of the state expectations.

Stimulating Teacher Learning

In addition to serving as support for data collection and analysis related to writing scientific conclusions, the standards and the test-related documents served as critical competitors, providing teachers with comparison points for their own values and beliefs about what was important to teach their students. In this way, these documents stimulated teacher learning. As they analyzed the anchor papers, the teachers worried that they could train the students to successfully write a WASL conclusion, but that this would be meaningless to the students. They expressed concern that the students "have no science content" to make the conclusion meaningful, as opposed to the authentic purpose underpinning a scientific conclusion: "Because as a scientist, you're stating what you know to be facts as they come off your data, but you're also making a case for your hypothesis, for it or against it" (PLC meeting, April 25, 2006). Andrea summed up this common concern when she stated, "[The test essentially says], 'Let's erase the chance for critical thinking and recopy the whole data table and that way they'll get a point.' " As such, a number of PLC participants used the state-provided guides and samples heuristically, asking questions of their students' responses and of their classroom activities that pushed them to think more deeply about the nature of scientific writing in conjunction with age-appropriate expectations for their students. Jessica clarified that while the state test dictated, to some extent, their inquiry process, the state standards were aligned with and useful in informing their teaching practices and learning goals:

We're looking at the GLEs not so much to just figure out, "How can we help our students take the test well?" but because we're like, "Okay, this is an important way to look at science. This is an important way to think about the world." . . . I don't feel as a new teacher that [the state standards and WASL] are a chain around my neck. Like a bad thing. It's, you know, I think what we're pursuing would be good if those standards and WASL weren't there at all. I think we would still be trying to reach similar ends. (Interview, April 5, 2007)

Their numerous conversations over the years of this study reflected continued refinement of their understandings of both the state's expectations and their own. At the beginning of the 2008 school year, they collected diagnostic student data in the first week of school. They used a scoring rubric they had developed themselves in the previous year, and devoted their first two PLC meetings to refining their understanding of the rubric and their interpretation of student answers. After they individually scored one student's response, they compared and discussed how each assigned value points:

Leon: So if a kid just talked about the low range and the high range and never talked about this peak they still get four points?

Nancy: I'm hearing no.

Hugh: The first question is they need to attack that, that's what scientists do though. They bracket. You know? We're looking for a result so we're going to use a condition that we know would give a low result and then the furthest out condition that we can test to and then if the results fall somewhere in between with better results, well, it would be nice if they could identify that, too. (PLC meeting, September 10, 2008)

Hugh's response reflects the consideration given to the scientific rationale for asking students to include particular types of information in their conclusions. His reasoning is not grounded in the state's scoring rubric, but in how scientists design experiments.

In PRiSSM, the construction of a common vision of high-quality learning and teaching was identified as an initial step in the inquiry cycle (see Figure 4.1). The three years of conversation amongst the Grays Bay teachers helps us understand that this vision is negotiated over time in response to critical competitors to teachers' beliefs. Initially, the released test items, scoring rubrics, and sample student papers (anchor papers) provided on the state's science WASL website provided that critical competitor. In the small, voluntary PLC group in the first year, the teachers moved rapidly from the anchor papers to collectively examining their own students' work. In this way, competing ideas came from each teacher's interpretation of one student's response to a conclusion-writing prompt. The following excerpt from a long conversation about one student's paper shows how they negotiated their understanding of student work in the context of the state expectations:

Corinne: Say that again, you're not addressing the "how."

Leon: Right. They're just reading the question as does the amount of light, and they're answering that yes or no.

Corinne: Yeah but they're not addressing the "how."

Leon: The "how"?

Andrea: So, are we guilty of writing labs for them that way? Without the [how]? . . . So this, "The grass with two hours of light grew only 1 cm per week but the six hours and the twelve hours grew 2 or more a week?" That's nothing?

Corinne: It's not specific, there's no [unintelligible] because it's not derived all the way or not.

Andrea: What if they end their whole thing, "So, the longer the grass was in the sunlight the taller the grass grew"?

Leon: That's answering something.

Andrea: Yeah, but they didn't address it at the beginning.

Leon: You know, it's such a hard one because.

Andrea: Would you give one for.

Katherine: I would give them a point because—somewhere in that.

Andrea: So, I would say zero for the explanatory language?

Brooke: Well, but they said, the first thing, the prediction was correct and the prediction said the grass that receives more light will grow the tallest. So, is that acceptable?

Leon: Yes. Because they either have to answer the investigative question or tell whether the hypothesis is correct or incorrect.

Andrea: Well, that's for that one, because, that's what they were answering. (PLC meeting, December 6, 2005)

Through ongoing dialogue such as this, teachers began to construct a collective understanding of the state expectations for student responses on conclusion-writing scenarios and also to construct a common vision of their own (higher) expectations. The following comment by Nancy was oft voiced by the other most active PLC teachers: "I would agree that we need to increase the skill. The state is just a bottom line. Everybody needs to hit this bottom line and I don't think we need to lower the bar that far" (PLC meeting, September 10, 2008) .

In significant ways the teachers generated knowledge valuable to their own teaching and to their colleagues in the district and in the state. The work of the Grays Bay teachers on conclusion writing led to their participation in creating district-wide benchmark assessments and scoring rubrics that held students to higher standards than those of the state scoring guides. Information gleaned from these classroom-based assessments helped the teachers make decisions about their next teaching moves. For example, the eighth-grade teachers found that the students came to them with much improved conclusion-writing skills, and decided to shift their targeted instructional efforts from conclusions to the planning of scientific investigations (PLC meetings, May 2008 and September 2008). Additionally, the positive results of their first year's collaboration influenced the Bay principal to actively incorporate collaborative inquiry across the school. While this was also a district-level implementation, this principal explicitly valued the process and even wrote an article for an administrator's professional journal that tied the teachers' inquiry to student achievement. These latter examples clearly evidence the directional interface of the PLC work to educational contexts outside the PLC; while external contextual factors such as standards impacted the work of the teachers, the PLC work simultaneously influenced a variety of broader educational contexts.

Despite the challenges the PLC faced when they expanded to 11 members, there was a core group of six who continued to pursue questions about the interpretation and application of the standards (such as systems and models) in their middle school classrooms, and who continued to wonder about "what do we do for the students who aren't learning?" (Jessica, PLC meeting, April 16, 2008). These types of questions evidenced the inquiry stance held by some of the PLC members. In a less critical fashion, the PLC members began to more explicitly negotiate the values in and meanings of the scoring guides they were modifying. For example, in the latter half of the third year and in the beginning of the fourth, teachers who had previously been less active participants in the PLC dialogue began to contribute. At the first meeting of the 2008 school year, Micah, a teacher who had remained relatively quiet over the past two years, distributed a sample exemplar student response he had constructed for the "Grass is Greener" scenario administered by the group as a classroom-based diagnostic assessment. This was the first conversation since the PLC expanded in the fall of 2006 in which *all* eleven of the teachers participated. The following excerpt shows the negotiating that occurred:

Micah: This is what I personally think should earn them the points. . . .
Jerri: For that explanatory math language though you could have just had the last sentence.
Nancy: Right. Could just have the last one.
Micah: Any of those three would work. Is what I personally think.
Andrea: Really?
Nancy: Oh, I would think that the first two have to be together.
Jerri: Yeah, you'd have to have the first two.
Margaret: You'd have to have both of them together or.
Nancy: Because you have to have both conditions. Yeah.
Margaret: Or you have the last one. . . .
Nancy: Here now we're going to have a debate on that. Because they do show explanatory but I think it's supposed to compare the two. So if you only talk about one you're not going back and comparing.
Leon: Yeah, well, yeah. I mean the state says it's supposed to explain how the data supports your answer.
Nancy: Yeah. So I would say these two together or the third one by itself.
Micah: Well, that's good feedback for me to know. (PLC meeting, September 10, 2008)

Micah's contribution was made at a point in the conversation when the group was struggling to explicitly define what a strong student conclusion would look like; they had student samples that were challenging their collective understandings about the rubric they had developed. His exemplar provided them with the critical competitor they needed to come to an understanding about the student work at hand. His willingness to share his ideas reflected his increased understanding of the common learning goals about conclusion writing and his trust that his contribution wouldn't "sound stupid" (personal conversation, April 2008).

While teacher learning was not always collective in the two years of the expanded PLC, Andrea talked about how even a frustrating year contributed to her professional growth:

> I personally took stuff away from that kind of disaster year with the models question. Because what I'm finding is that I'm starting to ask hopefully more thought-provoking questions. So when we do use a model, I actually stop and I'll either have the kids write or I'll ask them verbally to tell me what are the good things and bad things about this model—what are the limitations, whatever. And so I took stuff away from there that I'm using even though we didn't really get to that point with our PLC work. It's changed the sorts of questions I'm asking the kids. (Interview, September 17, 2008)

In their attempts to make meaning of the GLEs and broader standards and to clarify their own expectations for student learning in the context of the test-related documents, the Grays Bay teachers collectively or individually constructed new understandings that translated into their work with students.

CONCLUSIONS

For the Grays Bay PLC, the state science standards and test-related documents were, in many ways, useful support structures. The state test results helped them ground their inquiry focus in an area that was meaningful to them and also deemed important by the state. The released test items and accompanying anchor papers provided resources the teachers could adapt for their classrooms and use in the construction and negotiation of their collaborative inquiry process. The use of these test-related items, whether as released by the state or modified as the teachers' understandings deepened, provided them with classroom-based data that informed subsequent teaching actions. However, these actions were grounded in hours of collaborative reflection and data analysis by the teacher group. When these test-related documents were unavailable, the teachers were less able to come to a common understanding of the learning goals, as in the case of systems and models. Without these documents, the teachers struggled to construct classroom-based assessments and to agree upon common teaching actions. Based upon their continued negotiation of the meanings in the state standards for conclusion writing and planning an investigation, as well as their inability to define what the state expectation for students' understandings about scientific models meant, it became apparent that the meanings of the individual grade level expectations were not self-evident. The teachers' close examination of one aspect of the standards and assessment (conclusion writing) stimulated ongoing reflection on and dialogue about their own understandings and expectations and helped them focus their teaching. While extremely powerful to the teachers' professional growth trajectory, a significant amount of time was required for the teachers to construct a common understanding in just this one area.

Initially, low student scores on the high-stakes state test provided motivation for teachers to evaluate current practices, but for many, this was not enough. The more teachers explored the resources provided by the state, the more they came to understand the limitations of those assessment tools. The teachers learned that the high-stakes test could not provide the kind of diagnostic data that they craved. Teachers' initial frustrations about the lack of available data that contained specific information about what students could and could not do, or what they did or did not know, led them to modify existing test items and develop new tools that could provide them with the diagnostic information they wanted. Teachers also learned how difficult it is to develop diagnostic assessments. Through experience, they discovered that assessment writing is an iterative process, that student responses need to be analyzed in terms of intended learning targets, and that items need to be tested and revised. Their learning trajectory toward a deeper assessment literacy moved them closer to Stiggins's (2005) conception of assessment *for* learning as they began to use "summative assessments in formative ways" (p. 326) and, more importantly, engaged students in understanding for themselves the standard on conclusion writing and their own progress toward attainment of that goal. Collaborative inquiry provided the Grays Bay teachers with opportunities to build increasingly sophisticated understandings about the purposes and uses of classroom-based data, and how these data can or cannot inform instructional practices.

The teacher group's three-year examination of conclusion writing is testament to their dedication and collective ability to deconstruct pedagogical issues in a fine-grained manner. The teachers were adamant about negotiating this common understanding and making use of their collective strengths to better utilize state guidelines as supports for their classroom instruction. Further, over the three years, many of them reiterated a strong sentiment against teaching to the test. The time devoted to making meaning, grounded in their classroom data, of the standard on conclusion writing helped them to question and come to understand what was important scientifically about conclusion writing and to challenge their instructional approaches in order to help all their students improve. Their collaborative inquiry processes and stance toward inquiry, when supported with resources that helped advance their understandings, stimulated learning on an individual and collective basis.

IMPLICATIONS

Since the standards movement began in the 1980s in the United States, it has become increasingly tied to high-stakes tests and the standardization of student learning goals. These developments are key contexts for the work of the Grays Bay PLC teachers. Their collaborative inquiry focused intently upon making sense of state standards and translating these understandings into classroom practices that could help their students attain the standards-based learning goals. As they negotiated interpretations for the student learning outcomes intended by specific standards statements, they found a way to reconcile a fear that they might be merely teaching to the state test with their increasingly explicit understanding of the scientific value inherent in the given standard. In this way, the Grays Bay PLC provides a model of how collaborative inquiry can promote teacher *and* student learning. This model serves as a counterexample to fears that PLCs may be, as Hargreaves (2008) states, designed as "totalitarian training sects" where "analysis of student work and results is undertaken only in the context of literacy and math" (p. 179) and the purpose of the group is to "simply elevate scores on high-stakes test" (p. 176).

The challenge for teachers engaged in collaborative inquiry with a focus on standards is to resist the movement toward standardization while recognizing—and critically analyzing—the support that can be found in standards and related documents. As was noted in the introduction, standards can be used generatively, as guidelines for teaching, content, assessment, and professional development (National Research Council, 1996), or they can be used prescriptively, as could have happened with the Grays Bay teachers if they had not continued to question their own values and beliefs in relation to the test specifications and scoring criteria from the state-released items. The purpose of SCTI is to provide a space for professional learning that is derived from intentional and collaborative research on classroom practices and student learning. Louis (2008) asserts that "a mandated focus on data analysis and raising test scores conflicts with the core of PLCs, which involve trusting, shared solving of problems of classroom practice" (pp. 45–46). Hargreaves (2008) underscores the importance of a collective stance toward inquiry in moving this work forward, stating that "At their best, members of professional learning communities deliberate intelligently about what kinds of learning count as achievement, and courageously question, challenge, and subvert imposed prescriptions that diminish that learning" (p. 189). The Grays Bay PLC's three-year investigation of conclusion writing was motivated by a desire to utilize state standards and test-related documents as supports for their classroom practice and students' learning. Their successes were due in large part to the inquiry-oriented nature of their investigation that led them to continually question how these standards related to the students in their own classrooms.

Schools are currently immersed in using data from high-stakes tests to shape instructional decisions and, as such, teachers, administrators, and parents need supported and sustained opportunities to develop deep understandings of the standards upon which these tests are based. From this perspective, our findings suggest that deconstructing the meaning within standards may be an important element of teachers' collaborative inquiry. The American Federation of Teachers concluded in 1995 that:

> Without professional development school reform will not happen . . . The nation can adopt rigorous standards, set forth a visionary scenario . . . but unless the classroom teacher understands and is committed to the plan and knows how to make it happen, the dream will come to naught. (as cited in Hawley & Valli, 1999, p. 129)

Teachers need to individualize, through connections to their own practice, the broad student learning goals and large-scale tests put forth by states and other agencies. Unfortunately, these learning goals, which are intended to support teachers in thinking about curriculum and instruction, can be difficult for teachers to generally understand and connect to their learners and immediate classroom contexts. Collaborative teacher inquiry is one form of professional development that can provide a supportive environment for teachers to deconstruct and negotiate understandings of standards, grounded in their own students' learning data. But as evidenced in this case, deep reflections on standards can be quite difficult to conduct and require enormous amounts of time. When this inquiry is grounded in the larger school, district, and state foci on standards, teachers' efforts are authentically aligned with other forces impinging upon them. Perhaps more importantly, their resultant learning can contribute to shaping these external forces. SCTI, even in the context of high-stakes tests, holds promise for enabling teachers to recognize content standards as grist for reflections on their own practice and in becoming the instructional supports they are intended to be.

REFERENCES

Carroll, C., & Mumme, J. (2005). Leadership for change: Supporting and developing teacher leaders in Mathematics Renaissance K–12. Retrieved June 30, 2006, from http://www.te-mat.org/carroll.aspx#1

Cochran-Smith, M., & Lytle, S. L. (1999). Relationships of knowledge and practice: Teacher learning in communities. In A. Iran-Nejad & P. D. Pearson (Eds.), *Review of research in education* (Vol. 24, pp. 249–306). Washington, DC: AERA.

Cohen, D. K., & Ball, D. L. (1999). *Instruction, capacity, and improvement* (CPRE Research Report No. RR-043). Philadelphia: University of Pennsylvania Consortium for Policy Research in Education.

Cohen, D. K., Raudenbush, S. W., & Ball, D. L. (2003). Resources, instruction, and research. *Educational Evaluation and Policy Analysis, 25*(2), 119–142.

Fullan, M., Hill, P., & Crevola, C. (2006). *Breakthrough.* Thousand Oaks, CA: Corwin Press.

Garmston, R. J., & Wellman, B. M. (1999). *The adaptive school: A sourcebook for developing collaborative groups.* Norwood, MA: Christopher-Gordon Publishers.

Glaser, B. G. (1969). The constant comparative method of qualitative analysis. In G. J. McCall & J. L. Simmons (Eds.), *Issues in participant observation* (pp. 216–227). Reading, MA: Addison-Wesley.

Hargreaves, A. (2008). Leading professional learning communities: Moral choices amid murky realities. In A. M. Blankstein, P. D. Houston, & R. W. Cole (Eds.), *Sustaining professional learning communities* (pp. 175–197). Thousand Oaks, CA: Corwin Press.

Hawley, W. D., & Valli, L. (1999). The essentials of effective professional development: A new consensus. In L. Darling-Hammond & G. Sykes (Eds.), *Teaching as the learning profession* (pp. 127–150). San Francisco: Jossey-Bass.

Keeley, P. (2005). *Science curriculum topic study.* Thousand Oaks, CA: Corwin Press.

Louis, K. S. (2008). Creating and sustaining professional communities. In A. M. Blankstein, P. D. Houston, & R. W. Cole (Eds.), *Sustaining professional learning communities* (pp. 41–58). Thousand Oaks, CA: Corwin Press.

McLaughlin, M. W., & Talbert, J. E. (2006). *Building school-based teacher learning communities.* New York: Teachers College Press.

Merriam, S. B. (1998). *Qualitative research and case study applications in education.* San Francisco: Jossey-Bass.

Miles, M. B., & Huberman, A. M. (1994). *Qualitative data analysis: An expanded sourcebook.* Thousand Oaks, CA: Sage.

National Research Council. (1996). *National science education standards.* Washington, DC: National Academies Press.

National Research Council. (2003). *What is the influence of the National Science Education Standards? Reviewing the evidence, a workshop summary.* Washington, DC: National Academies Press.

Office of Superintendent of Public Instruction. (2005). *Science K–10 grade level expectations: A new level of specificity.* Olympia, WA: Author.

Office of Superintendent of Public Instruction (2007). Using results to improve student learning: Science grade 8 2007 released scenarios and items. Retrieved September 30, 2008, from http://www.k12.wa.us/Assessment/WASL/testquestions.aspx

Office of Superintendent of Public Instruction. (2008). A brief history of Essential Academic Learning Requirements and the Washington Assessment of Student Learning. Retrieved September 14, 2008, from www.k12.wa.us/assessment/WASL/MathPracticeTests/AppendixA-HSmath.pdf

Pedulla, J. J., Abrams, L. M., Madaus, G. F., Russell, R. K., Ramos, M. A., & Miao, J. (2003). *Perceived effects of state-mandated testing programs on teaching and learning: Findings from a national survey of teachers.* Boston: National Board on Educational Testing and Public Policy, Lynch School of Education, Boston College.

Stiggins, R. (2005). From formative assessment to assessment FOR learning: A path to success in standards-based schools. *Phi Delta Kappan, 87*(4), 324–328.

Strauss, A., & Corbin, J. (1998). *Basics of qualitative research: Techniques and procedures for developing grounded theory.* Thousand Oaks, CA: Sage.

Wells, G. (1999). *Dialogic inquiry: Toward a sociocultural practice and theory of education.* Cambridge, UK: Cambridge University Press.

5 Dialogue as Support in Teacher Collaborative Inquiry

Elizabeth Bondy and Pamela Williamson

University of Florida and University of Cincinnati

Scholars have suggested that professional development embedded in every-day classroom experience may help teachers explore problems of practice in meaningful ways (Cochran-Smith & Lytle, 1999; Little, 2003). Although there is considerable enthusiasm in the professional development literature for enabling teachers to talk with one another about their problems of prac-tice, there is less known about the features of talk that facilitate collab-orative inquiry. In their memorable discussion of "coblaboration," DuFour and colleagues (2006, p. 89) point out that some forms of talk, though enjoyable for teachers, are unlikely to lead to improvement in teaching or student learning.

Some light has been shed on the nature of dialogue that supports collabor-ative inquiry. For example, Strahan (2003) found that dialogue about student performance data facilitated the development of shared values and beliefs about instruction that enhanced student achievement. Snow-Gerono (2005) pointed out that a sense of psychological safety was important in promot-ing the wondering and uncertainty needed for inquiry to flourish. However, Supovitz (2002) noted that safety without a focus on teaching and learning was insufficient. Hollins, McIntyre, DeBose, Hollins, and Towner (2004) found that use of a five-step protocol for examining literacy instruction pro-vided a structure that helped teachers to collaborate to improve their under-standing and use of effective instructional strategies. Little (2003) noted a number of features of dialogue that impeded the collaborative inquiry needed to examine and address perplexing problems of practice. Still, the features of dialogue that promote productive collaborative inquiry are unclear. Further efforts to examine more closely the "black box" (Little, 2003, p. 915) of teacher talk in these groups certainly are warranted.

In this chapter we report on an exploratory study of the nature of talk among educators at a low-income, high-minority elementary school. The study focused on a weekly meeting, called Inclusion Meeting, that was cre-ated to assist teachers as they grappled with the inclusion of students with disabilities in their classrooms. Inclusion Meetings were not formally identi-fied as opportunities for collaborative inquiry. Rather, they were viewed as a setting in which teachers could collaborate to address pressing concerns about teaching and learning. Indeed, they gave educators a chance to exercise the skills of inquiry that they were developing as part of a professional development effort at the school.

PROFESSIONAL DEVELOPMENT AT HOPEWELL ELEMENTARY

Hopewell Elementary School (a pseudonym) is a K–5 facility of 425 students located in a city of 108,000. Hopewell has 95% of students who receive free or reduced-price lunch and a similar percentage who are African American. Since the 2000–2001 school year, the first author, Elizabeth, has worked closely with the school in a position called "professor-in-residence." In that role, she has spent at least one day per week at the school, working with the leadership team, consulting with teachers, facilitating professional development, overseeing research efforts, and coordinating student teaching activities. In short, Elizabeth has been a school partner who has worked closely with the school over time to improve the education of children and the learning of educators, including the university students and faculty who spend time there. In the 2003–2004 school year, the school joined a large, endowed partnership dedicated to helping schools become professional learning communities (PLCs). A PLC was defined as a collegial group of educators (including administrators) who work and learn collaboratively, make their practice public, study their own practice, share a vision of the kinds of practice that lead to student learning, and participate in decision making about the conditions that support excellent teaching and learning (Hord, 1997). The goals of a PLC include reducing teacher isolation, improving teacher learning and commitment to students, and academic gains for students. Elizabeth served as the facilitator for this work.

In that same year, Hopewell did not achieve adequate yearly progress for the students with disabilities, nearly one third of the student population. The principal determined that those students must be included in general education classrooms in order to have better access to the curriculum that they are expected to have mastered for the annual high-stakes tests. Teachers clearly needed support in order to facilitate inclusion. The blossoming effort toward becoming a school-wide professional learning community that had many task-specific subcommunities had laid the groundwork to help teachers rise to the challenge. Although the school could not yet be characterized as a PLC as defined earlier, teachers had begun to practice the collaborative teaching- and learning-focused interactions at the core of this kind of community. With the help of the facilitator, existing school structures, such as the monthly faculty meeting and weekly grade-level team meeting, were being transformed to provide opportunities for professional collaboration. In addition, new structures were designed to help educators raise questions about and study their own practice.

One such structure was ripe for supporting the professional development of Hopewell's teachers, who were now called on to include students with disabilities. Called "Teacher Fellows" (or Fellows, for short), the community was inquiry-oriented, teacher-directed, and during the year this study was conducted, included a year-long professional development focus on inclusion. Elizabeth, the first author of this chapter, facilitated these meetings. Participation in the Teacher Fellows community was open to all educators at Hopewell, and 21 out of 35 joined. The group held monthly two-hour meetings, and members were compensated with funds from the endowed partnership for their participation.

During the first year of Fellows, Elizabeth introduced the group to the concept and practice of inquiry as described by Dana and Yendol-Hoppey (2009). The authors summarize the inquiry process as including "articulating a wondering, collecting data to gain insights into the wondering, analyzing data, making improvements in practice based on what was learned, and sharing learning with others" (2009, p. 14). At the monthly meetings, Fellows learned about the inquiry process and helped one another pursue their individual wonderings over the course of the school year (in the following year, Fellows pursued collaborative rather than individual inquiry). In a typical Fellows meeting, Elizabeth provided some instruction related to an element of the inquiry process (e.g., how to find a wondering, kinds of data a teacher might collect, ways to analyze data). Instruction frequently included the use of a protocol from the National School Reform Faculty (n.d.) to facilitate discussion. For example, Fellows used various text-based protocols to structure conversation about excerpts from the Dana and Yendol-Hoppey text and student work protocols to help them examine and learn from student-produced material. Then, Elizabeth organized Fellows into small groups where they helped one another with their inquiries. This generally meant using a set of questions to guide the conversation. For example, questions for discussion in a January meeting included:

- What is your question? Why is this important to you?
- What steps have you taken to this point?
- What have you learned to this point?
- What has been challenging to this point?
- What help do you need?
- What step could you take tomorrow?
- What kind of data have you/will you collect?
- How are these data helpful to you in this inquiry?
- Do you see a new question emerging? What is it?
- If you see a new question, what steps will you take to begin to inquire into it?
- If you don't see a new question, what steps will you take to move your inquiry along?
- How have we (the team consulting with you) been helpful to you?

Fellows meetings typically ended with the completion of Individual Monthly Action Plans (IMAPs), borrowed from the National School Reform Faculty, in which Fellows specified what they intended to do in their classrooms between meetings. In particular, Fellows specified the change they would make in their practice, why they would make this change, how they would initiate the change, what supports they might need to make the change, and how they would know if they had made progress. Fellows submitted their IMAPs to Elizabeth, who provided written feedback and often face-to-face feedback as a means of facilitating the Fellows's inquiries.

The year concluded with an Inquiry Showcase in which Fellows and student teachers from partner schools presented the inquiries they had pursued during the year. Fellows also wrote abstracts to represent their work, and these were made available on the website of Center for School Improvement (n.d.).

Inclusion at Hopewell began the following year, and the Fellows shifted their focus to inclusion and collaborated on inquiry teams to study their commonly held questions about how to help diverse learners excel. For example, inquiry teams were formed around questions related to the differentiation of math instruction, ways to challenge advanced readers in kindergarten, the use of positive strategies for improving classroom social climate, and strategies for fostering homework completion. These topics became urgent to teachers as they grappled with the increasingly heterogeneous student bodies in their classrooms. For example, how could teachers provide math instruction that was appropriate for the wide range of achievement levels now represented in their classrooms? How could they ensure a supportive environment for learning among students who were unfamiliar with one another's needs and idiosyncrasies?

To provide support for teachers faced with inclusion, another structure was developed at Hopewell. Referred to as "Inclusion Meeting," dialogue within this structure is the focus of the study reported in this chapter. Inclusion Meetings occurred weekly for an hour following student dismissal, with membership shifting from week to week. Grade-level teams of teachers attended Inclusion Meetings on a rotating basis (i.e., kindergarten met the first week; first grade met the second week) throughout the year. Permanent members (i.e., those who attended each week) of the Inclusion Meeting were the principal, behavior resource teacher, curriculum resource teacher, reading coach, guidance counselor, school psychologist, and Elizabeth, the professor-in-residence. Members of the resource team (teachers of art, music, physical education, drama, dance, media) also rotated attendance.

Inclusion Meetings were organized around teachers' dilemmas related to student learning. That is, each teacher was invited to identify a student about whom he or she had serious concerns. Together, the group discussed and attempted to define the problem and identify appropriate action steps. Although these were loosely structured conversations, Elizabeth relied on several strategies to encourage participation and collaboration. These included reminding teachers to describe their observations of students with observable rather than judgmental language, prompting for details about the learner and the context, inviting participation of all teachers at the table, asking for articulation of precise action plans, and making explicit the expectation that the follow-up meeting (in 6 weeks) would begin with a review of progress made with each student for whom a plan was developed. In reporting student progress, teachers were asked about the evidence on which they based their judgments. Evidence might include test scores, homework completion, number of behavior referrals, or whatever kind of data represented student performance in the targeted area.

Inclusion Meetings, therefore, provided an opportunity for teachers to engage in an unusual kind of collaborative inquiry. Teachers moved quickly from identifying a question or wondering to pooling their wisdom in order to develop an action plan. They then implemented plans and came together again to report on the impact of those plans. Depending on the evidence reported, the teachers were thrown into another cycle of raising questions, developing plans, implementing plans, and reporting on progress—or they concluded that they would continue to implement the original action plan.

At the conclusion of that year, the authors of this chapter conducted focus groups with educators who participated as Fellows to gain insight into their experience of inclusion. That investigation made clear the teachers' nearly unanimous appreciation for the support they found in Fellows and in Inclusion Meetings. Comments such as the following were typical:

> I tend to think of faculty meetings as a lot of monologuing and grandstanding where we have to sit and we have to listen . . . (but) I felt empowered by (Fellows) because we were active participants in . . . solving the problems, and that's exciting. We learned, we did what we did, we worked hard, we were given challenging problems to solve . . . real stuff that's going on in our school that we need to think about, real problems with inclusion, real problems with kids, real problems with management or curriculum . . . and then we felt like our input mattered.

The teachers' enthusiasm for Fellows and Inclusion Meetings led us to wonder about the nature of interaction in those meetings. What exactly was going on that helped teachers feel genuinely engaged with problem solving and even "excited" and "empowered" by the experience? We knew from our own observations that some Inclusion Meetings seemed to go better than others—that sometimes teachers appeared to be excited and empowered and other times they left deflated. We decided to look closely at the interactions among participants in Inclusion Meeting to gain insight into the details of talk and the implications of those details for the quality of inquiry. We chose to study Inclusion Meetings because they included all teachers over the course of six weeks, and they were a typical school structure embedded within the school day. They had not been strategically organized to promote inquiry, yet sometimes they achieved the spirit of collaborative inquiry—and sometimes they definitely did not. We asked the question "How does dialogue shape teachers' problem solving opportunities during Inclusion Meetings?"

METHODS

To examine the talk during Inclusion Meetings, dialogue from eight separate meetings was transcribed verbatim and analyzed using discourse analysis as described by Fairclough (2003). Since discourse analysis is performed on samples of data, a data-sampling strategy must be developed (Fairclough, 2003) to ensure that all data are well represented by the analysis (Hatch, 2002). Thus, follow-up interviews with 21 of the 35 teachers who participated in the meetings were conducted. Teachers were purposely selected for interviews for maximum variation in both roles at the school (e.g., grade levels, subjects taught) and perceptions of the meetings (e.g., felt meetings were helpful, felt meetings were not helpful) that they freely shared with the researchers. Analysis of teacher interviews suggested that teachers viewed "productive" meetings as those that moved them toward classroom-level solutions. Thus, samples of meeting dialogue were selected for analysis if they included discussion of classroom-level solutions. To address our research question, we analyzed meeting dialogue for the following discourse features: (a) speech functions, (b) statement and question modalities, and (c) who was activated as responsible for the problem or proposed solution.

Speech Functions

Speech functions are important to identify, as speech functions suggest the underlying purpose of dialogue. There are two basic speech functions—knowledge exchanges and activity exchanges (Fairclough, 2003). A knowledge exchange consists of statements and questions, and the purpose of a knowledge exchange is to share information about a given topic under discussion. In our data, knowledge exchanges frequently occurred as teachers used evidence, such as test scores and classroom performance data, to construct an understanding of the concern. Activity exchanges consist of demands for action and offers, or acceptance of the demand for action. Unlike knowledge exchanges, there is a presumption that words will facilitate some kind of action on the part of speakers (Fairclough, 2003). In the case of Inclusion Meetings, one would expect activity exchanges to occur as participants planned what to do about the student cases that were presented.

Modality

Modality is a complex aspect of meaning conveyed through word choice and suggests the degree of certainty and authority the speaker has in their utterance (Fairclough, 2003). All parts of both knowledge exchanges and activity exchanges can be modalized. As noted earlier, knowledge exchanges consist of questions and statements. Questions elicit the commitment dialogue partners have to the truth of an utterance. For example, if a question is constructed as "Isn't your classroom too stimulating for students?", the speaker is seeking a highly committed answer compared to a different construction, such as "Might your classroom be too stimulating for the student?" The way in which statements, the other half of a knowledge exchange, are constructed suggests the speaker's certainty, or commitment to the truth, to what he or she is saying. For example, if a speaker says, "The student has a disability," the speaker is highly committed and speaks with authority that indeed the student has a disability. On the other hand, if the speaker suggests, "The student may have a disability," the speaker is neutral to the proposition and claims no commitment to this truth or authority.

Also noted earlier, activity exchanges consist of demands, a type of statement, and offers, also a type of statement. Unlike knowledge exchanges, demands reflect the initiating speaker's commitment to the necessity of their demand, whereas the offer, or response to the demand, reflects the receiving speaker's commitment to act according to the demand. For example, if a speaker says, "Call the parents," that speaker is highly committed to the demand as compared to a speaker who says, "Maybe you should call the parents," which can be interpreted as a suggestion that could be adopted or rejected. If the offer is undertaken (e.g., I will call the parents), the speaker is highly committed to responding to the demand, compared to the construction "I will not call the parents," wherein the speaker is not committed to act in response to the demand.

Importantly, all speech can be modalized to reflect uncertainty or tentativeness on the part of the speaker. In Table 5.1, we present representations of both kinds of speech functions (knowledge exchanges and activity exchanges), and examples of how parts of speech functions (statements, questions, demands, offers) can be modalized or not. By identifying speech functions and the concomitant modalities embedded within the functions, interpretations about speaker motivations and intentions can be made.

Who was Activated

Activation in discourse analysis tells who is responsible for getting things done (i.e., activated) and who is affected by the process (i.e., passivated) (Fairclough, 2003). It is a representation of the agency of members involved in the interactions. On the importance of being active or passive, Fairclough explains:

> The significance of 'activation' and 'passivation' is rather transparent: where social actors are mainly activated, their capacity for agentive

action, for making things happen, for controlling others and so forth is accentuated, where they are mainly passivated, what is accentuated is their subjection to processes, them being affected by the actions of others. (p. 150)

In short, the identification of the actor as activated or passivated indicates his or her agency in the interaction. This aspect of discourse analysis in Inclusion Meetings reveals who feels or is viewed as responsible and perhaps not responsible for taking action related to teaching and learning dilemmas.

Once relevant discourse features within each excerpt were identified and labeled, interpretations of the meaning of those features for the dialogue were written. From these interpretations, patterns of dialogic support for inquiry within a problem-solving context emerged. Although we also

Table 5.1 Speech Functions

Knowledge Exchange	
Statements: The actor's commitment to truth	
Assert	The student has a disability.
Modalize	The student may have a disability.
Deny	The student does not have a disability.
Questions: The actor elicits the other's commitment to truth	
Nonmodalized positive	Is your classroom too stimulating for the student?
Modalized	Might your classroom be too stimulating for the student?
Nonmodalized negative	Isn't your classroom too stimulating for the student?
Activity Exchange	
Demand: The actor's commitment to the obligation/necessity	
Prescribe	Call the parents.
Modalize	You should call the parents.
Proscribe	Don't call the parents.
Offer: The actor's commitment to act	
Undertaking	I will call the parents.
Modalized	I may call the parents.
Refusal	I will not call the parents.

Note: This table was adapted from Fairclough (2003).

identified features that appeared to shut down inquiry, we have chosen to refer to them only as they are related to the discussion of supportive discourse features.

FINDINGS: SUPPORTIVE TEACHER TALK
IN AN INQUIRY COMMUNITY

Inclusion Meetings, though not defined by the faculty as an inquiry community, provided the opportunity for educators to articulate a wondering, collect and examine data (including the wisdom and insights of colleagues), make improvements in practice based on what was learned, and share learning with others (at the next meeting). Established in response to the inclusion of students with disabilities at Hopewell Elementary School, Inclusion Meetings brought educators together to examine and address problems of practice. Our findings suggest that collaborative wondering, discussion of data and insights, and consideration of actions to be taken were facilitated through the use of three features of dialogue: tentative (modalized) speech, the activation of individual and collective teacher agency, and maintaining dialogic focus on the teaching/learning problem at hand.

Use of Tentative Speech

In her study of professional development schools, Snow-Gerono (2004) found that teachers needed "safe communities" that afforded "uncertainty" through dialogue (p. 253) in order to examine problems of practice collaboratively. In our study, safety was achieved dialogically through tentative or modalized speech, which by definition is uncertain (Fairclough, 2003). For example, when Lexa, an art teacher, discussed the behavior difficulties of one of her students, one of her colleagues asked, "I wonder if the space is difficult for some children to manage?" The question prompted Lexa to reflect aloud about the influence of the wide-open classroom space on the student's behavior. Lexa agreed that the space was causing some difficulties for the student, which led her to consider other instructional factors, such as the way she structured lessons, as potential influences on the student's behavior. Words such as "I wonder," an example of tentative or modalized speech, appeared to invite teachers to consider broadly their questions about their students and, in turn, the possibilities for improved practice.

On the other hand, teacher interviews suggested that sometimes meetings were "tense," which appeared to close down teacher wondering. Knotek (2003) cautioned that during problem-solving discussions, teachers are often in the "inherent bind" (p. 7) of having their own performance evaluated, which causes teachers to blame students rather than consider what they might do to improve the conditions for learning. Our analysis suggests this occurred when teachers were "grilled" or asked nonmodalized negative questions (see

Table 5.1). For example, a primary teacher brought forth a concern about a particular student with behavior problems whom she described as "making no progress." After a lengthy knowledge exchange about the ineffective use of point sheets with this student, a member of the leadership team and the teacher engaged in the following exchange in which Andra's nonmodalized question and statement appeared to erect a brick wall that brought the dialogue to a screeching halt:

> Andra: When there was an intern there with you and she had more of the control with all of the other children, *were you not* kind of one-on-one with him at that time? That was a good time to give him more attention during that period of time.

> Mary: Well yes, that *yes, but* that's not happening now.

The teacher responded with a "yes, but" statement, which appeared to be an attempt to defend herself rather than to continue to wonder about the perplexing matter at hand. Using modalized or tentative speech supports teachers' efforts toward problem solving, whereas nonmodalized speech was evaluative and judgmental and did not support an open-minded pursuit of insight and plans for improvement.

Activation of Agency

The discourse analysis revealed two kinds of activation that played important roles in supporting inquiry in Inclusion Meetings. These include self-activation and group activation.

Self-activation occurred when teachers represented themselves as agents of change in their classrooms and indicated a willingness to be open to changing their practice to ameliorate student learning problems. Dialogically, this was represented when teachers used "I" statements as they tried to define the problem or provide assistance in resolving the problem. For example, Alicia, an intermediate grade teacher, described her work with a student she characterized as "defiant." In the following excerpt, she discussed this concern with Terry, another classroom teacher, and Meg, a professional educator present at the meeting. Alicia explained that she was doing an inquiry project in Teacher Fellows on student defiance. The interaction continued:

Alicia: I just get stuck with her sometimes, because she refuses to move.
Terry: She does it in my room also.
Alicia: She does it in her reading class, she's done it in art, in music, and she's done it in the cafeteria. She holds up the whole class, and it's like a negotiation process. She's got all the power because here's the teacher and 16 other kids waiting on the one child, and if she

doesn't want to move, she doesn't have to move (laughing). *What am I supposed to do? Do I leave* her there and leave with the other 16 kids, or *do I just wait?* And um that, I think this is my most challenging issue, as far as behavior goes, because *I don't know how* to make her move, end of story. I tried you know bargaining, and that kind of stuff, and its like, 'whatever' (imitating the student).

In the very first line, Alicia takes responsibility for carefully considering the nature of the problem (i.e., I just get stuck with her), even though it is clear the student had similar issues in other classrooms (i.e., Terry's asserted statement and Alicia's asserted statements). Although Alicia felt as though this was a "most challenging" issue where the student had all the "power," she activated herself as responsible (i.e., What am I supposed to do, Do I leave, Do I wait?), and had even initiated a failed intervention (i.e., bargained with the student). Next, Meg initiated an activity exchange.

Meg: You have gone on-line and found some materials
Alicia: Yes
Meg: And I know you probably haven't had a chance to even look at them yet. I found a few things that I'm bringing to you all for Fellows next week. I'm not suggesting that that's going to solve all the problems, but sometimes you just need to read what some other people have said about defiance and how to work with it.
Alicia: mm hmm.
Meg: And maybe that'll provide some.
Alicia: Right, well that's the main goal. I'm hoping that with Fellows, I can figure out something to do with her.

Alicia's response to Meg's demand (i.e., You have gone online) suggested she was highly committed to the obligation (i.e., yes) of researching defiance. Importantly, Meg provided instrumental support for Alicia's efforts (i.e., I found a few things that I'm bringing to you) by activating herself as responsible for helping Alicia. In addition, Meg acknowledged Alicia's statement that the problem was challenging (i.e., I'm not suggesting that that's going to solve all the problems). Finally, Alicia noted that her "goal" was to find "something to do with her." At the end of the interaction, Alicia articulated her action plan as follows: "My plan for [this student] is to work through Fellows and come up with something to really practice and try, and that is my plan for her." Her self-activation and agency prompted Alicia to think about how to approach the problem in that she viewed herself as responsible for learning and taking action. Meg, too, self-activated and saw herself as responsible for helping Alicia.

On the other hand, when speakers viewed others, such as the parent or the student, as responsible for the problem, they did not talk about their practice in insightful and open ways. For example, Jane, a second-year intermediate math teacher, described a student she was concerned about as "very disruptive, can't sit still, always running everywhere; *he* just talks out." Linda, a member of the leadership team, maintained acti-vation of the student when she responded with the question "Is *he* in exceptional student education?" That is, she implied that the locus of the problem was within the student (i.e., that he had disabilities), to which Jane replied "no." Linda's question maintained a focus on the student as responsible for the problem rather than helping Jane carefully consider the dimensions of the problem (e.g., Under what circumstances does this student do well in your class?). Thus, the teacher's failure to self-activate and Linda's comment limited the teacher's agency to mitigate the prob-lem. Perhaps most notable was Jane's recognition during her interview that she likely contributed to the problem. When asked during her inter-view about other factors that contributed to the student's challenging behaviors, she responded:

> I hate to say it, the way that I teach. My teaching style is very, sort of loud and engaging. I'm moving a lot and so that kind of [gets that] student going, because they see me up there having fun, and it's like my stage. They want to be up on my stage, you know, and I like to crack a joke or two while I'm teaching, do something funny and stuff. There are kids that can't handle that. It's like it starts to snowball. They start to add in, they start to be funny; they start to act out.

It was interesting to find that Jane was indeed capable of the self-activation necessary to consider her own practice and its impact on her student. In the interaction with Linda, the absence of tentative speech and the location of the problem in the student appeared to "shut down" any wondering Jane was willing to consider. We see here an example of the kind of brick wall that can occur dialogically during problem-solving meetings when teachers are not encouraged to move toward self-examination.

Group activation refers to the invitation to group members to par-ticipate in the examination of the problem. When speakers at Inclusion Meetings invited group participation in the dialogue, frequently through the use of the "we" pronoun, more creative solutions to thorny prob-lems of practice were developed, and teacher interviews suggested this in turn produced feelings of social support among presenting teachers. Kruger (1997) explained that social support is realized when teachers "feel they can depend on others for assistance during difficult times" (p. 165). An example of this occurred during a kindergarten inclusion meeting. Nicole, a classroom teacher, brought up her concern about the behavior of Donald. Although Nicole and Donald had a good working relationship, he was uncooperative during his resource classes, so much so that he was in danger of suspension. This was an intractable case, particularly because all parties, including the family, worked hard to provide this student with a productive learning experience.

During discussion of this case, all meeting participants were activated in puzzling through this dilemma both during the construction of the problem and an action plan. This was accomplished by statements such as "I think *we* gotta think of some things for this child," and "*We* may a need an immediate plan, which wouldn't be, perhaps, a long-term plan, but if things are tough for him, for whatever reason right now, because he has to go off to resource; maybe we need to do something about that right now." Importantly, these kinds of statements (note the use of "we" in each statement) developed and maintained group agency, or group commitment to studying and solving the problem, through which Nicole experienced social support (Kruger, 1997), as she claimed in an interview. This interaction resulted in an activity exchange wherein the group figured out how Nicole and the resource teachers could collaborate more closely in order to make accommodations for Donald.

In another example, Sheila, a classroom teacher, was concerned about the lack of progress one of her students was making in reading. Nora, an administrator, doggedly engaged the group in problem solving with such questions as "Any other recommendations?" and "What can we do for this student?" After much discussion, the group discovered that this student was reading at the same level as the group receiving instruction from the special education teacher. Thus, the group decided to move the student to that reading group where she would receive more one-on-one attention. During her interview, Sheila updated the student's progress and reported, "She's doing fine now, and it's going to take time, but by the end of the year she should be on grade level with everyone else." Thus, the action plan put in place met what DuFour (2004) characterized as "Big idea #1: ensuring that students learn" (p. 8). Sheila felt supported and noted that "last year, it was more of what teacher was in charge of what. This year it's all across the board. We're all in this together."

Focus

When teacher talk in Inclusion Meetings stayed focused on the specific concern a teacher raised, thoughtful problem examination occurred. Some teachers were adept at maintaining focus, while others were not. In particular, questions that prompted clarification and elaboration of the issue fueled the dialogue about factors in the classroom environment that might explain the student's behavior. Examples of these questions included, "Does this happen all the time? When does it happen the most? When does it happen the least? What have you tried? How did she respond? Have you seen any progress? What is she good at? What motivates her?" Questions like these kept the dialogue squarely focused on the teacher's concern and appeared to help the teacher consider a variety of factors that could bear on the problem.

Frequently, however, the dialogue was not focused. In fact, one teacher noted during an interview that sometimes Inclusion Meetings were like "chasing rabbits." By that she meant that meetings sometimes veered off in many different directions. For example, in a discussion about the reading comprehension difficulties of one student, participants discussed the number of students on a waiting list for tutors, where funds to pay another reading tutor might come from, the implications of adding another tutor, and concerns about a classroom teacher's ability to properly assess students' reading. Although all of these topics were important, the teacher noted that she left the room "without an answer" to help her student.

Frequently, chasing rabbits occurred when off-topic questions were proffered. For example, when a teacher discussed the academic problems of one of her students who had recently come to Hopewell from a charter school, Janet, one of the school's administrators, asked about "charter school withdrawal procedures," a tangent that moved the discussion away from the student's academic problems. In short, when dialogue remained focused on the dimensions of the problem the teacher brought to the table, teachers were supported in examining and identifying potential solutions to the problem. When dialogue was unfocused, teachers reported feeling unsupported and frustrated.

IMPLICATIONS: SUPPORT FOR SUPPORTIVE DIALOGUE

The discourse analysis revealed marked differences in the ways participants in Inclusion Meetings interacted with one another. The interviews revealed the intersection between the nature of the interactions and teachers' assessment of the value of the encounter. Specifically, some kinds of talk—tentative speech, individual and group activation, focusing speech—were related to teachers' descriptions of Inclusion Meetings as helpful and productive and other kinds of talk were related to less positive assessments. In other words, some dialogue supported collaboration to define problems and consider action while other talk appeared to shut down the inquiry. The findings of the discourse analysis point to a number of ways in which educators can provide support for supportive dialogue in communities of inquiry.

Name the Features of Supportive Talk and Make Them Public

In our experience, most educators intend to be collaborative and supportive with one another. In fact, those educators in our study whose talk typically shut down dialogue and inquiry did not realize that they were having that effect on others. It is helpful, therefore, to be very specific with colleagues about the features of talk that tend to support inquiry. This can be done in a very straightforward and nonthreatening way by listing the kinds of talk and providing examples of each. At Hopewell, we did this with the entire faculty during preplanning week before the start of the next school year. We made a handout that listed kinds of talk to increase and kinds of talk to decrease in order to accomplish the goal of teacher and student learning. In addition, we began each Inclusion Meeting by reminding teachers of these kinds of talk with prompts written on a poster: Use tentative, speculative language; ask questions related to the topic; use collective pronouns; invite each person's participation; clarify plan of action; stay focused on the speaker's concern; express openness to new ideas. Included on the poster was a list of sentence starters to provide further scaffolding for teachers: I wonder if . . . ? Do you think that he . . . ? Is it possible that . . . ? What do you think, Ms. X? So, we have agreed that . . . ? Tell us more about . . . ?

Midway through the year, as the state-mandated tests grew closer and teachers' anxiety levels increased, we revised the poster to remind teachers of the purpose and the process of Inclusion Meetings. The new poster included a list of four tasks for Inclusion Meetings: We focus on student learning; We ask, "What can WE do to address the problem?; We rely on one another; We talk in ways that invite our best thinking. Again we included the features of supportive dialogue presented in the form of prompts. By making the features of talk explicit, we may enable teachers to move beyond their good intentions toward dialogue that facilitates rather than impedes collaborative inquiry.

Use Protocols to Help Structure Conversations

The discourse analysis revealed that when dialogue remained focused on the problem, teachers were supported in examining and identifying potential solutions to the problem. On the other hand, "chasing rabbits" did not support teachers' collaborative wondering and problem solving. The use of protocols helps educators to keep their eyes on the prize of student learning. As DuFour, DuFour, Eaker, and Many (2006) highlighted, "The fact that teachers collaborate will do nothing to improve a school. The pertinent question is not, 'Are they collaborating?' but rather, 'What are they collaborating about?' "(p. 91). Protocols can be borrowed from outside sources, such as the National School Reform Faculty, or they can be created to serve the particular purposes of the group. As explained on the NSRF website, protocols are agreed-upon guidelines for a conversation. This type of structure permits very focused conversations to occur. Protocols may be used for looking at student and adult work, giving and receiving feedback, solving problems or dilemmas, observing classrooms or peers, to push thinking on a given issue, and to structure a discussion around a text (see National School Reform Faculty, n.d.).

The NSRF has provided a variety of protocols to help educators focus on student work. These are especially useful in fostering collaboration instead of coblaboration because the guidelines point participants toward the analysis and discussion of student-produced material. Asking clarifying and probing questions are common elements of these protocols as are periods of listening without speaking. The goal is to encourage listening, reflection, equitable participation, and an openness to new ideas—in a psychologically safe environment. A facilitator, who can be a teacher or any other colleague with some knowledge of the protocol, leads the way by explaining, modeling, and monitoring the process. This kind of structure can support the use of supportive language because it gently and explicitly guides educators to collaborate in the study and improvement of student learning.

Talk About and Practice a Willingness to be Disturbed

Our analysis of teacher talk in Inclusion Meetings revealed that certainty was anathema to inquiry. That is, speakers who insisted that they already knew the problem and its solution were not open to collaborating with the group. Their thinking was "closed"; their minds were made up. Instead, the more tentative speech, referred to as modalized speech, opened the door to collaborative wondering and problem solving. In addition to modeling modalized speech (e.g., I wonder if he understands the directions in the textbook), facilitators can address directly with teachers the power of uncertainty by discussing a popular essay by Wheatley (2002). A reading teacher explained the power of this stance:

> You know, sharing with people is very powerful because you might have one way of looking at something, and somebody else comes in and says, "Okay, this is a different way of looking at it. Have you ever thought of that?" And you have to be willing to change and say, "Well, I'll give it a try." That was very, very powerful.

Hopewell teachers became familiar with the essay because they read it with the professor-in-residence in the Fellows group. It became clear that a single reading was unlikely to transform teachers' perspectives. While some responded instantly and enthusiastically, others needed multiple readings and opportunities to discuss the notion of being willing to be disturbed. Said one teacher,

> The whole idea of being willing to be disturbed changed my thinking. For instance, I realized I could ignore some behavior. Just flat out ignore it. And I hadn't done that before. And I started to ask myself why a child was doing what he was doing. You know, you could actually be rewarding the behavior and making it worse.

Her point is that by allowing herself to entertain ideas that she had never considered—being willing to be disturbed—she gained new insights into her own teaching and her students' behavior. Feeling comfortable with uncertainty appears to help teachers engage in the wondering and tentative talk that fuels inquiry. Encouraging and modeling a willingness to be disturbed is likely to support the supportive dialogue needed for collaborative inquiry.

Practice Supportive Dialogue in Multiple Settings

Habits are often hard to break, and new behaviors require practice if they are to become internalized. It is not surprising that educators need opportunities to practice new ways of talking with one another. One overview during preplanning week and a quick review during periodic Inclusion Meetings do not provide enough exposure and practice for teachers who need to learn new ways of speaking with one another. At Hopewell we have begun to shift the focus and structure of several traditional components of teachers' lives in order to foster more collaborative dialogue. Two examples of these adjustments include the monthly faculty meeting and the weekly team meeting.

For years Hopewell's monthly faculty meetings followed the traditional format in which administrators delivered information to teachers. Rarely was there an opportunity for teachers to talk other than to ask for clarification of that which had been presented to them. Many teachers would have agreed with the teacher quoted earlier who bemoaned the "monologuing" that characterized the monthly faculty meetings. In an effort to facilitate collaboration and a focus on teaching and learning, faculty meetings were renamed "Best Practice Meetings" and transformed to provide teachers with opportunities to present and discuss practices with one another. For example, an art teacher and a classroom teacher might present examples of their attempts to infuse art into math lessons, an individual teacher might present instructional strategies that she has found effective in improving students' expository writing, and the school psychologist might lead a discussion about how to be responsive to students with Asperger's syndrome. In each case, the goal is to stimulate discussion among teachers and challenge them to try new approaches to instruction. While Hopewell must continue to monitor the Best Practice Meetings so that they do not become merely another occasion for monologuing, the shift in approach does hold promise for promoting collaboration.

Similarly, Hopewell has taken steps to restructure the weekly grade-level team meeting. Traditionally, the team meeting has been an opportunity for the team leader to pass along information from administrators and perhaps review some issues related to curriculum. The team was required to turn in a form identifying the topics addressed in the meeting. In an effort to facilitate collaboration, team meetings were reconceptualized as opportunities for inquiry into problems of practice. The reporting forms were rewritten to prompt teachers to discuss teaching and learning. The three questions on the form are as follows: (1) Name one student about whom you have serious concerns. What is the nature of the concern and what action steps will you take to address the concern? (2) Name one student about whom you have had concern but who has made progress. Bring evidence of this student's progress and discuss what strategies contributed to this progress. (3) List the other issues the team reviewed at this week's meeting. Each week, one teacher on the team is responsible for Question 1 and another teacher is responsible for Question 2. Hopewell continues to work on the new approach to team meetings and has revised the reporting form twice in response to teachers' feedback.

Although Best Practice Meetings and team meetings have not achieved an ideal state of collaborative dialogue and inquiry, they represent an attempt to replace habits of coblaboration with new habits of collaboration. Certainly it matters who facilitates these meetings. Leaders who are sensitive to the features of supportive dialogue are likely to be more effective at encouraging inquiry and improving the quality of collaborative problem solving.

Normalize Problems of Practice

Insights from the discourse analysis of talk during Inclusion Meetings are useless to educators if they are unwilling to voice their questions and concerns about their own teaching. Sadly, many teachers have feared letting their colleagues know what goes on behind closed doors. As an experienced second-grade teacher commented, "I was the kind of teacher who was very scared of what other people would know about what goes on in my classroom." Educators must feel safe from judgment if they are to engage in open and honest collaboration with one another. One teacher explained, "Everybody has problems, and it's normal to talk about them." The normalizing of problems—everyone has them—is an essential part of establishing the environment in which supportive dialogue can flourish.

How does one accomplish this? At Hopewell, some teachers appeared to find support in a story told by the professor-in-residence about "naming the rhinoceros." Often told as the story about the elephant in the room, this story was made more dramatic and unforgettable by the detailed description of the bloody rhinoceros head resting on a platter in the middle of the dining table. According to this gory tale, the dinner guests cannot avoid seeing the frightful sight on a platter in the middle of the table. Still, no one says a word. "Will you please pass the salt?" says one, as she reaches around the platter to receive the salt shaker from her friend. While the teachers groaned and laughed at the tale, they also nodded knowingly when asked if teachers ever pretend that something quite obvious is really not there. Thus began the admonition to "name the rhinoceros," or "just say it" to encourage teachers to voice issues and seek solutions. They agreed that everyone had a rhinoceros, or two, or twelve in their classrooms and naming the beast was the first step in taming it. When educators view problems as normal and to be expected, they are more likely to make theirs public. This sense of safety is crucial for inquiry.

CONCLUSION

Dialogue among educators can be a thread in the web of support for teacher collaborative inquiry. It can also be the brick wall that stops inquiry in its tracks. A discourse analysis of dialogue in a loosely structured inquiry group revealed that several features of talk appeared to promote collaborative wondering about teachers' problems of practice. These features may be remembered best as follows:

- Making speech tentative ("modalized"): Expressing uncertainty keeps the problem "open" and invites input into its definition and potential actions to be taken.
- Making everyone responsible for problem analysis and resolution: Encouraging all the players to be "activated" helps them view the investigation of problems of practice as the responsibility of the group.
- Maintaining a clear focus on the problem: Keeping the group on point facilitates careful consideration of the matter at hand.

Certainly, some teachers intuitively use these features, and some intuitively do not. Therefore, it is important to consider how to support the use of language that in itself supports collaboration. We have provided some suggestions to consider, and readers will no doubt have additional ideas. Without this support, teacher talk will undoubtedly flourish. The question at hand, however, is will it be the kind of talk that will bear the fruit of new visions of teacher practice and improved opportunities for all students?

REFERENCES

Center for School Improvement (n.d.). Retrieved October 3, 2008, from The University of Florida's Center for School Improvement, http://education.ufl.edu/webapps/csi/search/index.php?pid=905&dc

Cochran-Smith, M., & Lytle, S. L. (1999). Relationships of knowledge and practice: Teacher learning in communities. *Review of Research in Education, 24,* 249–305.

Dana, N. F., & Yendol-Hoppey, D. (2009). The reflective educator's guide to classroom research (2nd ed.). Thousand Oaks, CA: Corwin Press.

DuFour, R. (2004). What is a "Professional Learning Community"? *Educational Leadership, 61*(8), 6–11.

DuFour, R., DuFour, R., Eaker, R., & Many, T. (2006). *Learning by doing: A handbook for professional learning communities at work.* Bloomington, IN: Solution Tree.

Fairclough, N. (2003). *Analysing discourse: Textual analysis for social research.* London: Routledge Taylor & Francis Group.

Hatch, A. (2002). *Doing qualitative research in education settings.* Albany, NY: State University of New York Press.

Hollins, E. R., McIntyre, L. R., DeBose, C., Hollins, K. S., & Towner, A. (2004). Promoting a self-sustaining learning community: Investigating an internal model for teacher development. *International Journal of Qualitative Studies in Education (QSE)*, *17*(2), 247–264.

Hord, S. M. (1997). Professional learning communities: Communities of continuous inquiry and improvement. Austin, TX: Southwest Educational Development Laboratory.

Knotek, S. (2003). Bias in problem solving and the social process of student study teams. *Journal of Special Education*, *37*(1), 2–14.

Kruger, L. J. (1997). Social support and self-efficacy in problem solving among teacher assistance teams and school staff. *The Journal of Educational Research*, *90*, 164–168.

Little, J. W. (2003). Inside teacher community: representations of classroom practice. *Teachers College Record*, *105*(6), 913–945.

National School Reform Faculty (n.d.). National School Reform Faculty Harmony Education Center Protocols. Retrieved October 3, 2008, from http://www.nsrfharmony.org/protocol/protocols.html

Snow-Gerono, J. L. (2005). Professional development in a culture of inquiry: PDS teachers identify the benefits of professional learning communities. *Teaching and Teacher Education*, *21*(3), 241–256.

Strahan, D. (2003). Promoting a collaborative professional culture in three elementary schools that have beaten the odds. *The Elementary School Journal*, *104*(2), 127–146.

Supovitz, J. A. (2002). Developing communities of instructional practice. *Teachers College Record*, *104*(8), 1591–1626.

Wheatley, M. J. (2002). *Turning to one another: Simple conversations to restore hope to the future.* San Francisco: Berrett-Koshler, Inc.

6 New Teachers' Collaborative Inquiry in Rural Schools
Challenges and Opportunities

Kerri J. Wenger and Jan Renee Dinsmore

Eastern Oregon University

Zumwalt & Craig (2005) note that in recent decades, new, first-time teachers represent an increasing proportion of the teaching force. Additionally, available studies indicate that new teachers tend to find their first jobs in lower performing schools with high numbers of minority and low-income students (Zumwalt & Craig, 2005). This is certainly the case for graduates of our university in the Pacific Northwest. Most accept first-time teaching positions in hard-to-staff, rural schools with high linguistic and cultural minority populations in Oregon and western Idaho. Furthermore, data indicate that many new teachers leave the profession during their first three years of teaching (Ingersoll, 2001; National Center for Education Statistics, 2007), making support for beginning teachers even more important.

In the current educational landscape, professional development for teachers is viewed as critical to increasing student achievement and improving school quality (Borko, 2004; Wilson & Berne, 1999). Our long-term work with preservice and in-service rural teachers suggests that professional development and support of rural teachers in their induction years (typically described as the first three years of teaching) is critical not only to combat attrition, but to improve instruction in rural schools.

In our region, the top five factors for teachers to leave Oregon schools are (a) the high demands of teaching; (b) lack of planning time; (c) lack of time to attend to students' needs; (d) lack of support by school administrators; and (e) level of rigor demanded of teachers (Ankeny & Zanville, 2002). The same report notes that while Oregon's supply of teachers for Oregon school districts remains strong, some rural areas like the ones in this study experience difficulties in recruiting and retaining teachers despite the supply pool. Rural schools in Oregon experience particular financial burdens, struggle to meet "Adequate Yearly Progress" goals required by the No Child Left Behind (NCLB) Act of 2000, and have very diverse student populations. Despite this, the attrition rate for teachers in rural Oregon remains close to the national average of about 37% turnover per year (Oregon Association of Colleges of Education, 2007; Zanville, 2006).

Given this context, there is clearly a need to support beginning teachers who are able to meet linguistically diverse students' needs, and who can adroitly negotiate the complexities of working and living in rural communities while working toward educational quality. As teacher educators, we have lived and worked in these rural communities for several decades. We remain in close contact with many of our graduates and, at their urging, sought to provide professional development in the form of collaborative inquiry groups across rural communities.

TEACHER PREPARATION FOR RURAL INLAND NORTHWEST COMMUNITIES

Eastern Oregon University's (EOU) baccalaureate program graduates approximately 180 teachers a year. These graduates become a high percentage of the teachers who serve rural eastern Oregon and western Idaho. Using a cohort-model approach to teacher education, we prepare teachers who come from mostly rural areas in Oregon and Idaho and who generally wish to work in rural inland Northwest schools. These schools are high poverty and linguistically diverse, with English and Spanish as the predominant languages.

In our undergraduate teacher preparation program, the preservice teachers experience a constructivist-based program where they build strong relationships with their peers and with us, their teacher educators.[1] They get used to working collaboratively with 15 to 20 peers to design curriculum, to develop a range of assessments of student learning, and to reflect on their teaching (Davenport, Jaeger, & Lauritzen, 2006). As student teachers and as beginning teachers, they tend to thrive in schools where they can also build strong relationships with their cooperating teachers (Dinsmore & Wenger, 2006). One student teacher put her delight in the collaborative relationships she was building in her high-poverty, linguistically diverse K–5 school this way:

> The entire grade level has taken me under their wings and have been just great to share their ideas, answering questions, encouraging me to "try it" but giving some alternative methods if it doesn't go just so. They all want to know what I am doing for my lessons so they can assist me any way they can . . . should it come as lending me their teaching treasures, giving me their ideas, quizzing me about the set-up . . . I feel there is a genuine interest in what and how I am doing. I find it hard to fail when I have that much support.

The level of support for this student teacher was clearly superior. Each school is unique, however, and each school's community context influences teaching practice. In the ten years that we have graduated teachers who have pursued their teacher-education program at the branch campus, about 80% take jobs within a fifty-mile radius. As their former teacher educators, we have a great deal of access to our former students as they embark on teaching careers. We visit their schools and classrooms regularly throughout each school year.

In the wake of NCLB, many schools where our graduates are hired provide little support for teacher-driven collaboration, especially with respect to curriculum development (Davenport, Jaeger, & Lauritzen, 2006). In contrast to a school where the student teacher is encouraged to try a variety of methods and supplementary materials, some districts with very high percentages of English-language learners (ELLs) have adopted quite rigid, time-consuming literacy and math curricula. One new teacher put it bluntly: "Choice? Oh, yes, I had a choice: Either use this highly structured reading program just as it's written, or don't work here." This teacher was frustrated because she felt that the curriculum did not address the needs of many of her young learners, but she was not permitted to deviate from the chosen curriculum and its methods: "It's like this: Here is the book. The words in blue, the script for the teacher, are the ones you read. And that's how you teach."

Another new teacher, working in a community of about 700, wrote that her school was "very workbook-oriented," and that she wanted to develop better materials in order to engage her students:

> I'm sure that some workbooks can be beneficial yet my heart tells me that dragging out the same text for the same subject over and over again throughout the year would not be very stimulating. Possibly this is true, as the cupboards are filled with partially completed workbooks from years past.

However, some beginning rural teachers in our inland Northwest schools experience nearly overwhelming freedom: "Yes, I'm in the land of teacher autonomy!" wrote one beginning teacher in a community of 2,500 people. More typical, however, is an emphasis placed on new teachers' responsibilities to master specific adopted curricula, under the oversight of school- or district-based mentors who are there to help teachers with implementation of the curriculum and analysis of student assessment data gathered as part of curriculum delivery.

Clearly, these rural teachers experience a wide variety of contexts and challenges. An expectation that most of our graduates share, however, is that they will collaborate with other teachers to help them meet the needs of their students. Graduates of our program e-mail and call each other frequently across geographically distinct communities, but many wanted more consistent contact as they were learning their craft. When a critical mass of our program's graduates came to us asking us to "find a way for us to work together again—we miss our cohorts!" we began to explore the possibilities of a collaborative inquiry group, tailored to beginning teachers across a range of schools and small communities within a fifty-mile radius.

As the work of researchers like Patrick (2003) and Howley, Theobald, and Howley (2005) suggests, there is a need to find out, from beginning rural teachers themselves, how they experience the professional, political, social, and cultural issues that they face in their induction years.

This chapter provides a picture of our two-year attempt at supported collaborative teacher inquiry (SCTI) with six interested beginning teachers in rural schools. We will try to paint a picture of the participants, describe our modest aims, and report on what we did together. We consider several questions about SCTI in a rural context: What were the most effective supports for SCTI in this context? What context-based challenges were encountered by this group of beginning teachers regarding their collaborative inquiry? What were the challenges for us, as university-based participants, in supporting them?

A VOLUNTARY INQUIRY GROUP: PARTICIPANTS AND AIMS

The Teachers

A snapshot of the teachers we worked with reveals a group of dedicated beginning teachers with a range of diverse ages, interests, and challenges. Each of these new teachers had an experienced teacher in their schools assigned to them as a mentor by their districts, and they reported varying degrees of assistance from these mentors when they needed help or had questions about teaching. Six beginning teachers took part in the volunteer inquiry group in the first year, and three of the six continued participation over both years. All were in their first, second, or third years of teaching. Pseudonyms are used throughout.

Even though these teachers had not all graduated in the same cohort group, they all knew each other, as most teachers in our small communities do. Their families, their networks of friends, and their experiences over years of growing up and living in the area all serve to bind them together in a web of multilayered connections. They all had the common experience of taking at least several university courses together, and they all had experienced the same program at our branch campus. Even though they lived and worked in different towns, they were familiar with each other's schools, having spent practicum time in a variety of schools across the region as part of their teacher preparation program. All came to the inquiry group with well-developed interpersonal skills with regard to peer support and collaboration.

While they wrote and discussed struggling with teaching in their induction years, all these teachers received high performance evaluations from their districts. They were interested in professional development as part of an inquiry group not because they were afraid of failing as teachers but because they were invested in student success in each of their different contexts. Table 6.1 provides information about notable characteristics of the teachers, their schools, and what they perceived as their biggest challenges when they began their work in the inquiry group.

About Us

As the university-based participants in the group, we have a combined thirty years experience in working with K–8 teachers in the content areas. Our work in a field-based program requires that we spend a great deal of time in schools within fifty miles of us, working with preservice and in-service teachers. Jan's particular area of expertise in mentoring in-service

Table 6.1 Inquiry Group Teachers

Teacher/Teaching Context	Biggest Challenges
Gail/Grades 3–5 (Teaches in same school as Marlys) Mostly European-American & middle-class students, with increasing language diversity; scripted reading and math programs; new & well-equipped building.	"Fitting in my own lessons around required curriculum"; teaching writing.
Marlys/Grades K–2 (Teaches in same school as Gail) See Gail's context above for further details.	Classroom management; getting kids to improve reading scores.
Sandy/Grades 3–5 Extremely high poverty; scripted reading program; high teacher turnover; nearly 50% English-language learners; old and dilapidated building.	Teaching writing; managing the workload and long workday; other required duties besides teaching; students with very low skill levels; pressures from state tests.
Rob/Middle school mathematics (Teaches in same school as Patty) High poverty, hard to staff school; had not met AYP for past three years when Rob was hired; lack of books and resources; dilapidated building.	Lack of resources; "Am I really at the right grade level for me as a teacher?"; "difficult" parents and perceived lack of support from administration or school policies; student motivation, "especially with the new no-promotion policy."
Patty/Middle school English (Teaches in same school as Rob) See Rob's context above for further details.	Motivating students to succeed in school and stay in school; keeping up on correcting student writing; being able to conference effectively with students about their writing.
Ruth/Grades K–2 High poverty; 60% of students speak Spanish at home; scripted reading program; fairly new and well-equipped building.	Getting students to read well and score well on weekly assessments; scheduling time for subjects other than reading and math; finding engaging materials to supplement curriculum.

teachers is content-area instructional improvement and classroom community building; Kerri's is in development of strategies for supporting ELLs. We believe we have developed the skill sets that Stein, Silver, and Smith (1999) suggest are important for professional developers, including an ability to match appropriate strategies to individual teachers over their developmental trajectory; experience in helping teachers critically evaluate curricula and their own implementation of it; and an ability to deal with interpersonal relationships while working for school improvement. Finally, especially important to this collaborative inquiry group, we had strong and mutually respectful relationships with the teachers. We knew them, and they knew us, well.

Aims for Teacher Collaboration and Inquiry

Our aims for SCTI were modest. These aims were based on listening to teachers' concerns in their induction years. We had learned that beginning rural teachers in our area were likely to have idiosyncratic, context-based needs; there was probably no "one size fits all" approach to supporting them as new teachers (Wenger & Dinsmore, 2007). But these beginning teachers, who were doing well in their classrooms, still felt pressure and were asking for help. One teacher put it: "I don't want to be just a whiner and a complainer in the faculty lounge at lunch. I'd rather be solution-focused." We entered into this process of building an inquiry group with an understanding of the diverse needs of individuals and a common desire to work together and discuss problems of practice.

As university-based participants, we believed that a situated view of teacher learning (Borko, 2004) would inform our desire to create a collaborative inquiry group with beginning teachers. Lave & Wenger (1991) note that the situated nature of learning requires particular attention to learners'—in this case, teachers as learners—social contexts. We were able to pay particular attention to these contexts, using our long-term knowledge about these schools and communities to inform our discussions of teaching in different rural schools. We felt that members of our inquiry group would profit from stories of each other's varied settings, helping them to develop new understandings of the sociocultural practices and contexts in their own schools.

We also believed that these teachers wanted to conduct classroom research that helped them improve their teaching. We wanted to support them as they worked on classroom-based investigations to enhance their practice by providing opportunities to discuss their ideas with people they trusted. Working from a situated perspective, we believed that if they had a way to talk together across the miles, to collaborate with and support each other, they could articulate their challenges and crystallize plans for investigating their own practice (Zeichner & Noffke, 2001). Finally, we wanted them to be recognized for, and supported in, their predispositions to inquiry early in their teaching careers. We hoped to support these emergent teachers in their development of inquiry as a habit of mind.

METHODS

Because we were interested in identifying and documenting what processes were helpful to this kind of teacher inquiry group, we conducted a systematic study of the group over time. In this qualitative study, we conducted videotaped interviews with each participant during the first school year. In addition, an online survey was developed and administered to help participants articulate common issues and experiences in their teaching contexts, and to describe aspects of their school- or district-based mentoring programs. Data sets also included the teachers' reflections and Web-based conversations, posted as part of a common Blackboard Internet classroom website; field notes from monthly group meetings; written "think pieces" produced by teachers during meetings (e.g., "I need help from other experienced teachers in learning how to . . ."; one focus-group interview (Krueger & Casey, 2000) after all teachers had taught for one full year or more; and field notes from two or more scheduled observations of each teacher. All data sets were analyzed using content analysis (Krippendorf, 1980) and constant comparative analysis to create coding categories, to generate themes, and to represent the data (Patton, 1990; Creswell, 1998).

The multiple roles of the two university professor participants in this study (mentors, researchers, and former professors of the beginning teachers) increased the need for member checking. Analyzed survey data, narrative analyses of Blackboard forum data, and drafts of research reports were presented to the teachers for review. When we presented data from this study at conferences, we previewed planned presentations with the teachers. Finally, a research colleague from another institution served as "critical friend" throughout data analysis.

AN OVERVIEW OF OUR PROFESSIONAL DEVELOPMENT

Getting Started

In the first year, we quickly learned that we were going to have to provide at least two kinds of support: first, finding a physical and cyberspace location for our work, and second, providing the kind of assistance that teachers would need to conduct collaborative inquiry. By the second year of the inquiry group, we were able to offer graduate credit, at very low cost, for ongoing inquiry projects developed by the participating teachers. Neither the teachers nor we had release time or payment for this voluntary work, although the university provided the use of the Blackboard shell, assisted with negotiations for classroom space, and engineered the registration procedure for graduate credit for the teachers.

Our first order of business as university-based participants was to get the word out about a possible inquiry group. To do this, we simply let two interested teachers know that we were amenable to starting a group, and let the rural grapevine handle recruitment. In the first six months of the group, we organized our meetings in a coffee shop in a centrally located small town. Once it became clear that we needed a quieter space, with better facilities for presentations and small-group work, we were able to use a rented classroom space at a local community college. The teachers quickly decided that inquiry meetings once a month after the school day were quite demanding on their time and energy due to driving time and afterschool demands. We decided to turn to cyberspace to support our conversations and created a university Blackboard site soon after our first meeting.

It fell to us as university-based participants to provide some formal guidance and support in helping the teachers with their inquiry. Since we already knew each other, and since the teachers were used to collaboration around teaching challenges from their teacher preparation program, there was a strong level of trust among the group. Nevertheless, we opened every face-to-face meeting with connection time and icebreaker activities. For example, at the beginning of one meeting we asked teachers, in pairs, to create and share a commercial jingle that summed up the teaching day they had just finished. We made one up, too, about our day with our preservice teachers. After much laughter and bad singing, we settled down to analyze one teacher's plans for student writing improvement.

As we listened to the teachers, we discussed what we perceived as a shared desire to do practitioner research. During face-to-face meetings, we planned ways for them to hone their big challenges into focused inquiry projects. In our first meeting, teachers engaged in wide-ranging discussions of common and individual worries and challenges in teaching. In response, at our second meeting, we asked teachers to sit quietly and draw something (in any format, be it cartoon, abstract, concrete, a series of images) that represented their biggest challenge in teaching. They then shared their drawings, and added details or words to their work. We then asked them to sit quietly and draw something that showed themselves successfully addressing a small piece of that challenge, as if they had unlimited time and resources at their disposal. In the ensuing discussion, we asked them what they might add to this drawing, and how they might use it to focus ideas for their classroom-based inquiry project. We wound up the meeting with a request that the teachers organize their thoughts into a short proposal for an inquiry project that they believed was useful and doable, to be posted in a specific discussion thread on Blackboard.

We then provided individual feedback, but posted this as part of the general discussion forum. Group members also responded to each other. As the months went on, we offered various suggestions about data collection and what materials and resources they might consider. For example, we asked many of them to read sections of Johnson's (2002) *A Short Guide to Action Research* and other descriptions of classroom-based data collection and analysis. We also corresponded behind the scenes with the teachers about their projects in personal e-mail communications and visited them frequently in their classrooms.

The Nature of Our Inquiry Work

While it was not our original intention to take on the overt role of guides, we did provide the majority of direction and facilitation at both face-to-face meetings and online in the first year. We had no formal agenda for a group inquiry cycle, nor did we begin our group with a clear idea of what important supports for teachers might be. We made decisions together as the work progressed. Particularly in the first six months, we generated whole-group topics (after listening to the teachers) for online discussions that we felt would assist them with their individual inquiries. The teachers gave input about workable deadlines and meeting times, and badgered each other and us for research literature as they investigated their areas of interest and reviewed their practice. Online, they mostly told a great many stories about their practice and their ongoing inquiry projects, sharing ideas and tips with each other. To a more limited extent, and always guided by us, they posted drafts of their investigations and examples of data, collaborating by responding to each other's analyses. In the face-to-face meetings, teachers brought ongoing analyses of their data, student artifacts, and questions for us as guides.

Three teachers, Ruth, Patty, and Sandy, continued in the inquiry group over both years. By the second year, the teachers were more practiced at honing their questions, and they developed inquiry project proposals and started data collection on their own. We were also more versed in what teachers were likely to need as they progressed with their projects, and we developed clearer expectations for the group as a whole. We required more reading by the whole group about inquiry, and we provided assistance with website analysis for those who were acquiring much of their information from Web-based resources. We posted online guidelines regarding deadlines and requirements for online posts, drafts, and presentation times. We explained our rationale for these more specific procedures, noting how we had used what we learned the first year to help us develop those supports.

An Example of Teachers' Inquiry Work

Sandy used an action research process to guide her second-year inquiry project (Johnson, 2002). She discovered a problem: Her students didn't like social studies, were disengaged in class, and were rarely successful on assessments. Her goal was to implement lessons that engaged students in social studies and increased learning.

She first reviewed her class ethnicity and noted that 65% were Hispanic and spoke Spanish at home, 25% were Caucasian, and 10% were other ethnicities. A survey was given to her students to determine what their preferences were for learning and why they were so bored. Students reported that they hated reading their social studies textbook, found the discussions after reading the text not very helpful, and disliked book-centered experiences. On the other hand, they reported enjoying social studies videos, discussions after videos, and stories about Oregon history. Prior to the implementation of her project, the class average on her test scores was 68%.

Sandy determined that implementing video and pictures via a mimeo (an interactive whiteboard) might enhance the students' interest in the topics studied in social studies. She then used various online search engines to obtain images and videos and create presentations about Oregon's climate, natural resources, population centers, and more. After the lessons and assessment, her average test score increased to 84%. While the content assessed was different, the trend in test scores continued to rise as Sandy continued to implement this format for instruction. After analyzing field notes on student comments and daily assessments as well as a second survey on students' attitudes toward social studies given after the lessons, Sandy concluded that there had been a dramatic change in her students' opinions of social studies. Sandy was quite proud of student comments such as "We like learning about history by seeing it!" and "Social studies isn't boring anymore."

Sandy continues to utilize the mimeo to enhance her instruction. She shares websites with other teachers and encourages students to find websites of Oregon history at home and during computer time. She plans on taking additional courses in technology to improve her teaching and increase student engagement and learning. In reflecting on her inquiry project, Sandy noted:

> One thing is true, there is no going back. There is only going ahead, so I am sharing websites with other teachers in my school. I am encouraging students to find websites and great pictures of Oregon during computer time, and other teachers are noticing. . . . I feel like a pioneer. A very tired pioneer . . .

Sandy had learned that her inquiry, exhausting as it was, made her feel she was teaching in more engaging, successful ways. She had identified and built on student preferences during her lessons and was happy that her students' social studies scores were improving. She was motivated to share her ideas with other teachers in her building, many of whom were not happy with their limited resources for social studies instruction.

SUPPORTING COLLABORATIVE INQUIRY
GROUPS ACROSS DISTANCES

With our modest goals for SCTI, we learned some important lessons about supporting inquiry with beginning rural teachers. In this section we discuss the benefits of online discussion as a usable forum for teacher collaboration. We then discuss the ways we came to understand the teachers' needs and contexts. We conclude with a discussion of the importance of guidance from us as professional developers to support deeper reflection, and how our knowledge of teachers' common understandings can help them build on what they know as they encounter new contexts and challenges.

Benefits of Online Discussion

We found that regular, guided online discussions were the best way to give the teachers time and space for reflection and collaboration. Because inquiry group members were working in geographically distinct areas, we needed multiple modes of communication. We learned, through trial and error, the necessity of having regular posting times (weekly worked best) in order to facilitate quality interaction and response. Such structure proved helpful to the teachers, but also to us as teacher educators. While we encouraged first responses by a certain date, teachers kept the conversations going for many weeks beyond the first threads in the asynchronous discussion forum.

Ruth, in the first year of the inquiry group, said that trying to combine collaborative inquiry with the first year of teaching was "like hanging onto the tail of a runaway horse!" Sandy echoed these concerns in a Web-based discussion when she wrote:

> My great challenge comes from my arch nemesis, TIME. . . . I do not have the time that I need to find valuable interventions for my struggling students. . . . I need interventions for ADHD students, sight readers, and kids who, simply put, have no number sense at all, even though they have played with manipulatives until their fingers cramp. I need TIME to locate my silver bullets and execute them. As I write, I am losing minutes.

For rural teachers interested in collaborative inquiry, Web-based discussions provided a good framework for "talking" to learn. These teachers wanted to discuss problematic cases and compare their successes, but opportunities for such interaction during busy teaching days were few. The online discussion forum was an avenue for overcoming this limitation.

Additionally, the online discussion forum became essential for encouraging group members' honest reflections about their teaching, telling stories, and raising and discussing teaching dilemmas. One example of a dilemma came from Ruth, early in the group's two years together. Ruth was teaching in a high-poverty school with a large percentage of ELL learners and scripted language arts and mathematics programs. In a Web-based discussion forum, she discussed the tension between her desire to implement a constructivist pedagogical approach and district requirements.

> The lack of constructivism in my teaching is probably one of my most frustrating challenges. I have given it some thought and realize that I have encouraged constructivism mostly in math through some of the helps in the teacher's guide—even though my mentor teacher told me to put it away and just use the student workbook. . . . Unfortunately, we are gearing up [for] standards and promotions tests which means we have to give out a lot of worksheets that encourage practice but not a lot of authentic learning. Any suggestions?

Patty, a third-year, eighth-grade language arts teacher in her district's sole middle school, sympathized with Ruth's case and e-mailed a shared concern to the group. Her e-mail included:

> This was hard for me to realize, but I think I've become a question, teacher-response, question, teacher-response type of teacher! Yuck . . . [But my students] start talking and disturbing others. I guess I'm operating on a bit of teacher-directed teaching. Embarrassed, Patty.

After discussions in the inquiry group, responding to suggestions from us and from their peers, both Ruth and Patty chose to conduct inquiry projects on how to make math and reading, respectively, more student-centered while still using district-approved curriculum. For these teachers, the online discussion forum supported the construction of an inquiry focus.

The teachers relied heavily on each other's encouragement and specific suggestions in their Web-based discussions. For every question posed to each other in a discussion forum, each participant had an average of three responses from other beginning teachers, generally with specific suggestions, names of people who might be able to help, and teaching materials. The following post from Gail to Sandy is typical:

> Your post made me smile . . . I do not have any brilliant ideas, but we had G.H., an author one of our teachers knows from Utah, come and speak to our kids this week, and he had some good ideas about stories . . .

Gail's post continued for two more paragraphs, with tips from this author, how she was trying those with her young writers, and with the author's contact information.

An analysis of the content of the teachers' postings indicates attributes of a collaborative inquiry group, albeit an emerging one. Teacher dialogue was focused on exchanging ideas with little evidence of deep reflection on learning or teaching, and the leadership of the work was driven by university faculty, rather than shared amongst the participants. This exchange between Sandy and Ruth, which took place over 11 days, typifies the nature of the online dialogue:

Sandy: Hi Ruth!! Long time, no see. I still can't believe you are teaching small people. They scare me. You sound an awful lot like me. I too have poured over Beers' book [*When Kids Can't Read: What Teachers Can Do*] and what you are really speaking of are interventions. I am on the math task force for our school district, and touch math is one of the interventions that we plan on adopting. Our special ed teacher is going to do a little presentation on it, I think, during a staff meeting this Thursday. I will give you all that I know on Thurs. People seem to like it.

Ruth: Hey Sandy it was great to get your feedback (my first I might add on this thread—Jan and Kerri are you out there?). After reading about your trials at your school, I'm feeling better about my own. You always have a great way of putting things. You're a hoot! Lately I've been bummed because after working hard for 8 months, I realize time is running out and half my class is not making it. My frustration levels are high, especially during math. To help prevent student abuse, I had to switch math from the afternoon to the morning, partly to have students that weren't dozing off and partly to keep the beast in check (my temper). Well enough of confession, did you find anything interesting about Touch Math at your meeting? I'd love to try it but it's so expensive and our school is not using it. Any suggestions?

Note that Sandy sympathizes, validates their shared study of a teaching resource (Kylene Beers' book on literacy), and promises to provide information, which she later did. But Sandy asks no critical questions about Ruth's current practice, or the way she is structuring or delivering math activities. We also see that Ruth not only wants to hear from Sandy in this conversation, but explicitly attempts to draw the professors into the thread.

The online discussion forum became a usable, open space for teacher interaction. Its asynchronous nature afforded on-demand communication opportunities in the midst of the participants' hectic lives, and its online nature created a space for this geographically dispersed group to collaborate. The discussion forum evolved into a space for telling stories, reflecting honestly about teaching, and raising teaching dilemmas. However, analysis of the teacher interactions revealed the limited degree to which the teachers critically pursued the dilemmas being raised. It became clear to us that the group needed specific supports for engaging in more critical conversations, which we discuss in detail in a later section.

Teachers' Needs and Contexts

An important knowledge set that helped us support these beginning teachers' individual inquiries was our ability to link their questions back to resources they had encountered in their teacher education program. Because we knew their prior (and fairly recent) experiences, we could easily remind them of texts, articles, and suggested lesson activities that they might have forgotten or not had a chance to explore fully. We were, in short, able to build on what they knew. For example, when teachers experimented with a new classroom management strategy or integrated literacy instruction into their attendance-taking procedures, we were able to link these actions back to specific experiences in their recently completed teacher education programs.

In terms of our support for collaborative inquiry, we looked for themes that emerged during online discussions and face-to-face meetings, and worked to facilitate deeper dialogue in these areas. In the following section we will discuss three of these themes: (a) utilization of rural contexts in constructing student-centered lessons, (b) administrative and collegial supports and constraints, and (c) the impact of scripted curricula and high-stakes tests on instruction and self-efficacy. Throughout this section we will also discuss what we learned about the supports teachers needed from us and the ways in which we provided them.

Utilizing Rural Contexts in Student-Centered Lessons

In addition to asking questions about teaching, the inquiry group shared success stories about their practice. A number of these stories revolved around the ways that teachers used resources and people from their communities to authentically engage students in the topics they were studying. As leaders, we knew that these stories could lead to new understandings about teaching in rural areas. We tried to push for further understanding about rural contexts, as when Kerri posted this online prompt for discussion:

> When we talk to you in your classrooms and as we read your posts, we've noticed that when you bring your different communities and what is special about them into your teaching, kids are really engaged. How are you bringing your communities into your schools?

This prompt led to several more success stories and descriptions of ways that community members and visitors made contributions to classroom instruction. For example, one teacher used her visits to children's homes to build on students' and families' interests as she planned some of her lessons, and another teacher designed a science unit that integrated the dissection of a wild cougar carcass donated by a parent. Gail wrote specifically about how she was trying to infuse her ideas for community visitors into her inquiry project goals:

I invited my grandpa, a veterinarian, to come talk about being a vet. I was excited to have him come, and so my students were excited, too. Now one of my students wants to be a vet! I also invited a local children's book author to come read to my class. The father of one of my students helps at the Idaho Extension Office and is coming after spring break to talk to my students about plants. I will let you know how that turns out. All this helps me make more engaging ties to my lessons, since these visitors are talking about what students are interested in or know about.

From their online discussions, and as we watched these teachers teach, we found that teachers in our inquiry group drew consistently on "the meanings inherent in rural lives" (Howley, Theobald, & Hawley, 2005) in order to enrich curriculum in meaningful ways for students.

Our work together gave us a picture of what teachers in our rural schools needed in order to plan engaging, community-based lessons. These teachers knew their rural communities so well. For example, Gail made use of community visitors from rural industries; Patty developed unit lessons that encouraged her middle school students to investigate the *Brown v. Board of Education* case and relate the implications of this to racism between Whites and Hispanics at her school; and Marlys incorporated her students' favorite video games into her writing instruction. These are all good examples of beginning teachers' abilities to build on their rural students' interests and experiences to engage and to motivate learning. These teachers initially did not think their ideas were worthy of mention or development, especially if they were teaching in schools where mandated curriculum programs took up much of the school day. They had not considered the extent of their expertise and the networks on which they might draw to plan student-centered instruction, nor how they might use those networks to enrich curriculum and to motivate students. Through our facilitation of teachers' discussions we were able to highlight the value of these community resources.

Administrative and Collegial Supports and Constraints

Teachers in the inquiry group received mixed messages from school leaders about their development as professional educators. On the one hand, each of the teachers in the inquiry group was reviewed positively on district measures of their performance. They had all participated in a state-mandated district mentoring program and, in the districts' views, these teachers were doing just fine. On the other hand, mentoring programs did not result in collegial relationships or opportunities for inquiry (Wenger & Dinsmore, 2007). Additionally, there was a strong cultural tendency in the schools to view any questions from teachers about materials or procedures as rocking the boat. This made teachers in the inquiry group feel that their collaborative efforts for professional development were not valued in their schools.

These mixed messages were also present in the way teachers were brought into the school culture. Our earlier work (Wenger & Dinsmore, 2007) indicated a high degree of welcome for new teachers in rural schools, although support for teacher learning in collaborative situations was rare. In an interview near the end of the study, Sandy discussed her perception of a lack of collaboration in her building:

> My friend Cleo from my undergraduate days is wonderful about shar-
> ing, and we call and correspond on a regular basis. But overall, our
> school district would do itself a real favor if they stressed collaboration
> with their schools a lot more. They think mapping curriculum is doing
> the job, and it is not. . . . Either you learn on your own, and share with
> a few friends, or not. We have a wealth of people, but no infrastruc-
> ture. Everyone is very nice, mostly, but we are islands unto ourselves.

The teachers also noted specific examples of a lack of support from school administrators throughout their collaborative inquiry efforts. Four of the teachers reported that requests made for resources to support their data-driven inquiries were regularly refused. These included additional books for the classroom library and time to work with other teachers on topics of their choosing during district in-service days. Teachers were also refused minor departures from normal school procedures, such as Sandy's attempt to collaborate with a primary-grade colleague on a voluntary partner-reading activity, with the principal citing concerns about time constraints and the necessity to maintain an established reading diagnostic testing schedule. What surfaced as important to the inquiry group was not necessarily important to their administrators. For example, school leaders did not provide any special support for the kind of community-based practices described in the previous section.

The teachers desired support for the ongoing learning that helped them relate students' needs and contexts to their curriculum and instruction. They were committed to their jobs and had strong ties to their students and communities, yet their need for supported professional development was not being met. Sandy stated she was more than just a "warm body to deliver curriculum" and saw collaborative inquiry as a positive force in her development as a teacher:

> Collaboration is *very* important because I need the fresh influx of
> ideas, problem-solving strategies, and just need to know that others
> are experiencing the same dilemmas that I am. My school does NOT
> support teacher collaboration—they feel inservice once a month about
> something they want is good to go!

Sandy's words underscore the frustration that many of these teachers felt in their schools. Sandy's expression of being a "warm body to deliver curriculum" is not a good context for teacher growth, discovery, and professional development. Nor is the feeling that collaborative inquiry must take place, as Sandy put it, "under the radar."

As teacher educators in this rural context, we are invested in maintaining strong relationships with our local administrators, and appreciate the huge challenges that they face. Cash-strapped local schools are facing real pressure to improve student test scores in several content areas. While we were not attempting to create fiery change agents in our collaborative inquiry group, we did recognize the importance of providing support to teachers in schools where they simply do not have much autonomy. At the same time, we were saddened by what we perceived as a lack of administrative support for these teachers in their selected inquiry projects.

Scripted Curricula and High Stakes Testing

Every teacher in the inquiry group agreed with the teacher who wrote anonymously on her survey "We just need fewer scripted programs!" Gail wrote on a Web-based discussion forum about the difficulty of making scripted programs her own as she taught her primary students: "Our curriculum is pretty structured, so I do not create a lot of lesson plans . . . but I try different anticipatory sets to different lessons." Gail followed up this online discussion during a monthly meeting:

> With reading, I just hate it—some of the scripted lessons. It's like you know really smart things that help kids really read, but because of the program taking all your time, then you *can't* do those things. It's just so frustrating. You're just hoping for a smart class, so you can ride the crest and have them all get good (district-mandated reading test) scores and stay in teaching!

The teachers were frustrated by some of their districts' programs, which they perceived as limiting their ability to differentiate instruction for both struggling learners and high-achieving students. The necessity to implement standardized literacy and math programs was viewed by the teachers as a barrier to real collaboration with other teachers. Sandy and others characterized their attempts to "work around" and modify scripted programs as a kind of covert resistance for which there was not much school support.

The pressure to have students succeed on district- and state-mandated tests was also felt by all the beginning teachers. Gail, in particular, cited pressures related to helping her first graders make benchmarks as limiting her participation time in the second year of the inquiry. For example, one of her e-mails included this story about her practice:

> I just had to brag on my kids for a second. . . . Remember when we acted out a poem about stuff in our pockets [in the teacher preparation

program]? Well, my kids were learning a poem about George Washington, and it was thinking about whether he had stuff in his pockets. So, we acted out the poem. We added props, and had a person introduce the poem with a scroll, and on and on and on. They had a lot of fun! They kept wanting to do it for other people: "Can we say it for the PE teacher?" . . . Well, just thought you'd like to know that our fun in children's lit is being passed on to the next generation—in between tests, more tests, and "how fast can you read" tests.

In this passage, Gail shared her ability to modify scripted programs and "work in her own teaching" in order to implement reading strategies that she had developed in her inquiry project. The teachers' perceptions of problems with scripted curriculum initiated most of their individual inquiry foci. The collaborative inquiry group's conversations bolstered teachers' self-efficacy and provided a vehicle for exploring and sharing enhancements to each of their curricula.

Final Comments.

As stated before, the teachers came to us with a strong desire to collaboratively inquire into their practice. However, for all their goodwill, we found that beginning teachers need a reward for their efforts, especially if they are not receiving any recognition or reward in their school settings. By the end of the second year, the teachers listed (a) enjoyment of ongoing contact with their group, (b) the opportunity for graduate credits at a very low cost, and (c) improved instruction for their students as their three main reasons for participating. By far, the biggest challenges for our group were contextual, and these challenges were profound. In fact, only three of our original group chose to continue into the second year of the collaborative inquiry; we see that the challenges rooted in their teaching contexts overwhelmed their desire or perceived ability to participate.

Supporting Reflective Practice

Building a Community of Inquiry.

One of the lessons we learned early on was that we needed to guide the inquiry processes more than we had anticipated. This was especially true of the online discussion. Perhaps because these were beginning teachers struggling with an array of challenges, or perhaps because they were simply used to us being the teachers, we found that online discussion was nonexistent unless we initiated a thread with a specific prompt. For example, in the beginning of the second year, we encouraged teacher reflection and discussion using prompts such as "How do you want to improve your practice this year?," "What do you want to do to enhance your teaching?," and

"How do you plan on reaching this goal?" However, once a prompt was up, we didn't need to demand interaction; the teachers had much to say to each other.

We also found that face-to-face meetings served as much a motivational purpose as an analytic one. Especially helpful were "share the learning" meetings during which teachers presented inquiry project results and implications for their practice. At these events, teachers came with well-designed PowerPoint presentations, student artifacts, and short written summaries about their inquiry projects. While the original purpose of these meetings was to provide moments of reflection and celebration, they also served as an accountability mechanism for moving the inquiry work forward and as a community-building event.

The challenge for us, then, became trying to build on these strong relationships to push teacher learning. Generally speaking, the teachers were adept at cheerleading and giving ideas to each other, but not as adept at asking critical questions about difficult cases and specific acts of teaching. A review of all the Web-based discussions over the two years of the study shows that we were, indeed, more likely to push more critical thinking and reflection about teaching than were the teachers (about three fourths of our posts were aimed at encouraging reflection about a teacher's specific practices). As the group's guides, we became the participants who offered explicit supports for deeper inquiry. For example, Jan's question to Rob is representative here:

> Great thoughts Rob! You can see why we are called "practitioners"— practice, practice, practice! It is great that you use your colleagues to problem solve—they are a valuable source of knowledge and experience to draw on in order to remain solution focused rather than problem focused. Just a question I thought of . . . you said you try lots of new things and that some work and some don't—Is there a difference in how you explain or present the new plan or idea—what makes some things work and some flop? Usually my stuff flopped when I didn't either follow through on the implementation of my great idea OR I didn't buy into it 100% myself.

As the conversation between Jan and Rob continued online, Jan became more directive about the fact that he needed to rethink the "how" of his lessons on mathematical concepts for eighth graders. In one lengthy post in response to some of Rob's complaints about what he perceived as a lack of motivation in his students, Jan's comments included:

> Just so you know—teaching a bunch of "stupid" (to use your words) or "boring" math lessons probably won't get the job done. Are you up for the challenge? You know, another outside source who would probably LOVE to offer some advice would be RW. If you go to her

with an outline of your lessons—she may be able to help you find the best WAYS to teach them and the most interesting activities to have the kids do. I know that you could think of these by yourself but if you want to run it by another expert . . . I think you are going to end your year with a smile on your face and successful teaching!

When we reviewed all the Web-based conversations, we also noticed that we tried to articulate and to identify what was good about their analyses of others' work in our posts, and to link these analyses to the broad purposes of our collaborative inquiry. For example, Kerri wrote a message to the whole group late in the first year that included:

You have been posting good, critical questions on our discussion boards. Keep up the interaction! Hilda Borko writes: "For teachers, learning occurs in many different aspects of practice"—from hallway talks with other teachers to a one-on-one with a struggling teen—Like many of you who have noted that learning about teaching comes from teaching, we need to find ways to steal time to think about our teaching and how to make it better, while supporting each other.

As the inquiry progressed, we continued to try to help the teachers become more critical and questioning in their comments. Using examples from their practice and our online conversations, we also tried to lead them towards deeper reflection about their practice, as in this post from Kerri:

One thing we've noticed as we've seen you teach, and as we've had conversations with you, is that when you bring kids' community knowledge—their interests and their families' interests—into your lessons, the kids are very engaged. Marlys's example of treating writing like a video game is a good example . . . we should talk more about this.

In this case, while the teachers did take up the invitation to talk more and to ask more probing questions of each other's practice, they continued to rely on us for guidance.

If we look at this from a situated learning perspective, we see that strong relationships before beginning the collaboration were important building blocks in the group discussions. There was a level of trust established that enabled the teachers to dive into some substantive questions about teaching and learning. Because they knew each other, they trusted each other enough early in their inquiry processes to ask questions and brainstorm ideas for inquiry projects together. We also believe that our ongoing attention to providing connection time in face-to-face meetings, coupled with liberal doses of humor during online discussions, helped to maintain a culture of collaboration and a shared focus on working hard together to improve our practice. In addition, we provided individualized advice to teachers about how they might collect data, frame inquiry questions, and locate relevant research materials beyond those that they had found. This collection of professional development activities set the stage for the inquiry work of the teachers.

IMPLICATIONS

So what have we learned from this work? Our research suggests that there are a number of challenges and opportunities inherent in supporting rural beginning teachers. In this section we will discuss three major implications:

1. Collaboration can be a means for increasing job satisfaction.
2. Collaborative teacher inquiry with beginning teachers requires active facilitation from someone who knows the teachers and their learning trajectories.
3. Web-based structures can support ongoing dialogue and reflection.

Collaboration and Job Satisfaction

The biggest challenges for teacher inquiry in our group were some of the same challenges cited as reasons why teachers leave Oregon schools: (a) the high demands of teaching; (b) lack of planning time; and (c) lack of support by school administrators. These challenges can be extremely difficult to overcome. One critical implication of the contextual roadblocks to teacher collaboration of any kind—let alone deep and sustained collaborative inquiry—is increased job dissatisfaction. None of the teachers in our inquiry group left teaching during their induction years, but they all experienced deep feelings of frustration over these challenges.

Research suggests that professional development is most effective in supporting teacher learning and improving instruction when it is long-term, school-based, collaborative, and focused on student learning (Darling-Hammond & Sykes, 1999; Garet, Porter, Desimore, Birmant, & Yoon, 2001; Knight & Wiseman, 2005; Walker, Edstam, & Stone, 2007; Zeichner, 2005). We had, arguably, these aspects in place as we attempted to support collaborative inquiry for these rural teachers. But faced with many demands on their time and a lack of local support for sustained inquiry of their own choosing, some teachers in the group sometimes viewed SCTI as an add-on rather than a foundational experience in their professional development. However, their enjoyment of being a part of the inquiry group, and their interest in each others' work, kept them involved.

Snow-Gerono & Franklin (2007), working in Idaho schools near our area, have found high dissatisfaction in mentor teachers in elementary schools. They note that this dissatisfaction seems to be due to a lack of teacher agency as a result of one-size-fits-all curriculum adoptions in response to NCLB. We agree with these teacher-researchers when they note that teacher education in our current time period "must be about preparing thoughtful, inquiring educators who consider meaningful learning opportunities for themselves and their students" (Snow-Gerono & Franklin, 2007, p. 111). We would also argue that this implies that professional development as SCTI should be about building on school-university connections in order to increase rural teacher job satisfaction, increasing the agency of new teachers in their schools to improve student learning opportunities according to their own strengths as teachers, and informing teacher educators' work with preservice teachers who will be entering these contexts. This work is challenging because it takes a great deal of time, and because it requires professional developers who are experienced in supporting new teachers in a range of classroom contexts with a wide range of individual needs.

Need for Active Facilitation

During the two years of our inquiry group work, we were quite well suited as university professors to provide ideas for data collection strategies and critique. But we have heavy teaching loads and many demands on our time. We found that supporting collaborative inquiry, even with a very small group of committed beginning rural teachers, is at least as time-consuming as teaching an extra graduate class each term.

In keeping with a situated perspective on teacher learning, we attempted to work with each teacher's individual needs and interests, and to teach (sometimes successfully, sometimes not) them to support each other's inquiry and reflection about their teaching. We were trying hard to *activate* teacher learning, rather than *deliver* it (Wilson & Berne, 1999). But this long-term approach takes a great deal of time. In the absence of external funding, or institutional support in terms of special Web-based forums that are not tied to traditional course enrollment structures, we continue to find that keeping up with the demands of collaborative inquiry are overwhelming for us as well.

Stein, Silver, & Smith (1999) note that "collaboration does not mean that everyone contributes the same amount, in the same way, at the same point in time" (p. 261). These authors stress development over a long period of time and that different members will support and contribute different skills along the way. Certainly there is a value in simply creating and sustaining a permanent space (on the Web, in our case) for teachers to connect and critically reflect, to share stories of their practice, and to seek advice from peers and professional developers. But guidance is necessary. As different stories are shared over time, different individuals' expertise can be called into play, when requested by inquiry guides who know the participants well.

It can be argued that the support we were able to give the inquiry group in the Web-based forums and the monthly facilitated meetings over two school years provided a kind of learning ground that may prime the participants for future sustained collaborative inquiry with groups of committed teachers working on a common area of inquiry. We have some data to suggest that this is the case. Patty is now working with another teacher in her building on integrating literature workshop time into their language arts curriculum to help increase Hispanic students' motivation and interest. She is interested in pursuing her master's degree, and plans to use her beginning inquiry in this area as a springboard to a major literacy research project.

Web-based Forums can Support Teacher Dialogue

It seems clear that other professional developers in rural areas might make good use of Web-based supports for collaborative inquiry. We would suggest the creation and use of a permanent discussion forum on the Web, easily accessible to all teachers in the group. Beginning teachers, especially, might make good use of the asynchronous and ongoing discussion opportunities provided through a Web-based approach. Beginning teachers are dealing with a host of survival issues that can interfere with regular attendance at face-to-face inquiry meetings, but asynchronous discussions with peers are able to be fit into a hectic school day. The Web-based forum provides a framework for sharing apprenticeship stories in a risk-free way, with ample time for reflection. Professional developers who participate in these discussions are ideally placed to give gentle nudges toward deeper, more sustained inquiry. Asynchronous discussions also give professional developers time to personalize necessary mentoring for teacher learning. These conversations might be an important part of the developmental trajectory of new teachers working across geographic distances ("baby steps" into SCTI, if you will). Also, simple is best for uses of technology in many rural areas; most of us in our group have, at best, dial-up Internet connections. Complicated graphics or pictures that take ages to download each time a new discussion thread is started are not necessary.

CONCLUDING REMARKS

A view of teacher learning as situated was useful to us as we approached collaborative inquiry with beginning teachers. Professional developers and inquiry groups might benefit from building on this perspective as they nurture an inquiry stance in their groups. Other universities whose graduates are teaching in geographically isolated rural areas could make use of some of the aspects of the collaborative inquiry processes that grew organically out of this group's work, such as online discussion boards led by program graduates or university program teaching supervisors. If teacher educators become professional developers, and their inquiry group members are volunteer teachers, creative means of compensation could be explored. Release time for professional developers, graduate credits and/or release time for teachers, and the possibility of districts' paying for teacher credit might be valuable considerations. If a university is able to track its graduates' first-hire positions, online inquiry groups could be set up in advance of beginning teachers' induction experiences. Such online collaborative inquiry groups could be tailored to meet the needs of beginning teachers and to keep them in contact with a peer cohort of beginning teachers across a variety of contexts.

Our work suggests a need for external guides who were sensitive to the contexts of these beginning teachers. In the absence of such professional developers, experienced teachers or district-based professional developers could guide this kind of inquiry group, with its face-to-face meetings and online discussions.

Finally, it appeared that collaborative inquiry processes, though limited in scope by some profound contextual challenges, were useful for rural beginning teachers. The teachers enjoyed, in Marlys's words, "being connected" with their group online and during face-to-face meetings, and they felt that the group helped them engage in continuous learning about their craft. Their desire to share ideas and problems with their group members remained strong throughout their induction years in rural schools, in spite of overwhelming workloads and many demands on their time. If finding ways to support collaborative inquiry for beginning teachers in rural schools gives them a sense of professional support and satisfaction about their career choice, SCTI can be worth the effort.

NOTES

1. Cohort members at our branch campus are typically non-traditional-aged students who have lived and worked in rural communities for most of their lives, and who find access to higher education at a site near their small towns essential if they wish to pursue a teaching degree. During their three undergraduate cohort terms, preservice teachers engage in over 260 hours' service in local rural schools, in addition to a 16-week full-fledged student teaching experience (see Wenger & Dinsmore, 2005; Dinsmore & Wenger, 2006, for a full discussion).

REFERENCES

Ankeny, M., & Zanville, H. (2002). *Oregon Research Report for Oregon Quality Assurance in Teaching.* Oregon Department of Education.

Borko, H. (2004). Professional development and teacher learning: Mapping the terrain. *Educational Researcher, 33*(8), 3–15.

Creswell, J. W. (1998). *Qualitative inquiry and research design: Choosing among five traditions.* Thousand Oaks, CA: Sage.

Davenport, M. R., Jaeger, M., & Lauritzen, C. (2006, April). *To inquire or not to inquire? Examining the impacts of inquiry-based cohort teacher preparation on preservice and in-service teacher practice.* Research paper presented at the American Educational Research Association (AERA) annual meeting, San Francisco.

Darling-Hammond, L., & Sykes, D. (Eds.). (1999). *Teaching as the learning profession: Handbook of policy and practice.* San Francisco: Jossey-Bass.

Dinsmore, J., & Wenger, K. J. (2006). Relationships in preservice teacher preparation: From cohorts to communities. *Teacher Education Quarterly 33*(1), 57–74.

Garet, M. S., Porter, A. C., Desimore, L., Birman, B. F., & Yoon, K. S. (2001). What makes professional development effective? Results from a national sample of teachers. *American Educational Research Journal, 28*(4), 915–945.

Howley, C. B., Theobald, P., & Howley, A. (2005). What rural education research is of most worth? A reply to Arnold, Newman, Gaddy, and Dean. *Journal of Research in Rural Education, 20*(18). Retrieved 07–28–2006 from http://www.umaine.edu/jrre/20–18.pdf

Ingersoll, R. (2001, Fall). Teacher turnover and teacher shortages: An organizational analysis. *American Educational Research Journal, 38,* 499–534.

Johnson, A. (2002). *A short guide to action research.* Upper Saddle River, NJ: Pearson.

Knight, S. L., & Wiseman, D. L. (2005). Professional development for teachers of diverse students: A summary of the research. *Journal of Education for Students Placed at Risk, 10*(4), 387–405.

Krippendorf, K. (1980). *Content analysis: An introduction to its methodology.* Beverly Hills, CA: Sage.

Krueger, R. A., & Casey, M. A. (2000). *Focus groups: A practical guide for applied research* (3rd ed.). Thousand Oaks, CA: Sage.

Lave, J., & Wenger, E. (1991). *Situated learning: Legitimate peripheral participation.* Cambridge, UK: Cambridge University Press.

National Center for Education Statistics. (2007). Teacher attrition and mobility: Results from the 2004–05 Teacher Follow-up Survey. Washington, DC: U.S. Department of Education.

Oregon Association of Colleges of Education. (2007). *Draft statement in support of funding a program to mentor new teachers in Oregon,* 1/27/2007.

Patrick, R. (2003, November 30). *Where are beginning teachers' stories about learning to teach in culturally and socially diverse secondary school classrooms?* Paper presented at the annual conference of NZARE/AARE, Auckland, New Zealand. Retrieved 28 December 2005 from http://www.aare.edu.au/03pap/pa03300.pdf

Patton, M. Q. (1990). *Qualitative evaluation and research methods.* Newbury Park, CA: Sage.

Snow-Gerono, J. L., & Franklin, C. A. (2007). Accountability systems' narrowing effect on curriculum in the United States: A report within an elementary education teacher certification program. In Louise F. Deretchin & Cheryl J. Craig (Eds.), *International research on the impact of accountability systems: Teacher education yearbook XV* (pp. 97–112). Lanham, MD: Rowan & Littlefield Educations.

Stein, M. K., Silver, E. A., & Smith, M. S. (1999). The development of professional developers: Learning to assist teachers in new settings in new ways. *Harvard Educational Review, 69*(3), 237–269.

Wenger, K. J., & Dinsmore, J. (2007). *Constructivist teaching practices: Building achievement bridges in rural Oregon and Idaho schools.* Research paper presented at the Association of Teacher Educators (ATE) annual meeting, San Diego, CA, February.

Walker, C. L., Edstam, T., & Stone, K. (2007, April). *Two years, three kinds of educators, and four schools: Improving education for English language learners.*

Research paper presented at the Annual Meeting of the American Educational Research Association, Chicago, IL.

Wilson, S. M., & Berne, J. (1999). Teacher learning and the acquisition of professional knowledge: An examination of research on contemporary professional development. In A. Iran-Nejad & P. D. Pearson (Eds.), *Review of Research in Education* (pp. 173–210). Washington, DC: AERA.

Zanville, H. (2006). *Educator supply and demand: Implications for staffing Oregon schools.* Salem, OR: Oregon Department of Education.

Zeichner, K. (2005). A research agenda for teacher education. In M. Cochran-Smith and K. Zeichner (Eds.), *Studying teacher education. The report of the AERA Panel on Research and Teacher Education.* Mahwah, NJ: Lawrence Erlbaum Associates.

Zeichner, K. M., & Noffke, S. E. (2001). Practitioner research. In V. Richardson (Ed.), *Handbook of research on teaching* (pp.298–332). Washington, DC: American Educational Research Association.

Zumwalt, K., & Craig, E. (2005). Teachers' characteristics: Research on the demographic profile. In M. Cochran-Smith & K. M. Zeichner (Eds.), *Studying teacher education: The report of the AERA panel on research and teacher education* (pp. 111–156) . Washington, DC: AERA.

7 Resource Networks for Collaborative Teacher Inquiry

David Slavit, Wendi Laurence, Anne Kennedy, and Tamara Holmlund Nelson

Washington State University Vancouver

Evidence exists that teachers engaged in meaningful inquiry into their practice require supportive resources (Ball & Cohen, 1999; Putnam & Borko, 2000). Numerous researchers also assert that particular resource needs arise amongst teachers working in collaborative inquiry contexts (Gamoran, Anderson, Quiroz, Secada, Williams, & Ashmann, 2003; McLaughlin & Talbert, 2006; Louis, 2008; Wilson & Berne, 1999). This chapter examines specific resources that can influence teachers' development and enactment of collaborative inquiry. We discuss the notion of a resource network as an analytic tool for operationalizing the theoretical discussion of support found in Chapter 1. To illustrate this approach, we discuss the nature of a dynamic resource network that influenced the trajectory of the work of two collaborative inquiry groups, drawing upon data from the PRiSSM professional development project (see Nelson et al. in this volume). We give particular attention to those resources which surfaced as supports for the collaborative inquiry process and also discuss resources that were not present but identified as potentially useful by the participants or the researchers (Table 7.1).

In the context of supported collaborative teacher inquiry (SCTI), we define *resource* in a broad sense to include tangible and intangible objects and expertise capable of supporting the collaborative inquiry process. Although, by definition, a resource is potentially helpful, it does not automatically, or even necessarily, transcend to the level of support. The mere provision of resources to teachers engaged in inquiry does not ensure positive impacts, or any impact at all. Cohen, Raudenbush, & Ball (2003) address this with respect to instruction:

> The effects of resources depend on both access and use: students and teachers cannot use resources they don't have, but the resources they do have are not self-acting. Simply collecting a stock of conventional resources cannot create educational quality, for quality does not arise simply from such attributes. (p. 122)

Similarly, in order to understand the nature and level of support that resources provide to teachers engaged in SCTI, it is insufficient to merely

Table 7.1 A Collection of Resources that Can Support the Functioning and Work of Collaborative Teacher Inquiry Groups

	Resource as Support	
Internal	*Internal/External*	*External*
Teachers' skills, knowledge, and perspectives.	Group facilitation and leadership.	Funding.
Knowledge obtained from teachers' prior professional experiences.	Time.	Trust in the teachers and their inquiry work by administrators.
Concurrent, relevant, and accessible professional development experiences.	Access to and use of research literature or other relevant information.	Awareness, valuing, and promotion of the inquiry work by administrators.
		State and national content and professional standards.
		Professional organizations.

review lists and descriptions of potential and actual resources. For example, multiple resources can be mutually supportive and provide opportunities or information that a single resource cannot (Gamoran et al., 2003; McLauglin & Talbert, 2006).

However, there is value in carefully looking at specific resources; analysis at the individual resource level can inform specific, targeted impacts on SCTI. Such analysis could consider the resources' locus of origin, timeliness and level of availability, degree to which the resource meshes with the inquiry goals and perspectives of the teacher researchers, the resource's real and potential impacts, and the absence of other potentially useful and related resources. However, researchers seeking to understand the totality of the relationships between resources and collaborative inquiry processes must move to a coordinated analysis of the existing resources that, taken as a whole, comprise a network from which teachers engaged in collaborative inquiry draw, are unaware of, or fail to utilize either by choice or inaccessibility (Figure 7.1). Thus, we place resource networks at the center of our analysis.

Two cases from the PRiSSM project will be utilized in our discussion of resource networks. The Alder Creek case (all names of people and locations are pseudonyms) will examine the construction of a resource network as supports for teachers engaged in collaborative inquiry, and the Cedar Grove case will focus on a resource network that supports teachers who become leaders of professional learning communities (PLCs).

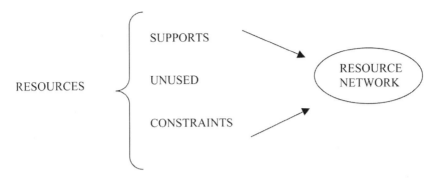

Figure 7.1 Compilation of resources and their real or potential impact as part of a resource network.

METHODOLOGY

The two cases discussed here are based on long-term case studies (Merriam, 1998) of five PRiSSM PLCs. These cases have been developed since 2005; for this analysis, we draw predominantly from qualitative data collected during the 2006–2007 school year, the third and final year of the PRiSSM project. Some details of the methodological approach, including specific data collection and analysis techniques related to PRiSSM, are described more fully in Nelson et al. (this volume). Details of the analytic techniques pertaining to resource networks follow. For these cases, we focus on the ways in which teachers conceptualized the notion of support in the form of specific resources, the presence or lack of these resources in their professional development context, the convergence of individual resources into a resource network, and the impact of a particular resource network on the work of the two collaborative inquiry groups.

Audiotapes of PLC meetings and video recordings of classroom instruction, teacher and group interviews, numerous e-mails, and other informal contacts represent the bulk of the data set. A thematic analysis focused on deriving units of meaning from patterns embedded in the data corpus (Taylor & Bogdan, 1984). The interconnectivity of resources emerged as a salient theme in the case of Alder Creek, and the influence of resources in the development of leaders emerged in the case of Cedar Grove. For both cases, analyses of resources focused on (a) their supportive nature, particularly from the perspective of the participants, as well as factors that influenced their potential and real impacts, (b) the identification of their locus of origin, and (c) missing resources that may have been useful to the teachers' inquiry work. A discussion of the specific analytic techniques related to the first two of these areas is found in the subsequent sections.

Relationships between Resources and Supports

An assumption of our analysis is that every resource, if accessed, has the potential to be either a limiting factor, negligible influence, or support in a given collaborative teacher inquiry context. While we define resource as being capable of supporting the inquiry process, we recognize that not all resources actually move the inquiry work forward. Therefore, in analyzing the nature of a resource as real or potential support, we explore the interplay between resource, inquiry context, and inquiry process (Figure 7.2).

First, the inquiry context and inquiry process can have significant bearing on the supportive nature of a given resource. Specifically, the existence and availability of some resources are completely dependent on the educational context in which the inquiry activities occur, while their selection and utilization are largely dependent on the nature of the inquiry process. For example, teachers in a school containing a literacy coach have that potential resource available, but may choose to not utilize this resource because their focus is on mathematics. Second, inquiry context can define various aspects of the inquiry process, including the inquiry focus. Context can also influence and perhaps determine how a given set of resources is available to and used by teachers in a collaborative inquiry group. For example, teachers in a school who have undertaken a content literacy initiative may be led (by the administration or their own interests) to include this

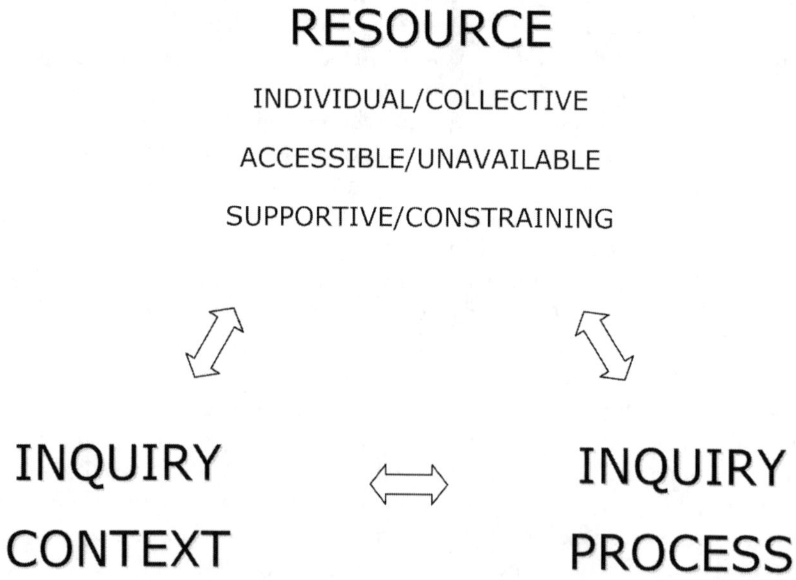

RESOURCE

INDIVIDUAL/COLLECTIVE

ACCESSIBLE/UNAVAILABLE

SUPPORTIVE/CONSTRAINING

INQUIRY
CONTEXT

INQUIRY
PROCESS

Figure 7.2 Analytic framework regarding the impact of a resource or resource network on collaborative teacher inquiry.

as part of their inquiry focus, and to also make use of the literacy coach and selected research in this area. Third, it is clear that the inquiry process is grounded in context and dependent on available resources. Therefore, the supportive nature of a given resource or resource network is highly dependent on the context and specific inquiry focus of a teacher group. The cases that follow provide specific examples of the interplay between these three important features of collaborative inquiry, with specific attention to how resources surface and are utilized in a specific inquiry setting.

Locus of Origin

Some of the resources identified as impacting, or potentially impacting, the collaborative inquiry process are directly related to the teachers themselves and can thus be viewed as internal to the collaborative inquiry group. These include, among other things, the intellectual and knowledge resources teachers bring with them to the inquiry group process. Like McDuffie (this volume), we will differentiate between resources that emanate from the immediate context of the teacher group (including those emanating from or related to individual teachers) from those with a more external locus of origin. However, while McDuffie uses work inside or outside the teacher's classroom as the separation between internal and external support, we will use all aspects of a teacher's or teacher group's past and current experiences as the demarcation between internal and external resource that supports collaborative inquiry work. Hence, in this chapter, internal support refers to resources derived from the individual members' lives and educational experiences that they use to move the collaborative inquiry work forward. Specific examples include prior teaching experience, professional experience as a research scientist, and experiences as a professional development facilitator. On the other hand, some resources emanate from individuals or forces outside the teacher group and are thus defined as external resources. Examples include school and district initiatives that relate to the inquiry work, state and national curricular recommendations and benchmarks, and available funding. All of these have a locus of origin that emanates from outside the teacher group's immediate environment. Finally, some resources can be difficult to categorize in this framework, such as a group facilitator, who has identity and presence both in and out of the collaborative inquiry group.

Concluding Analytical Comments

Analyzing a resource network, not merely the isolated impact of an individual resource, allows the researcher to better understand the educational context in which the collaborative inquiry progresses and the source and nature of the supports that shape the group's inquiry trajectory. While specific individual resources are discussed, our analysis focuses on the collective nature of the resources present and their overall role in the functioning of the collaborative inquiry group. From this broad perspective, our analysis of data focuses on the totality of the resource network present, with detailed attention to a small collection of key resources (Table 7.1). This approach allows for a macroanalysis of the overall resource network, which incorporates an internal/external framework for discussing the locus of origin of each resource, while also providing microanalyses of the resources in regard to the factors mentioned earlier.

CASE 1: ALDER CREEK HIGH SCHOOL

The Alder Creek PLC case study highlights the intellectual and knowledge resources that six high school science teachers drew from, and hoped for, to support their collaborative inquiry. Analysis reveals that the teachers' capacity to do their work was increased through internal and external sources of support that resulted in a complex resource network. The Alder Creek case provides a glimpse into how resources were accessed and shared by teachers during supported collaborative inquiry.

Group Composition and Focus

Two factors that can impact the work of a PLC are membership and interest. Early work at Alder Creek was driven by a small group of teachers who had agreed to work voluntarily on a shared problem of practice. Cheryl, the leader of the Alder Creek PLC, first joined PRiSSM as a lead teacher midway through Year 1 (2004–05). For the next 18 months she worked closely with school colleagues as well as mathematics and science teachers from other schools and grade levels to explore strategies for eliciting more targeted and conceptual questions from students. In an interview, Cheryl shared examples of how this work impacted the ways in which she interacted with students in her classrooms, and generally expressed positive views of her inquiry during this period:

> I mean, isn't it great that you could spend two years on this one question if you felt like it needed it? Or you could stop it in November of next year and go on to the next one. You really get a self-directed idea, and you have a smaller group so you can really get your fingers into something instead of, "Okay, we're going to read this book and we're all going to go to this seminar, and we're going to like it."

An important aspect of collaborative inquiry for Cheryl was that teachers had control over who was involved with PLC work, what they were researching, and how they were conducting the research. This seemed to provide both motivation and sense of efficacy to the work.

As the 2006–07 school year began, Alder Creek's school district decided to mandate PLC participation for all teachers in all schools. Alder Creek teachers were asked to re-form their PLCs by discipline, although teachers had choice as to the formulation of subgroups within their discipline. Motivated by early positive experiences in PRiSSM, Cheryl actively engaged in recruiting teachers into her collaborative inquiry group. Her enthusiasm for conducting research on classroom practice attracted teachers with a collective interest in looking more deeply at student learning. At the end of the year, Cheryl reflected on her recruiting process and mind-set as she went about finding new PLC members:

> The year before [2005–06] we just dropped an email and said, "Who wants to be in PRiSSM?" We only had 4 people. So last year [September, 2006] I went to individuals and said, "This is what PRiSSM is about, these are some things we can do." And kind of sold them into the idea. And then when the people who are on board came, we're like, "Yeah, we're really jazzed about PRiSSM." We started looking at data and just very driven to have seen research.

While Cheryl spent a good deal of physical and mental energy in the recruitment process, she was enabled in this work by an unrecognized and complex network of resources that created the context for the eventual formation of the PLC. Dan Tobin, the district's science manager and an active leader in the overall development and implementation of PRiSSM, spent many hours behind the scenes helping to identify and recruit teachers to Cheryl's PLC, including discussions with school administrators. Cheryl's story of recruiting demonstrates a recurring phenomenon amongst PLC teachers who may be unaware of the totality of the resource network that supports their work.

The reconstituted PLC now consisted of science teachers with varied experiences and backgrounds. Some early-career teachers were beginning their professional lives while others were entering the classroom from science-related positions in industry. The group also had a diverse array of educational backgrounds, with subject expertise that ranged from biology to chemistry, and bachelor's degrees to doctorates. As will be discussed, this group diversity was recognized and used as a source of internal support by the Alder Creek PLC.

Group Diversity as Support

Cheryl's story of recruiting also partly belies the underlying like-mindedness amongst the teachers, as each felt strongly about the importance of developing students' abilities to write scientific conclusions. These commonalities provided a bridge for the teachers to forge through difficult conversations and to develop a respect for each other's backgrounds. For example, in an early PLC meeting the group decided to "go away from the WASL [state achievement test]" and collectively understand "from a 'life in general' perspective what should go into a good conclusion." These discussions eventually led the group to formalize their inquiry focus on supporting students' scientific conclusion writing.

However, diversity within the group continuously surfaced and at times challenged Cheryl's facilitation skills. For example, later in this same meeting the group struggled to find specific ways in which they might analyze student work:

Ariel: I think we can talk about that [conclusion writing] and which way we want it to be, and that way we're not pretending we're WASL scoring these, per se, but that we are looking at the conclusion only and saying, "This conclusion has a mode, or blah blah blah among all the students." Or among each class can have their own [mode score], or how we're going to look at [disaggregate] the data.

Sophia: So what would that look like? I would say, "This overall conclusion is a three because . . ."

Ariel: Well, we might look at each of the data points, for example, add them up and the overall thing would be blah blah blah.

The preceding passage illustrates some of the different perspectives towards data, and research in general, that repeatedly surfaced inside the group. While Sophia was looking to engage Ariel in a discussion about specific aspects of conclusion writing, Ariel seemed more focused on generating numeric scores for descriptive analyses of student correctness. After Kaitlin, the PRiSSM facilitator, later offered guidance and examples that helped the group refine their inquiry focus and research design, Cheryl led a discussion that consolidated the group's collective approach towards data collection and analysis:

Emma: Yeah, and then we can use [agreed upon indicators] as a reference ourselves to . . . before we score though we should get together and say, "We agree that . . ."

Cheryl: Well that's what I was thinking. Was that at the next meeting, if we all bring in ten different examples, and we double score them. So I score it, you score it. Then we see if we're scoring the same thing and make sure we're on the same page. And then it might even be nice to not score your own kids.

Grace: Yeah.

Lauren: And I think we should do double scoring on every group. So that, like I might rotate to Lisa once and then another time rotate to Emma. So that, because they even do that on the thing they give to the kids coming up from middle school to decide if they're going to be pre-AP. They do double scoring on that, and that's less crucial, I think, than a . . .

Emma: Genuine study.

Lauren: And then we have to decide how we're going to record data and keep track of it too.

Cheryl: [Well and I love data]—

Lauren: [By class, by kid] by teacher, by . . .

Cheryl: I love data and so I don't mind running the data, I like to do statistics, so, I mean—

Grace: I can help you.

Fletcher: And I have, like, I have all this statistics software on my computer so if you want to use it . . .

Besides clarifying the precise nature of the group's inquiry focus and design, the preceding dialogue shows how the group members were quite interested in better understanding their learners from various perspectives using a variety of methodological tools. These included various quantitative approaches to data representation and analysis as well as introductory statements about discussing student work and getting "on the same page." Throughout the year, when discussing and enacting methodology, the teachers continued to utilize a complex and varied set of internal resources that included methodological perspectives from previous scientific careers, educational research textbooks, and other inquiry-related experiences from graduate education experiences. During these moments, Cheryl possessed the needed facilitation skills to segue through difficulty or allow for talents to be shared. These interactions were augmented by a group that valued their own diversity and saw it as a way to reach their common goals. These two factors, facilitation and the valuing of diversity, were the primary reasons why this set of methodological resources coalesced into a usable and important resource network with which the group could move forward.

Throughout the remainder of the inquiry process, the diversity within the group continued to provide depth to the internal resource network. After determining their inquiry question, the group moved to delegating specific inquiry tasks. Discussions during these meetings often centered on how the teachers' backgrounds might provide perspective on the pedagogic, content-related, and research aspects of the collaborative inquiry. For example, the early career scientists talked about contributing what they knew of writing conclusions in the field, and those who brought an education background offered to work on developing objectives. At the end of the year, Lauren reflected on her past experiences in this regard:

I come from a research background. That's what my previous life was, working as a research scientist at (a regional hospital). So, just by nature, I like research. I like having a question or problem and trying to find an answer to it. So I guess mainly it's something I want to do rather than something I'm being forced to do.

Each group member was prepared and willing to contribute their perspectives as they designed the methodology for their collaborative inquiry. As the year concluded and the teachers began a day-long retreat to look at their data, the differences in content and education were again leveraged to work as a resource for data analysis. For example, some teachers utilized spreadsheets to store and analyze the group's quantitative data, while others drew from their master's level work to code data qualitatively. Interactions such as these demonstrate how the combination of facilitation skills, group valuing of diversity, and the willingness of the group to share their backgrounds and experiences became a source of internal support for collaborative inquiry.

Concurrent and Relevant Learning Opportunities

An emerging pattern in the data analysis was the teachers' abilities to draw from resources that were timely, appropriate, and accessible (Laurence, 2007). The use of these resources supported individual and group learning opportunities. Access to these resources was facilitated by PRiSSM- and district-related opportunities, including targeted professional development experiences. These opportunities allowed group members to access a cafeteria plan of professional development activities and other resources in support of their inquiry work. In addition, graduate education experiences and completing the tiered licensure process were examples of individual learning opportunities that played a role in group interactions. Evidence of these individual learning opportunities appeared as the teachers analyzed data and interpreted their findings. For example, at the end of the year, Cheryl reflected on the role that advanced coursework played in their group dynamics and processes:

> We started looking at data and were very driven. We have one person who has their Ph.D. [in psychology] and one person who is in the middle of their Ph.D. [in adolescent behavior] so those two people really bring a lot. They have that background of how do we get kids to do things we need them to do? [Note: This is in addition to Lauren, who has a Ph.D. in science]. We're research driven. We're really interested more in that whole process and having the opportunity to explore that process than necessarily being a PLC.

As an example of group learning, Cheryl, Lauren, and Kaitlin attended a professional development event that targeted student assessment and analyzing student work. This opportunity, made possible by the two teachers' involvement in a research project with the authors, came as the Alder Creek PLC was developing a tool to collectively assess their students' conclusion writing. Using a framework introduced at this meeting, the two teachers spent the day designing what would become the group's primary data collection and analysis tool. The impact of this professional development opportunity was immediate and enduring, as the assessment tool was used again the following year. In addition, through Kaitlin's urging, this tool and some of the PLC's student learning results were shared district-wide, an action that served to validate the group's work and value.

The teachers' abilities to access learning opportunities and their participation in the PLC were also supported by funds provided by their school district, PRiSSM, and, in the case of Cheryl and Lauren, their role as co-researchers in a university project. Among other things, Cheryl was able to attend two national conferences during the school year that involved presentations on their inquiry work, and all teachers were able to use district and PRiSSM funds to work together as a group during PLC meetings, as well as the previously described professional development event focused on data analysis. Without the available funding, the support provided through these experiences would not have been possible.

Use of a Resource Network to Expand and Enhance Collaborative Inquiry

The Alder Creek PLC is an example of a collaborative inquiry group that cultivated the internal resources of the group, leveraged external resources, and allocated discretionary funds to create an expanded resource network. As the 2007–08 school year began, the teachers again had many questions about the form and direction of their PLC. However, the teachers' use of the expanded support network was demonstrated early on, as discussions of inquiry focus, data collection, and theoretical framework were derived from a wider network than the year before, despite the fact that PRiSSM funds were no longer available. For example, while the teachers began the previous year unaware of many professional conferences and science-education research societies, they were able to advance their inquiry progress by making use of theoretical frameworks and methodologies found in the proceedings of a conference attended by Cheryl.

By documenting which resources were accessed, we begin to understand the choices and factors that influence teachers' construction of a support network for collaborative inquiry. In the case of Alder Creek, internal and external resources enhanced the opportunity for the teachers to build a resource network and move the collaborative inquiry work forward.

CASE 2: CEDAR GROVE MIDDLE SCHOOL

Unlike the Alder Creek case, which focused on the relationship of a resource network and an entire inquiry group, this case explores the availability and use of a resource network by an individual teacher who participated in a collaborative inquiry process and served as the group's primary facilitator. While the analysis will center on Karen, the recognized leader of the group, we also include analyses of other group members, as appropriate, due to the shared leadership and overall strength of the group. The case provides insight into the nuanced ways in which teacher leaders need support for collaborative inquiry work, and the ways in which teacher leaders can perceive, receive, construct, and make use of such resources.

The Cedar Grove PLC consisted of a core group of four mathematics and science middle school teachers who chose to focus their inquiry on student engagement and higher order thinking. In addition to Karen, other members of the PLC included Kevin, a sixth-grade science teacher, and Pete and Perry, who taught mathematics. All four members of the PLC were respected leaders at Cedar Grove, and all but one completed or initiated efforts to obtain national board certification. Karen, an original teacher leader in the PRiSSM project, had prior experience as a content coach and had participated in or presented at a host of regional, state, and national professional development events. Data for this case are taken from the third year of PRiSSM, the same time frame as the Alder Creek case discussed earlier.

Developing Leadership and Facilitation Skills

While Karen was the leader of the Cedar Grove PLC, there was an intentional effort to establish distributed leadership throughout the group, in part due to a similar culture engendered by both PRiSSM and Cedar Grove Middle School. Late in the academic year, Kevin stated:

> We all pretty much share, and it's 100% give and take, all four of us come together. So there's no real leadership. The only thing Karen and I might do is do the paperwork.

Karen organized agendas and regulated discussion, but all group members attempted to provide initiative to both the community- and inquiry-oriented aspects of PLC activities. Hence, leadership was distributed in terms of group processes, but also in terms of determining the direction and focus of the work and daily interactions.

Ermonie, Cedar Grove's mathematics coach and member of PRiSSM's leadership team, served as the PLC facilitator provided by PRiSSM. She knew the teachers at this school quite well and recognized Karen and the other members of the Cedar Grove PLC as strong leaders who possessed advanced collaborative inquiry skills. As a result, she attended very few of the group's PLC meetings, devoting her limited facilitation time to other PRiSSM PLCs in the district. At the end of the year, when Kevin was asked to identify his PRiSSM facilitator, he stated, "I guess I don't know . . . I don't think there is one." Yet, as will unfold in this case, even skilled teacher leaders need the support of knowledgeable others at various times. In this case, Karen and other group members sought support from researchers (including the authors) who attended PLC meetings, as well as Andrew, the assistant principal, who attended most of the monthly meetings. Therefore, while the resource network related to supporting group leadership was quite healthy and immediate with regard to internal supports, the teacher group had a more complex challenge identifying and utilizing external sources of support in this regard. However, as will be seen, Karen and the rest of the group were quite successful in expanding their internally built resource network by making use of additional resources from external sources.

Support for Leadership and Facilitation Skills

PRiSSM professional development activities emphasized specific community-building techniques, with a focus on the need to develop interpersonal norms (Garmston & Wellman, 1999). While Karen did not make use of specific protocols or activities provided or modeled in PRiSSM, these general philosophies were apparent in her facilitation style and actions, particularly early in the year when community and norm building were foci of PLC activity. Karen had a significant, personal resource network on which to draw, some of which came from her involvement in PRiSSM and some from other professional development experiences. The latter included district and regional leadership experiences, participation on statewide curricular committees, and, like Cheryl from Alder Creek, presentations of her work with members of the research team at regional and national venues. Each of these experiences impacted her ability to lead PLC work. For example, the district- and state-level positions afforded leadership experience in professional development activities and firsthand exposure to curriculum, standards, and assessment work, while the national presentations allowed her to become increasingly articulate about the nature of her own PLC work and collaborative inquiry in general. In addition, Andrew and members of the research team provided occasional input into the PLC process. Therefore, while Karen's PLC leadership technique was consistent with and influenced by her PRiSSM experiences, numerous other supports were also present. The culminating resource network was a complex array of supports emanating from a host of internal and external sources.

Facilitation of Community and Group Processes

Karen made frequent use of her leadership and facilitation skills in supporting the group's development of community norms and interpersonal skills. For example, early in the year, Karen had a growing frustration with Perry's tendency to disregard attendance norms by arriving late as well as a perception that he tended to "dominate discussions." Karen spent time with researchers and Andrew to reflect on and think about strategies she might use to move the group forward. Drawing from her own experiences, she allotted significant meeting time to revising and rebuilding group norms during this period. Specific activities garnered from her PRiSSM experiences were used in this process, including the use of a framework for conceptualizing and developing specific norms of collaboration (Garmston & Wellman, 1999). Although difficulties remained throughout the year, the functioning of the group was not significantly impacted by further breeches of these norms. In this instance, the presence of a knowledgeable other with whom to reflect proved to be a useful form of support to reinforce or augment Karen's own knowledge, experience, and confidence in facilitating a collaborative inquiry group.

Like the Alder Creek case, the teachers at Cedar Grove also valued the diversity found within the group. At the end of the year, Kevin reflected on the benefits of the cross-disciplinary nature of the group:

> This experience has had a profound impact on my teaching. Camaraderie between the science and mathematics teachers within the PLC is rewarding in its own right. It has also opened my mind to new and different teaching strategies and tools that have been shown to increase student learning.

While the group's diversity was a definite strength, it also had negative consequences as the inquiry process unfolded. When viewed in terms of content focus, group diversity was not always a support. Specifically, group interactions were sometimes split by content focus and, when combined with the previously described breech in norms, nearly led the group to dissolve itself early in the year. In addition, the content-embedded differences in the group's inquiry focus often limited the depth of conversation across all four members, as illustrated early in the year:

Pete: And is that taking kids to that higher level of thinking?
Kevin: They have to evaluate. I mean, that would be Bloom's, right?
Pete: Well, yeah, I'm just, just—
Kevin: That would be higher on Bloom's?
Pete: You know, just wanting to get my mind around it. What's going on.

When the mathematics and science teachers engaged each other, the dialogue stayed at the general level displayed above. Specifically, whole-group discussions of student thinking tended to center on general notions of "higher levels" and "critical" than on specific student thinking grounded in mathematics or scientific content. Later in the year, when the majority of data analysis occurred, planned and unplanned dual conversations about student work would arise, which were separated by content. These conversations explored issues of student understanding and instruction that were embedded in the task-specific content. In essence, the group members found outlets to overcome the levels of generality in conversations like the aforementioned, and eventually were able to use rubrics and other analytic tools to specifically delve into their students' mathematical and scientific thinking. However, the diversity in content background frustrated the group's desire to use common assessments and hindered their ability to meaningfully collect and analyze data as a whole group. Throughout the year, Karen and the rest of the group members received very little support in regard to addressing the content-related dilemmas generated by the composition of the group. Support from a knowledgeable other to help increase awareness of relevant research, bridge content barriers, or guide them to useful but separate content-embedded conversations would have been helpful to the group's functioning and overall inquiry work.

Interfaces with External Resources and Contexts

School administrators, professional development, and the use of research literature were all part of a resource network that supported the group's ability to relate their PLC work to broader contexts. A key source of administrative support for the Cedar Grove PLC was Andrew, an assistant principal. Andrew chose to be a regular attendee at PLC meetings, having been assigned the oversight role for science instruction in the school. While Andrew was not an active member of the inquiry process, he provided support for securing and managing funds, informing and encouraging other administrators to attend various PLC events, and linking the work of the PLC to key school and district events and stakeholders. His regular presence was very much appreciated by the group as a significant sign of administrative support. Further, Andrew served as conduit between the PLC and Elaine, the principal at Cedar Grove, and he consistently communicated the goals and nature of the PLC work back to her. Elaine also attended most PRiSSM administrator events and had frequent conversations with PLC members about their work.

Karen and the members of the Cedar Grove PLC had a strong desire and vision for sharing their work beyond their PLC context. Andrew, who also shared this vision, gave time to Karen at the opening staff meeting to talk about the work of the PLC in the prior year. Karen expressed her appreciation of Andrew for this action, reflecting, "[In the past] we showed our work at the PRiSSM showcase [annual, regional display of PLC work to PRiSSM colleagues and administrators], but we deprived our own staff of knowing about the work we did." This desire to more broadly share the work was also expressed during PLC meetings:

Karen: Even in our own district, I show [other teachers] the [kids'] lab write-up and they're like, "What?" They're just blown away. But then again, that's a supplemental piece that we've developed at

Cedar Grove as opposed, and I've shared it with other buildings, it's not like it's our secret, we freely share it.

Kevin: But it shouldn't be just a Cedar Grove thing, it should be something that's more . . .

Karen: District-wide.

Kevin: State-wide. It should be on the [state education] website. This is how you should be scoring this. But they're not doing that. It shouldn't be one of those things that you need to go to River school district, and specifically Cedar Grove Middle School, in order to be successful.

Karen, Kevin, and Pete have all discussed their PLC work at regional and national educational conferences. These teachers have come to see their results valued beyond their own school context and have realized that their work as a researcher might have value and import not only to other teachers but to the educational community as a whole. As stated in the opening chapter of this volume, supports are often necessary to bridge collaborative inquiry work to broader educational contexts. The Cedar Grove teachers had a rich network of support that facilitated their ability to make these connections, enriching their own work as well as the broader educational contexts with which they connected.

Despite access to these supports, Karen expressed occasional displeasure with the support she was provided for two reasons. The previously discussed lack of facilitation support provided by PRiSSM was one source of frustration. All leaders, regardless of skill set, need a venue for sharing and reflecting on the successes and challenges of their work. Second, the PLC models and perspectives familiar to Elaine, many of which came from a district-wide PLC initiative, were somewhat different from those Karen experienced in PRiSSM. The reluctance of Elaine to delegate control of the agenda during "PLC time" and in all-school staff meetings, and Karen's perception that Elaine was attempting to exert too much influence on PLC focus and process, contributed to further frustrations for Karen. Although Elaine made numerous public displays of support for Karen and the work of the PLC, Karen felt a continuous tension with Elaine regarding both PLC direction and process that was never fully resolved. Towards the end of the year, Karen spoke specifically about her view of the administrative support she and her group received:

> I feel real supported. Our vice principal [Andrew] is . . . really involved with just being there and he's always asking, "What can I do to help you out? What can I do to support this?" He sees it as a real positive thing. Our head principal is starting to see it as something positive.

Karen also went beyond Cedar Grove in seeking administrative support. After hearing that Dan Tobin, the district science manager, would be attending their PLC meeting in October, Karen led the group in a discussion of needed resources, including funding for professional travel, as well as how they could clarify the manner in which the group's work could better connect with district goals. Dan was able to provide a small amount of additional funding for conference travel and successfully addressed the group's questions. This short period of access and relatively small display of support by Dan validated the group's work and expanded avenues for improvement. While Dan attended very few meetings, his communication and brief show of support were very important to the functioning of the group.

Karen and all members of the Cedar Grove PLC were quite cognizant of the importance of seeking out external resources, particularly articles from the research literature. Requests were made to Ermonie, Andrew, Dan Tobin, and members of the PRiSSM project staff. Karen reflected on the group's use of literature at the end of the year:

> The conversations are more rich. They involve research. We back up our statements with either things that we've done or things that we've seen or things that we've heard about or read about. Or if it's something that we're not familiar with, we'll find an article and we'll all read the article. It's more [pause] professional.

However, analysis of the PLC transcripts reveals little reference to the use of research, and specific research literature often came to the group without a thorough search. On the other hand, materials and information obtained from various professional development events were highly used. For example, midway through the year, Karen devoted approximately one half of an entire meeting to debriefing events at a local conference attended by all of the group's members. Themes and activities related to school and district initiatives were also commonly found in the analysis of PLC interactions.

Possible Supports Needed

Karen's support network regarding her facilitation of the collaborative inquiry efforts of the Cedar Grove PLC was much larger than is available to most teachers. Her school provided embedded time and a supportive climate for PLC work, she had a solid working relationship with school and district-level administrators, talented colleagues with whom to work, and many years of experience designing and supporting teacher learning opportunities. In addition, because of Karen's leadership qualities, her experiences in PRiSSM and other professional development contexts, and the strength of her group members, she only showed an occasional sign of needing support for developing and maintaining community and facilitating group processes.

The diversity within the group, particularly its cross-disciplinary nature, proved to be a significant challenge to the facilitation skills of Karen and the overall functioning of the group. For example, Karen could have benefited from additional facilitation support in relation to the data-related inquiry processes of the group, particularly regarding data collection and analysis. Further, while Karen was able to align and focus group conversations with individual meeting and overarching goals, the presence of an external facilitator could have enhanced the depth and focus of the group's dialogue by providing suggestions for additional resources and by acting as a critical friend for determining what kinds of facilitator moves might enhance group work. Opportunities for Karen to discuss this and other such issues with a knowledgeable other may have benefited the group.

Supporting Successful Leaders

There were several things that allowed Karen to be successful as a PLC leader over the year: knowledge and skills regarding the collaborative inquiry process, leadership abilities, strong group membership, administrative support, and a vision of external impact. Her inquiry knowledge and skills consisted of the desire and will to spend time discussing vision and focus early in the process, and the ability to connect common assessments to PLC inquiry goals. Her vision of external impact was clearly present in her approach to the work of the PLC, such as the ability to conceptualize the work for presentation at national venues. Support in the development of these leadership factors came from a host of experiences, including PRiSSM, and emanated from people who were trusted and available, or from resources that were particularly relevant and readily known.

The resource network Karen and the Cedar Grove PLC received provided multiple avenues for bridging their work with broader educational contexts in many ways and at many times. Personally, Karen's current positions as a district science coach and member of state-level standards-setting committees has put her into positions where she can better recognize and impact science education in larger contexts. Karen's move to this broader context locates her inside a resource network that will, among other things, allow her to provide supports to teacher colleagues that she herself found most helpful when engaging in collaborative teacher inquiry.

CONCLUSIONS AND IMPLICATIONS

The previous cases, both of which possess unique characteristics, collectively offer an important glimpse into various features of support for collaborative teacher inquiry. First, each case points to the need to recognize the inherent strengths and weaknesses of the membership of each teacher group to conduct collaborative inquiry, and then find ways of building on strengths and overcoming limitations. Second, attention must be given to how the people and systems outside the teacher group reinforce or challenge the teachers' abilities to focus on what they feel is important. These findings fit well with the theoretical notions of support expounded in the opening chapter of this volume.

In both cases, the need to attend to strengths and weaknesses is seen, among other things, in the ways that resources were identified and used in supporting leadership development, negotiating a vision of classroom teaching, accessing information, and conducting student-focused inquiry. In each case, groups actively constructed a resource network to support their collaborative inquiry process. For Alder Creek, the teachers were able to develop a personal and PLC consciousness of where and how to access information. Ultimately, this speaks to teacher professionalism and the ways in which teachers gain access to information they feel is necessary to improve student learning and classroom practice. This case is also an example of distributed cognition across a group, with specific supports being provided to make this possible. The presence of diverse content and experiential backgrounds, the use of various research techniques, and collaborative dialogic norms supported the group in their development and use of distributed cognition in pursuit of instructional questions pertaining to a specific content focus. For Cedar Grove, despite the limited presence of a formal PRiSSM facilitator, several knowledgeable others provided teacher leaders opportunities to think through critical needs for the PLC in terms of structure and function. This case also illustrates the need for and importance of validation of the efficacy of skills teacher leaders bring to inquiry processes and practices, such as shared leadership and attention to interpersonal norms. The resource network supported the groups' abilities to utilize their own distributed leadership tendencies and qualities in moving their inquiry work forward.

However, no matter what aspect of collaborative teacher inquiry we are considering, support cannot just focus on teachers, but must take into account the contextual interactions that emerge throughout the process. In the context of classrooms, Cohen et al. (2003) state that "teachers and students shape environments by what they notice and how they respond, but environments shape attention and response" (p. 127). Similarly, teachers engaged in supported collaborative inquiry are in an environment that both shapes and is shaped by what they notice and how they respond. As Figure 7.2 illustrates, each case is set in a particular time and presents teachers with a complex array of choices shaped by this moment in time. When professional developers consider the resources to recommend or provide, the interactions between what is available, what is needed, and what is selected by teachers must be recognized. Further, professional developers and school administrators must be responsive to how the choices that are made reshape or contribute to reshaping the context or environment. Both the Cedar Grove and Alder Creek cases highlight the need to nurture existing resource networks in order to align teacher, school, and district initiatives with respect to purposes, processes, and expectations. For example, the teachers in these cases were provided meeting time through support from both PRiSSM and helpful school schedules designed by administrators.

All teachers and teacher groups need support. When appropriate and timely resources are made available, collaborative inquiry has the potential to offer teachers a powerful and impacting professional development experience. But because specific aspects of a supportive resource network have their locus of origin in a wide variety of places, including those that are internal and external to the teachers, the identification and utilization of this network can be difficult for both the teachers and the professional developers seeking to assist in the process. Further, because the inquiry work is being conducted by a collection of individuals coming together as a whole, it might be necessary to identify and provide resources that tend to the needs of both the individual and the group. As seen in the two cases in this chapter, the roles and capabilities of the individuals within the group can influence professional developers' decisions about needed resources. Further, the teachers in these cases were resourceful, with a level of skill at accessing and leveraging resources on their own which may not be present in other groups. As Dan Tobin displayed, targeted communication and resources can sometimes overcome a support person's inability to regularly attend meetings.

Current educational reform calls for teachers to identify student needs and construct developmentally appropriate learning experiences that build on student strengths. Professional development for teachers should not have a different philosophy. Groups of teachers who devote the necessary time, energy, and emotion to opening up their practice and engage in data-based, student-centered inquiry deserve the supports we expect them to provide their students—supports that are timely, appropriate, build on their collective strengths, and attend to their collective weaknesses. As is the case for classroom instruction, there does not exist a one-size-fits-all model for supporting teacher collaborative inquiry.

REFERENCES

Ball, D. L., & Cohen, D. K. (1999). Developing practice, developing practitioners: Toward a practice-based theory of professional education. In L. Darling-Hammond & G. Sykes (Eds.), *Teaching as the learning profession: Handbook of policy and practice* (pp. 1–32). San Francisco: Jossey-Bass.

Cohen, D. K., Raudenbush, S. W., & Ball, D. L. (2003). Resources, instruction, and research. *Educational Evaluation and Policy Analysis, 25*(2), 119–142.

Gamoran, A., Anderson, C. W., Quiroz, P. A., Secada, W. G., Williams, T., & Ashmann, S. (2003). *Transforming teaching in math and science: How schools and districts can support change.* New York: Teachers College Press.

Garmston, R. J., & Wellman, B. M. (1999). *The adaptive school: A sourcebook for developing collaborative groups.* Norwood, MA: Christopher-Gordon Publishers.

Laurence, W .B. (2007). *Revisioning: A theoretical model of teachers' career choices.* Unpublished doctoral dissertation, Portland State University, Portland, Oregon.

Louis, K. S. (2008). Creating and sustaining professional communities. In A. M. Blankstein, P. D. Houston, & R. W. Cole (Eds.), *Sustaining professional learning communities* (pp. 41–57). Thousand Oaks, CA: Corwin Press.

McLaughlin, M. W., & Talbert, J. E. (2006). *Building school-based teacher learning communities*. New York: Teachers College Press.

Merriam, S. B. (1998). Qualitative research and case study applications in education. San Francisco: Jossey-Bass.

Putnam, R. T., & Borko, H. (2000). What do new views of knowledge and thinking have to say about research on teacher learning? *Educational Researcher, 29*(1), 4–15.

Taylor, S. J., & Bogdan, R. (1984). *Introduction to qualitative research methods: The search for meanings*. New York: John Wiley & Sons.

Wilson, S. M., & Berne, J. (1999). Teacher learning and the acquisition of professional knowledge: An examination of research on contemporary professional development. In A. Iran-Nejad & P. D. Pearson (Eds.), *Review of research in education* (pp. 173–210). Washington, DC: AERA.

8 Supporting Collaborative Teacher Inquiry

Anne Kennedy, David Slavit, and Tamara Holmlund Nelson

Washington State University Vancouver

In the United States, an exciting vision for student learning now exists. The increased focus on understanding student thinking in relation to well-defined learning goals or standards changes the nature of teachers' work. However, enacting this vision places new demands on teachers' knowledge, skills, and abilities. Teachers are being asked to be more deliberate and more systematic in constructing lessons and analyzing learning for all students. Individual responsibility for student learning in single classrooms is shifting toward collective responsibility, by groups of teachers and other leaders, for the learning of each child. Professional learning through supported collaborative teacher inquiry (SCTI) is a possible mechanism for influencing and navigating this change. SCTI affords teachers opportunities to reflect critically on problems of practice, to gain exposure to others' ideas, to evaluate how others' ideas differ from their own, and to uncover new meaning for their work.

Hiebert, Gallimore, and Stigler (2002) discuss the balance between practitioner and professional knowledge, with the former being private and directly linked to classrooms, whereas the latter is public, shared, storable, and subject to external verification. Dall'Alba & Sandberg (2006) describe a similar distinction through a focus on practice, stating that "understanding *of* practice must be integrated with understanding *in* practice to form a practical understanding that is both sound and skillful" (p. 402). SCTI, as described in this book, shows promise as one way to foster teachers' deeper understandings of the relationship between content, instructional practices, and student learning. The power of SCTI is that it provides a mechanism for teachers to come together to co-construct practitioner and professional knowledge.

This book explores supports needed and supports provided to enhance collaborative teacher inquiry. Just as classroom teachers wrestle daily with principles of equity and the realities of reaching all learners, professional developers likewise wrestle with the challenge of facilitating the growth of teachers with different needs. A question on which professional developers reflect is: Can *all* teachers be influenced to examine their instructional practices and the subsequent impacts on student learning? For this to occur, a variety of factors are desirable, including a conducive professional context for the work, adequate on-time and follow-up support, and teachers who are able, or have the potential, to consider the benefits of the professional development. By focusing on needed supports and resources, this book strives to open up a discussion that goes to the heart of what Fullan, Hill, and Crévola (2006) describe as the challenge for teacher learning:

> How, then, do we make deeper daily learning a reality for teachers? Replacing the concept of professional development with professional learning is a good start; understanding that professional learning "in context" is the only learning that changes classroom instruction is the second step. (p. 25)

Finding the best way to support SCTI is not simply a matter of tinkering with instructional habits by prescribing best practices or recommending new structures or processes to enhance group learning (Fullan, 2005; Hawley & Valli, 1999). We see the following as essential supports for collaborative inquiry that can lead to sustained changes in instructional practices: knowledge, process, and focus facilitation; an inquiry stance; teacher commitment through choice; teachers' data literacy; and aligned resources for the purpose of building coherence in the system.

THE ROLE OF THE FACILITATOR IN SUPPORTING COLLABORATIVE TEACHER INQUIRY

Facilitation plays a key role in supporting collaborative teacher inquiry. Facilitators (whether formally appointed or informally serving in this role) can provide various timely and appropriate resources, reinforcements, or recommendations that target specific group needs and allow teachers' inquiries to move forward purposefully and efficiently. In this volume, facilitators of SCTI included teachers, university faculty, content specialists, and professional development providers. In some cases, facilitation was shared amongst members of the group, with expertise distributed through a differentiation of roles and responsibilities. Looking across these cases, the different ways in which facilitators supported group learning is revealed. As a *knowledge facilitator*, leaders suggested or, in some cases, directed participants to use specific strategies for conducting collaborative inquiry or assisted them in surfacing relevant knowledge that informed their inquiry. *Process facilitators* paid attention to the enactment of structures and interactions in the group to ensure equitable participation and productive group work. Finally, *focus facilitators* served as direction keepers to ensure that inquiry teams maintained a productive, content-focused, and improvement-oriented stance toward SCTI.

Knowledge Facilitators

A knowledge facilitator supports the development of teachers' knowledge and skills for conducting collaborative inquiry (McLaughlin & Talbert, 2006). In the case of McDuffie, the facilitator directed teachers toward the use of modified forms of lesson study and video clubs based on the teachers' needs and interests, and directly and indirectly connected experiences drawn from the larger landscape of professional learning opportunities residing in the district. The selected strategies provided a venue for Ms. Rada to integrate learning from a variety of sources and to shine a spotlight directly on teacher and student interactions. What we learn from this case is that a facilitator can play an important role in matching specific collaborative inquiry strategies with teachers' readiness to benefit from the selected activities. In McDuffie's reference to Fernandez (2005), she points out that what teachers learn depends on the specific issues on which teachers focus, the tasks teachers use to structure lesson study work, and the nature of teachers' engagement in the work. As a knowledge resource, the facilitator can assess teacher development as both an educator and a collaborator in order to select appropriate strategies that best match the goals and purposes of the group. In the Slavit, Laurence, Kennedy, and Nelson case (this volume), Cheryl, the lead teacher, was able to exploit the internal expertise of the team and build a bridge between the goals of the group (understanding students' abilities to write conclusions) and analysis strategies derived from the team's own scientific understandings and those of an external professional development provider. In this instance, Cheryl acted as a knowledge facilitator to broker both internal and external resources. This allowed teachers to successfully find a way to analyze student learning data and led to an increased understanding of where their students were struggling. These cases illustrate two types of knowledge facilitation. The first case describes the toolbox of strategies and protocols that facilitators might use to enhance the inquiry process, while the second case describes the importance of deep subject matter knowledge needed to move the inquiry process forward. In both cases, facilitators were able to support the inquiry process because they had a knowledge base that allowed them to adapt the learning needs of the inquiry team to the intended purposes and outcomes of the inquiry.

Process Facilitators

Process facilitation refers to the actions that individuals take to develop the culture of collaborative inquiry groups. For example, actions might include the use of procedures that increase engagement and a collective sense of responsibility, or structures that build interpersonal relationships and group norms. In each of the cases there was at least one person who provided direction to their groups by producing agendas, preparing for group meetings, and attending to group interactions during meetings, whether online or face-to-face. Karen, in the Alder Creek case (Slavit et al., this volume), exemplified the often challenging aspect of process facilitation—what to do when people disregard group norms or when group processes break down—where the procedural slips into the interpersonal. Karen helped to build the group's culture by confronting what she perceived as counterproductive actions from one member (being late and dominating conversation) and by intentionally and directly facilitating the group toward more productive interactions. Similarly, the facilitator in the Lamb, Philipp, Jacobs, and Schappelle case provided direction and structure for the group, and her manner of working with the teachers served to build trust and a sense of community amongst teachers. She expertly moved from the role of professional development provider, to the role of colleague, to the role of learner, depending on what she saw as the teachers' needs. As a process facilitator, this flexibility in reading the needs of the group and selecting the right responses demonstrates both the subtlety and skill required for process facilitation.

Process facilitators can also help teams learn to talk together in different ways. Some kinds of conversations support open and honest *dialogue* that surfaces shared or misaligned understandings and can lead to a reconstruction of teachers' values and beliefs. Alternately, *discussions* are more results-oriented and move the group toward decisions (Garmston & Wellman, 1999). The discourse analysis described in the Bondy and Williamson case speaks directly to how dialogue shaped the nature of collaborative inquiry. They argue that teachers and other educators need structured learning opportunities that build knowledge and skills around ways of talking with one another in a manner that leads to an appropriate balance of dialogue and discussion. In McDuffie, Ms. Rada was supported in her thinking by caring and supportive colleagues who focused on positive aspects of her classroom instruction and asked high-level questions that helped her clarify her thinking and deepen her understanding. Such supportive discourse structures can be fundamental to the success of collaborative teacher inquiry.

Focus Facilitators

Focus facilitators attend to the direction and purpose of collaborative inquiry so that teachers stay focused on meaningful content, practice, and student learning. This kind of facilitation seeks to ensure that collaborative inquiry groups do not just work hard, but they work on what really matters. A drift from purpose can happen when issues or concerns ancillary to the work of the group get in the way of the real purpose of the work. Wenger and Dinsmore (this volume) describe an emerging realization by university researchers that beginning teachers needed help in finding and keeping their focus. These teachers were as much interested in sharing teacher stories as they were in addressing specific issues related to teaching and learning. The ability of the facilitators to maintain focus was central to moving their teachers towards data-based inquiry, but also toward more critical views of classroom practice.

NURTURING AN INQUIRY STANCE

A key consideration regarding the scope of impact for SCTI models of professional development is the nature of the inquiry stance of individual teachers, and the group as a whole. In Chapter 1, drawing on the work of Wells (1999), Cochran-Smith and Lytle (1999), and Jaworski (2006), the authors discussed an inquiry stance as a deeply internalized disposition, or way of being, that is conducive to pondering, questioning, and seeking to satisfy curiosities. The cases discussed in this book provide a contextualized view of the importance of nurturing an inquiry stance. Just as curricular materials can be enacted by a teacher with or without fidelity to their corresponding instructional philosophy (Senk & Thompson, 2003), an inquiry cycle (identifying the problem, making data-based decisions related to practice, and sharing learning with others) can be enacted with or without an inquiry stance (Nelson, Slavit, & Deuel, 2008). When an inquiry group possesses an inquiry stance, they are more able to explicitly examine the influence of various contextual elements on their pedagogical practices and learning goals for students. They are also more inclined to view their collaborative actions as steps in an ongoing process that can be evaluated, questioned, and advanced (Sirotnik, 1988). Through questioning, reflecting, and dialogically interacting with others, an inquiry stance positions teachers to move outside of their own paradigm and explore issues of practice from different norms and perspectives. As an example, Ms. Rada (McDuffie, this volume) was challenged in numerous ways by colleagues and materials which supported an entirely new way of thinking about how to mathematically interact with her students. Leon and colleagues (Nelson, Kennedy, Deuel, & Slavit, this volume) critically analyzed curricular recommendations during their collaborative inquiry process, and many teachers at Hopewell Elementary (Bondy et al., this volume) developed questioning tendencies around student dilemmas that led to an inquiry stance toward issues of inclusion. In each case, we see that an inquiry stance is manifested in the dialogue, but it can also be manifested, less visibly, in the reflective processes of the teachers.

We would assert that all teachers are capable of adopting an inquiry stance. But certain contexts may make this extremely difficult, or perhaps not even in the best interest of the teacher. For example, some teachers may not feel they have a license to question, as evidenced in Wenger et al. (this volume). Many of the cases discussed throughout the book also illustrate that teachers may lack the time to think and reflect that is necessary in developing and enacting an inquiry stance toward a problem of practice. The cases discussed in Lamb et al., McDuffie, and Nelson et al. (this volume) illustrate that deep content knowledge can support teachers in developing and enacting an inquiry stance toward teaching in a discipline. In any case, we have found that certain teachers come to the table with an inquiry stance, while others benefit from years of modeling, strategic scaffolding, and gentle prodding to develop such a stance toward practice. While not a requirement for participation in an SCTI model, an inquiry stance can facilitate a deeper examination of practice by redefining the notion of success and broadening the purpose of teacher participation.

LEVERAGING TEACHERS' COMMITMENT TO COLLABORATIVE INQUIRY THROUGH CHOICE

One of the critical, but somewhat hidden, supports for collaborative inquiry is teachers' choice in determining some aspect of the inquiry process. In our experience working with over 30 collaborative inquiry teams over the last five years, we have witnessed the movement of voluntary teacher collaboration teams to district-wide, mandated PLCs that direct teacher work in terms of focus, process, outcomes, or all three. We have watched as highly effective teams focused squarely on understanding critical aspects of teaching and learning turned into groups of teachers required to comply with external requirements such as curriculum alignment, common assessment or grading practices, or use of prescribed instructional practices. Alternately, we have seen teachers who have struggled to conduct collaborative inquiry on their own turn into productive teams when provided the structure, support, and, in some cases, focus and direction needed to move the inquiry process forward. In reviewing each of the cases in this volume, it became increasingly clear that the issue is really not about whether SCTI is voluntary or mandatory, but instead about what choices teachers are given in relation to inquiry work. Personalizing learning through choice and control engenders relevancy, responsibility, and ownership, supporting the shift from professional development to professional learning (Fullan et al., 2006).

Both Bondy et al. (this volume) and Lamb et al. (this volume) provide rich examples of the interplay between teachers' participation, either mandatory or voluntary, and choices in the inquiry process. Bondy et al. describe Hopewell Elementary as a school that aspired to become a professional learning community. Meetings in the school were restructured to provide different types of opportunities for collaboration, and there was an expectation that teachers would participate in these meetings. Weekly Inclusion Meetings (mandated) featured individual inquiries around specific students' needs, while Fellows meetings (voluntary) were organized around teachers' common dilemmas related to student learning. In both instances, planned efforts supported individual and team development for conducting collaborative inquiry and enhanced group interactions (knowing what dialogue supported collaboration or shut down the inquiry). The combination of teachers' freedom to select a problem they wanted to work on and the intentional scaffolding of the inquiry process provided the supports necessary for teachers to feel that their problems were important and that the collective expertise of the team could contribute to new ways of approaching teaching and learning challenges. As the authors note, at the study's conclusion Hopewell still required coaching in order for the school to function like a PLC, but were making progress in understanding the supports needed for teachers to feel genuinely engaged in solving problems of practice.

The case presented by Lamb et al. provides an example of voluntary professional development in a setting that initially provided teachers little choice about the nature of their inquiry. The authors articulate a framework for teacher learning that directed teachers to focus explicitly on children's mathematical thinking. Early in the program, teachers were given little freedom or flexibility to determine the nature of their inquiries with students or each other. As they progressed through the program and began to demonstrate evidence of an inquiry stance, they were encouraged to take more ownership over the nature and course of classroom and professional development inquiries and activities. The success of the program is evidenced by the number of teachers that chose to participate in these professional development activities over a number of years, and the degree to which teachers began to view themselves as researchers into their own practice.

When teacher choice is present and SCTI is grounded in teachers' personal questions and concerns, it provides motivation for and investment in the purposes and outcomes of the work (Darling-Hammond & McLaughlin, 1995). Yet, there is a larger issue here. The tension between teachers directing their own learning and the broader question of what learning goals and/or problems of practice are most important for improved student learning is a fundamental challenge for those who wish to support collaborative teacher inquiry. If teachers are to be empowered to determine significant aspects of their professional learning, then there needs to be sufficient knowledge resources available to propel the work forward. Similarly, these knowledge resources need to be consistent with student learning goals defined by the broader contexts (those beyond the teacher group) in which the SCTI operates (Palinscar, Magnusson, Marano, Ford, & Brown, 1998). For example, in the Wenger et al. case, teachers came to the inquiry work with a great deal of enthusiasm and each teacher was supported in pursuing inquiries based on personal interest and need. Teacher success was due in large part to the intensive and targeted intervention of the university professors who were able to support teachers collectively and individually, and focus the work on student learning. However, this case also demonstrates how SCTI can create dissonance with other professional development activities that differ in approach and purpose. The district-provided mentoring programs left some of the new teachers feeling that they had little control over either their professional learning opportunities or their professional practice. These inconsistencies served to significantly inhibit SCTI potential. We maintain that choice is important to the success of teachers' collaborative research; thus, consideration needs to be given to how teachers are encouraged to participate and are given control over the inquiry process.

CONCEPTIONS AND USES OF DATA

What Constitutes Data?

Teachers' conceptions and uses of data are inextricably linked to their dispositions regarding the purposes for conducting classroom-based inquiry. Many teachers engage in such inquiry to serve the purpose of convincing others, such as principals and parents, that they are reaching various student-learning goals. These teachers usually conceive of and use data to *prove* that their inquiry is accomplishing these goals. Such dispositions are often promoted by school and district initiatives and nurtured by the high-stakes testing environment predominant in the current U.S. educational system. On the other hand, teachers also engage in inquiry for the purpose of gaining information to help them resolve dilemmas of practice or explore areas in which questions or curiosities exist. In these cases, rather than trying to prove specific results to external stakeholders, teachers seek to *improve* their practice and their students' learning by exploring these dilemmas and curiosities. The aforementioned dispositions can have specific influences on teachers' conceptions and uses of data. For example, the use of experimental design, quantitative data sources, and summative assessment measures tend to be associated with a proving disposition, while qualitative methodologies and formative assessments tend to be related to an improving disposition (Nelson, Slavit, & Deuel, 2008).

The teachers in the SCTI groups in this volume tended to assume an improving disposition toward their work. Hence, these groups conceived of data as that which could better help them understand their dilemmas and address their curiosities. Student work emerged as the most common data source across the cases (Wenger et al.; Bondy et al.; McDuffie, this volume) and most teachers used this work to explore a question directly related to their practice. In addition, the teachers in the Lamb et al. chapter also made use of student work from other classroom contexts as provided in the professional development sessions. In McDuffie, Ms. Rada relied heavily on analyses of her own classroom teaching and interactions with students to supplement her analysis. While student work was explored, the teachers in Nelson et al. relied most heavily on state content standards and test-related documents as their primary data source. In most cases, the student work (and even the standards) served as a tool for exploring classroom-based issues for the purpose of improving practice rather than analyzing student achievement for the purpose of proving a specific educational result to external stakeholders. The underlying dispositions and choices of data sets seemed to have important implications on the learning trajectories of the teachers in these SCTI settings. Specifically, an improving goal served to inform teachers' understandings of students' thinking that afforded an immediate, and sometimes nuanced, instructional response.

Support for the Use of Data

The teacher groups discussed in this volume received a wide variety of supports for using data in their inquiry process. For example, in Nelson et al., the Grays Bay teachers made use of test-related documents and their own scientific understandings to better understand and critically examine state science content standards. In McDuffie, Ms. Rada drew on her National Board experience, the research literature, and most heavily on her interactions with the members of her collaborative inquiry team to pursue dilemmas of practice. The teachers in Lamb et al. utilized a structured professional development setting (Cognitively Guided Instruction) replete with evidence from research and opportunities to explore student classroom data. The impacts of these supports were a clearer understanding of state standards, new perspectives on teacher–student interactions, and more focused, deeper conversations about students' mathematical thinking, respectively.

Slavit et al. (this volume) discuss the importance of a resource network for supporting teachers through data-based explorations of their practice. While exposure to a variety of resources is important, it is perhaps more important that resources serve as supports that are both usable and relevant to the actual work of the inquiry group. It would seem that teachers engaged in SCTI can benefit from resource networks of this kind, as did the teachers in most of the cases contained in this volume. However, it is also important that the resource network mesh with the disposition toward research that permeates the teacher group. Teachers who seek to either prove student learning results or improve practice need resources that fit their purpose. A mismatch between support and teachers' dispositions can disrupt potential impacts of the support, even if the support is usable and relevant to the work at hand. Building teachers' skills in using data is essential, but, in the current climate of accountability, data discussions can easily turn to issues of standardization and increased test achievement while minimizing the "moral purposes of education," that is, caring about the growth and development of each individual student (Hargreaves, 2008). Those supporting collaborative inquiry need to remain attentive to those activities that support data literacy across a wide spectrum of experiences and opportunities in order to meet the specific resource needs of the teachers.

SUPPORT FOR RESOURCE IDENTIFICATION, INTEGRATION, AND UTILIZATION

Perhaps one of the greatest barriers to enacting SCTI can come from a misalignment of school-improvement initiatives as they relate to schools and individual teachers. Teachers may desire professional development in an area that is unrelated or tangential to their school's current developmental focus. In fact, a general challenge to teacher professional learning involves the various competing agendas that vie for teachers' time and attention. Alignment and coherency, in terms of school-improvement processes, structures, and philosophies, can become a key source of support for collaborative teacher inquiry. When lacking, teachers experience dissonance, frustration, and a lack of momentum for their work together. While alignment in and of itself may not change classroom practices, alignment of resources, mandates, and learning priorities can create some essential conditions for changes that have the greatest impact on schooling (Fullan et al., 2006).

The cases in this book present two perspectives for considering resource alignment that parallel the kind of support discussed in Chapter 1. At a microlevel, resources can be aligned within various aspects of a collaborative teacher inquiry, including the focus, data-based activity, and interactions. At a macrolevel, resources can also align with the goals and perspectives of the broader educational contexts in which this work occurs (such as district and school initiatives and state standards). We note that this broader kind of resource alignment is quite difficult to construct when the resource network that emanates from the broader educational context is itself internally out of alignment. From this perspective, we see that alignment of resources can have immediate impacts on the inquiry work of teacher groups. However, resource alignment can also be a multifaceted process with far-reaching impacts that can be difficult to see, anticipate, or even explain.

Teachers can identify resources on their own or be provided resources by facilitators, other members of broader educational contexts, or the system itself (such as state content standards). Support for resource identification could involve helping teachers make sense of their student learning goals, or how to make sense of what these goals would look and sound like in the context of looking at student work. Once a given resource is identified, its interplay with other resources can help determine the manner in which it is actually utilized. But this interplay is largely determined by the two kinds of alignments described previously. Hence, while other factors are present in a teacher group's decision to utilize a given resource, the manner in which it is identified and made available, as well as the manner in which it is aligned with other resources, is important in this decision.

The McDuffie case provides an example of how resources can be aligned within a specific inquiry context to create a synergy that allowed a teacher to change her practice. Here, Ms. Rada explored new forms of instruction that changed the way students interacted with each other, the teacher, and the content. The collaborative inquiry team (CIT) provided the catalyst for this breakthrough, but other specific sources of support provided the necessary intellectual stimulation and concrete strategies from which Ms. Rada could draw in changing her practice. For example, the curricular materials provided rich mathematical tasks that could be used to engage students of differing abilities into the content and discourse, and her participation in a book study provided validation for using new instructional approaches as well as practical strategies for improving questioning techniques and understanding student thinking. While each resource was powerful in and of itself, it was the CIT that enabled Ms. Rada to move from a theory into practical application. Critical interactions amongst and between team members provided Ms. Rada a venue to connect learning of practice with learning in practice (Dall'Alba & Sandberg, 2006), and the consistent philosophical orientation presented by each source of support enhanced the alignment of resources and experiences that contributed to Ms. Rada's development, as well as the development of the CIT. While this case is only one example of how aligned resources can support collaborative inquiry, other cases, such as the Alder Creek teachers in Slavit et al. (this volume) and Bondy et al. (this volume), demonstrate similar results.

The Lamb et al. and Nelson et al. cases provide stark contrasts in the context of the broader level of resource alignment discussed earlier. The teachers and schools in the Lamb et al. case eventually aligned curricular materials around the Cognitively Guided Instruction (CGI) professional development model. The CGI model provided a broader context and a coherent, useful set of resources for the inquiry work of the teachers. These included a framework for thinking about students' mathematical thinking, samples of student work, relevant research, and a process by which teachers could engage in constructive dialogue around their own student work samples. Administrators also aligned with this framework, as the model may have been unsuccessful had the administrators failed to intellectually and monetarily support the program at key intervals during its evolution. On the other hand, the Grays Bay teachers (Nelson et al.) turned to the broader context of state content standards for support. However, the state supplied only the test-related documents to support the teachers in making sense of these materials. The Grays Bay teachers brought to bear their own educational and scientific perspectives in attempting to make sense of the materials.

Relationships between the lens through which teachers view and use resources and the theoretical orientation that frames the resources are other important considerations in resource alignment. In the Lamb et al. case, teachers became more attuned to students' mathematical thinking in direct alignment with the CGI framework. Because CGI is based on solid evidence, the teachers found this to be useful to their students. The Grays Bay teachers brought a more critical lens to the state standards and developed pedagogic and content-related understandings of conclusion writing that were useful to their students, but not necessarily consistent with the state's vision. The presence of a collective inquiry stance toward their work supported the Grays Bay teachers through this process and in their ability to develop usable knowledge about this specific student learning issue.

CONCLUDING REMARKS

Teacher Voice

This volume provides numerous examples of teachers striving to better understand their practice and student learning. In doing so, the teachers created theory and generated knowledge that was useful to them, and potentially to others. But for most teachers, this is usually where it ends, and the knowledge generated stays inside the teacher group; teachers receive very little support for transitioning their practitioner knowledge into professional knowledge. Imagine if the vast number of educational researchers who contribute to a specific knowledge base, such as those who researched children's mathematical thinking and created the knowledge base for CGI, had no systemic supports for sharing this knowledge. What would happen? What if the knowledge remained inside this group of researchers?

Classroom teachers, including many in this volume, are in a knowledgeable position to contribute to the research base, and hold the potential to do so. Teachers have access to students all day, all year, and many teachers have the drive to better understand their learners through inquiry. Some teachers, like those at Cedar Grove (Slavit et al., this volume), can be vocal about their desire to share their work in broader educational contexts. The cases in this volume provide a vision for teachers working with knowledgeable others to expand and enhance a broader, richer research network and a new agenda for educational research that emphasizes shared responsibility and actualizes teachers as principal investigators on important problems of practice. Unfortunately, some teachers must fight hard to put themselves into positions where they can have such influence, even though they may have the drive and ability to produce and share important knowledge. The numerous constraints within our educational system, particularly in regard to time demands, are difficult to overcome. Facilitation and other supports discussed in this volume are helpful to teacher groups in constructing (or understanding) important theory and practical applications. But additional supports are necessary to provide teachers with avenues for sharing their knowledge in broader contexts.

Future Work

We hope that teachers, administrators, professional development providers, and researchers are able to advance their thinking and knowledge base through reflection on the cases at hand. We also hope we have offered specific ideas for framing and addressing problems of practice, as well as ideas for researching into specific aspects of SCTI. This volume addressed many questions related to SCTI, but many others remain. We conclude with the following questions regarding directions for further work in the important area of SCTI.

Research questions:

> *What kinds of knowledge can be gained from a collection of SCTI cases?*
> *What is the nature of the interactions between SCTI work and broader educational contexts?*
> *How can we better understand the link between facilitation and SCTI processes and outcomes?*
> *How do teachers develop an inquiry stance towards practice?*
> *How do we better link SCTI to student learning outcomes?*
> *How do we systematically afford teachers opportunities to contribute to the literature base?*

Teacher professional learning questions:

> *How do we enhance the interface between teacher inquiry work and broader contexts?*
> *How do we sustain SCTI given the ever-changing environments in which it is enacted?*
> *How do we reach all teachers?*

REFERENCES

Cochran-Smith, M., & Lytle, S. L. (1999). Relationships of knowledge and practice: Teacher learning in communities. In A. Iran-Nejad & P. D. Pearson (Eds.), *Review of research in education* (Vol. 24, pp. 249–306). Washington, DC: AERA.

Dall'Alba, G., & Sandberg, J. (2006). Unveiling professional development, a critical review of stage models. *Review of Educational Research, 76*(3), 383–412.

Darling-Hammond, L., & McLaughlin, M. W. (1995). Policies that support professional development in an era of reform. *Phi Delta Kappan, 76*(8), 597–604.

Fernandez, C. (2005). Lesson study: A means for elementary teachers to develop the knowledge of mathematics needed for reform-minded teaching?. *Mathematical Thinking and Learning, 7*(4), 265–289.

Fullan, M. (2005). *Leadership and sustainability: Systems thinkers in action.* Thousand Oaks, CA: Corwin Press.

Fullan, M., Hill, P., & Crévola, C. (2006). *Breakthrough.* Thousand Oaks, CA: Corwin Press.

Garmston, R. J., & Wellman, B. M. (1999). *The adaptive school: A sourcebook for developing collaborative groups.* Norwood, MA: Christopher-Gordon Publishers.

Hargreaves, A. (2008). Leading professional learning communities. In A. M. Blankstein, P. D. Houston, & R. W. Cole (Eds.), *Sustaining professional learning communities* (pp. 175–197). Thousand Oaks, CA: Corwin Press.

Hawley, W. D., & Valli, L. (1999). The essentials of effective professional development: A new consensus. In L. Darling-Hammond & G. Sykes (Eds.), *Teaching as the learning profession* (pp. 127–150). San Francisco: Jossey-Bass.

Hiebert, J., Gallimore, R., & Stigler, J. W. (2002). A knowledge base for the teaching profession: What would it look like and how can we get one? *Educational Researcher, 31*(5), 3–15.

Jaworski, B. (2006). Theory and practice in mathematics teaching development: Critical inquiry as a mode of learning in teaching. *Journal of Mathematics Teacher Education 9,* 187–211.

McLaughin, M., & Talbert, J. E. (2006). *Building school-based teacher learning communities: Professional strategies to improve student achievement.* New York: Teachers College Press.

Nelson, T. H., Slavit, D., & Deuel, A. (2008). *Teachers' collaborative inquiry: Making sense of classroom-based data.* Paper presented at the National Association for Research in Science Teaching, Baltimore, MD.

Palincsar, A. S., Magnusson, S. J., Marano, N., Ford, D., & Brown, N. (1998). Designing a community of practice: Principles and practices of the GIsML community. *Teaching and Teacher Education, 14*(1), 5–19.

Senk, S. L., & Thompson, D. R. (2003). *Standards-based school mathematics curricula: What are they? What do students learn?* Mahwah, NJ: Lawrence Erlbaum Associates.

Sirotnik, K. A. (1988). The meaning and conduct of inquiry in school-university partnerships. In K. A. Sirotnik & J. I. Goodlad (Eds.), *School-university partnerships in action: Concepts, cases and concerns* (pp. 169–190). New York: Teachers College Press.

Wells, G. (1999). *Dialogic inquiry: Towards a sociocultural practice and theory of education.* Cambridge, UK: Cambridge University Press.

Contributors

Elizabeth Bondy is professor and director, School of Teaching and Learning, University of Florida. Her work focuses on elementary education, particularly in high poverty schools. She works in university/school and university/community partnerships in high poverty settings. Since 1999, she has been Professor in Residence at an elementary school where she works closely with teachers, administrators, and students as well as teacher education students and advanced graduate students who are engaged in field experiences and research at the school. Dr. Bondy's most recent research focuses on examining the concept and practice of the teacher as "warm demander" in the classroom community.

Angie Deuel is a research associate at Washington State University Vancouver. She received her doctorate in language and literacy using discourse analysis to study her 10th grade students' book club experience. Her research interests include understanding discourse processes within teacher inquiry groups and the stance teachers take towards their practice.

Jan Renee Dinsmore is an associate professor of education at Eastern Oregon University. She teaches at a branch-campus in a cohort-model teacher preparation program in rural eastern Oregon. Her current research focuses on constructivist teaching practices and teacher mentoring.

Victoria R. Jacobs is an associate professor of mathematics education in the School of Teacher Education at San Diego State University, co-director of a master of arts program focused on K-8 mathematics education, and a member of the Center for Research in Mathematics and Science Education (CRMSE). Her research interests focus on children's mathematical thinking and how to support teachers in using children's thinking as the foundation for instructional decisions. Her professional development work embraces these same ideas and often involves long-term collaborative relationships with teachers and school districts.

Anne Kennedy is the founding director of the Science and Mathematics Education Resource Center (SMERC), a partnership of Educational Service District 112, Washington State University Vancouver, and 30 southwest Washington School Districts. She is also active in supporting regional and statewide reform efforts in mathematics and science education. Her current teaching and research interests include school change, leadership, and sustainable program development and implementation.

Lisa Clement Lamb is an associate professor of mathematics education in the School of Teacher Education at San Diego State University, co-director of a master of arts program focused on K-8 mathematics education, and a member of the Center for Research in Mathematics and Science Education (CRMSE). Before coming to SDSU in 1998, she taught high school mathematics in California and Virginia.

Wendi Laurence was a research associate at Washington State University from 2006- 2008. Her research centers on developing learning support networks, teacher career decisions, teacher development, and policy analysis. She is particularly interested in how we prepare and sustain individuals as they take on difficult work. Dr. Laurence is now the Founder & Director of Create-osity, a company dedicated to developing, understanding and sustaining innovative learning. Her consultation activities include qualitative research methodology, learning assessment, curriculum design and community based learning.

Amy Roth McDuffie is an associate professor of mathematics education in the College of Education at Washington State University Tri-Cities. Her research and teaching focus on preservice and practicing teachers' professional learning and development in mathematics. Specifically, McDuffie incorporates and studies situated, practice-based approaches to teacher learning.

Tamara Holmlund Nelson is an associate professor in science education at Washington State University Vancouver. Her research interests focus on science teachers, professional development and the translation of new understandings into classroom practice. Her husband, two kids, and dog fill her life outside of work.

Randolph A. Philipp is professor of mathematics education in the School of Teacher Education at San Diego State University and a member of the Center for Research in Mathematics and Science Education (CRMSE). In his current research, he is working with the coauthors of this chapter to map a trajectory for the evolution of elementary school teachers engaged in sustained professional development. Randy started his educational career as a secondary school mathematics teacher in Los Angeles, California, and as a teacher in the Peace Corps in Liberia, West Africa.

Bonnie P. Schappelle is a research associate at San Diego State University's Center for Research in Mathematics and Science Education (CRMSE) working with the coauthors of this chapter on a project funded to study teachers' evolving perspectives over the course of long-term professional development. She has served as assistant to the editor of the *Journal for Research in Mathematics Education* and has been a researcher on numerous CRMSE projects since the 1980s. Before working at CRMSE, she taught high school mathematics.

David Slavit is professor of mathematics education and former director of the Masters in Teaching Program at Washington State University Vancouver. Through numerous federally-funded grants and the initiation of school-university partnerships, he has transformed his primary professional focus into analyzing teacher development at the classroom, building, and district levels. Other research interests include students' algebraic thinking and uses of instructional technology.

Kerri J. Wenger is an associate professor in literacy and ESOL education at Eastern Oregon University. Her research focuses on second language teaching and learning in multilingual rural settings and teacher professional development.

Pamela Williamson is an assistant professor at the University of Cincinnati with appointments in special education and The Center for Urban Education. Her research interests include teaching and learning in high poverty settings for students with disabilities.

Index